The New Testament in its Ritual World

What was life like among the first Christians?

The social and historical background of the New Testament is now a major focus of interest for New Testament scholars. Exploration of ritual is an important part of this focus on the communities behind the written text, yet to date there has been comparatively little work done in this area.

This lucidly written book starts from the premise that ritual was central to, and definitive for, early Christian life, as it is for all social orders, and explores the New Testament through a ritual lens. This approach takes into account the social environment, Roman social history and the archaeological records of the time, and does justice to a central but slighted aspect of community life. By grounding the exploration in ritual theory, Greco-Roman ritual life, and the material record of the ancient Mediterranean, Richard E. DeMaris, a leading researcher in the field, offers new and insightful perspectives on early Christian communities and their cultural environment, and outlines an alternative approach to the New Testament.

Richard E. DeMaris is Professor of New Testament Studies, Valparaiso University, USA. He is the 2008 Catholic Biblical Association Visiting Professor to the Pontifical Biblical Institute in Rome.

The New Testament
in its Ritual World

Richard E. DeMaris

Routledge
Taylor & Francis Group

LONDON AND NEW YORK

First published 2008
by Routledge
2 Park Square, Milton Park, Abingdon, Oxon. OX14 4RN

Simultaneously published in the USA and Canada
by Routledge
270 Madison Ave., New York, NY 100016

*Routledge is an imprint of the Taylor & Francis Group, an
informa business*

© 2008 Richard E. DeMaris

Typeset in 10/12pt Sabon by Graphicraft Limited, Hong Kong
Printed and bound in Great Britain by TJ International Ltd,
Padstow, Cornwall

British Library Cataloguing in Publication Data
A catalogue record for this book is available
from the British Library

Library of Congress Cataloging in Publication Data
DeMaris, Richard E.
  The New Testament in its ritual world / Richard E. DeMaris.
    p. cm.
  Includes bibliographical references (p.) and index.
  1. Church history–Primitive and early church, ca. 30–600.
  2. Ritual.   3. Rites and ceremonies.   4. Ritualism.   I. Title.
  BR162.3.D46 2008
  225.9′5–dc22   2007034644

ISBN10 0-415-43825-X (hbk)
ISBN10 0-415-43826-8 (pbk)
ISBN10 0-203-93079-7 (ebk)

ISBN13 978-0-415-43825-4 (hbk)
ISBN13 978-0-415-43826-1 (pbk)
ISBN13 978-0-203-93079-3 (ebk)

Contents

Acknowledgments   vi
Abbreviations   ix
Introduction: Ritual Studies and the New Testament   1

PART I
Entry Rites   11

1   Perilous Passage   14

2   Contested Waters   37

3   And the Greatest of These Is Death   57

PART II
Exit Rites   73

4   Paul's Omphalos   76

5   Jesus Jettisoned   91

Bibliography   112
Index of Ancient Sources   131
Index of Modern Authors   137
Index of Subjects   141

Acknowledgments

All books have a genesis and this one began during an extended period of research and reading outside the field of New Testament studies in the mid-1990s, while I lived in Germany. A member of the Protestant Theology faculty at the Eberhard Karls University, Prof. Dr S. Mittmann, was kind enough to orient me to the considerable resources of Tübingen, though I did not visit the library of the Theologicum nearly as often as the university's main collection and the archaeological library above the town in Hohentübingen. Thanks go to my longtime academic home, Valparaiso University, and to the Catholic Biblical Association for enabling me to make a foray into the literature of the social sciences, especially ritual theory.

I am also indebted to Timothy E. Gregory, director of the Ohio State University Excavations at Isthmia, Greece, and to many affiliated with that dig for educating me in the archaeological record of ancient Corinth and its environs. Such training was indispensable for making use of the material record of the Mediterranean world, which I do at several points in this book. Besides Tim, I learned an immense amount from Jeanne Marty, Richard Rothaus, Jayni Reinhard, and Scott Nash over the course of many summers under the blazing sun and crystal-blue skies of Greece. In addition to Valparaiso University and the Catholic Biblical Association, I am grateful to the National Endowment for the Humanities and the American School for Classical Studies at Athens for making travel to and residence in Greece possible. The NEH also supported a period of research at the American Academy in Rome, where I studied with John Bodel and Richard Saller. They, too, added to my knowledge of the ancient Mediterranean's archaeological record.

Once the ideas for this book were incubated and began growing into chapters, I needed a testing ground for them. Annual national and international meetings of the Society of Biblical Literature and the Catholic Biblical Association provided the opportunity to present several papers that have been revised and incorporated in this book. An even better venue has been the Context Group, a circle of biblical scholars that has pioneered the application of the social sciences to biblical interpretation, especially the New Testament. Group members have conducted rites of affliction for this book. Almost all of its content has run the gauntlet of their close reading and critique. (The trials have been conducted cordially except for an occasional simian flare-up.) Several deserve singling out for the generous help they gave me: Scott Bartchy, Doug Oakman, Eric Stewart, and Ritva Williams. I also benefited from very helpful comments and suggestions from Dennis Duling, Craig de Vos, Jack Elliott, Philip Esler, Anselm Hagedorn, Santiago Guijarro, John Kloppenborg, Jason Lamoreaux, Stuart Love, Carolyn Leeb, Bruce Malina, Steven Muir, Dietmar Neufeld, Lyn Osiek, John Pilch, David Rhoads, Dick Rohrbaugh, and Gary Stansell. Special thanks go to Jerry Neyrey for making valuable suggestions about the structure the book should take. Without doubt, it would be immensely weaker without the vetting the Context Group gave it. The flaws that remain originate with me.

In the course of writing I regularly queried several colleagues at Valparaiso University, who were patient with my inexpert questions and expert enough to set me straight. For Hebrew Bible matters I turned to Mark Bartusch and Carolyn Leeb, for Classics Mark Farmer, and for the church of late antiquity Lisa Driver. These friends and colleagues saved me time and trouble. Also at Valparaiso I worked closely with the inter-library loan officers at the Christopher Center for Library and Information Resources, Susan Wanat and Marcia Andrejevich, who have been unfailingly helpful and efficient. Other libraries that opened their doors to me were the Hesburgh Library at the University of Notre Dame and the University of Illinois library in Champaign, Illinois.

Most recently I benefited from the artistic skills of Danielle Ren Hertzlieb, who composed the two illustrations that appear in Chapter 2. She consulted a number of maps and plans to create Figures 2.1 and 2.2, and these deserve mention:

Gregory, Timothy E. (ed.) (1993) *The Corinthia in the Roman Period*, Journal of Roman Archaeology Supplementary Series 8, Ann Arbor, MI: Journal of Roman Archaeology, p. 32, Fig. 1.

Rothaus, Richard M. (2000) *Corinth: The First City of Greece: An Urban History of Late Antique Cult and Religion*, Religions in the Graeco-Roman World 139, Leiden: Brill, p. 24, Plan 4.

Small, A. (ed.) (1996) *Subject and Ruler: The Cult of the Ruling Power in Classical Antiquity*, Journal of Roman Archaeology Supplementary Series 17, Ann Arbor, MI: Journal of Roman Archaeology, p. 205, Fig. 2.

Williams, Charles K., II, and Nancy Bookidis (eds) (2003) *Corinth*, vol. 20: *Corinth, The Centenary, 1896–1996*, [Princeton, NJ]: American School of Classical Studies at Athens, p. xxviii, Plan V; p. 286, Fig 17.7; p. 289, Fig. 17.11; p. 295, Fig. 17.19.

Wiseman, James (1970) "The Fountain of the Lamps," *Archaeology*, 23, p. 131, unlabeled plan of Gymnasium Area.

I should also note that some of my earlier publications have, after revision, provided templates for portions of this book. Parts of the Introduction, Chapter 3, and Chapter 4 appeared in "Baptisms and Funerals, Ordinary and Otherwise: Ritual Criticism and Corinthian Rites," *Biblical Theology Bulletin*, volume 29 (1999). The article is used with permission. Likewise, part of Chapter 2 comes from "Cults and the Imperial Cult in Early Roman Corinth: Literary Versus Material Record," a chapter in *Zwischen den Reichen: Neues Testament und Römische Herrschaft*, edited by M. Labahn and J. Zangenberg and published by Francke-Verlag in 2002. This, too, is used with permission. Part of Chapter 3 appeared in the *Journal of Biblical Literature*, volume 114 (1995), as "Corinthian Religion and Baptism for the Dead (1 Corinthians 15:29): Insights from Archaeology and Anthropology." The Society of Biblical Literature let me know that that I hold copyright on this article, and I wish to thank the society for its speedy response to my permission inquiry.

These acknowledgments would not be complete without mention of my wife and academic colleague, Sarah Glenn DeMaris, who makes life a paradise. I dedicate this book to her, even though when I first told her that its subject matter was ritual, her Seinfeldian response was, "Oh, so this is a book about nothing."

Abbreviations

The abbreviation of ancient texts follows *The SBL Handbook of Style* for biblical and early church literature and *The Oxford Classical Dictionary* (3rd ed. rev.) for classical Greek and Latin literature.

AB	Anchor Bible
ABR	*Australian Biblical Review*
AJA	*American Journal of Archaeology*
AJP	*American Journal of Philology*
ANF	Ante-Nicene Fathers
ANRW	*Aufstieg und Niedergang der römischen Welt*. Edited by H. Temporini and W. Hasse. Berlin. 1972–
ATANT	Abhandlungen zur Theologie des Alten und Neuen Testaments
ATLA	American Theological Library Association
BA	*Biblical Archaeologist*
BBR	Bulletin for Biblical Research
BJRL	*Bulletin of the John Rylands University Library of Manchester*
BRLJ	Brill Reference Library of Judaism
BT	*The Bible Translator*
BTB	*Biblical Theology Bulletin*
BZNW	Beihefte zur Zeitschrift für die neutestamentliche Wissenschaft
CBET	Contributions to Biblical Exegesis and Theology
CNT	Commentaire du Nouveau Testament
ConBNT	Coniectanea biblica: New Testament Series
ConBOT	Coniectanea biblica: Old Testament Series
CSHJ	Chicago Studies in the History of Judaism
Dessau, *ILS*	H. Dessau, *Inscriptiones Latinae Selectae* (1892–1914)
ETL	*Ephemerides theologicae lovanienses*
EvQ	*Evangelical Quarterly*
ExpTim	*Expository Times*
FGrH	F. Jacoby, *Fragmente der griechischen Historiker* (1923–)
FRLANT	Forschungen zur Religion und Literatur des Alten und Neuen Testaments
GBS	Guides to Biblical Scholarship

GRBS	*Greek, Roman, and Byzantine Studies*
HNTC	Harper's New Testament Commentaries
HR	*History of Religions*
HTR	*Harvard Theological Review*
HTS	Harvard Theology Studies
HUT	Hermeneutische Untersuchungen zur Theologie
ICC	International Critical Commentary
IG	*Inscriptiones graecae.* Editio minor. Berlin, 1924–
Int	*Interpretation*
JAAR	*Journal of the American Academy of Religion*
JBL	*Journal of Biblical Literature*
JETS	*Journal of the Evangelical Theological Society*
JRitSt	*Journal of Ritual Studies*
JSNTSup	Journal for the Study of the New Testament: Supplement Series
JSOTSup	Journal for the Study of the Old Testament: Supplement Series
JSPSup	Journal for the Study of the Pseudepigrapha: Supplement Series
LCL	Loeb Classical Library
MTSR	*Method and Theory in the Study of Religion*
NICNT	New International Commentary on the New Testament
NIGTC	New International Greek Testament Commentary
NTS	*New Testament Studies*
OBO	Orbis biblicus et orientalis
PTMS	Pittsburgh Theological Monograph Series
RelSRev	*Religious Studies Review*
SBLDS	Society of Biblical Literature Dissertation Series
SBLSymS	Society of Biblical Literature Symposium Series
SNTSMS	Society for New Testament Studies Monograph Series
StPB	Studia post-biblica
TAPA	*Transactions of the American Philological Association*
Teubner	Bibliotheca scriptorum graecorum et romanorum teubneriana
ThesCRA	*Thesaurus cultus et rituum antiquorum*
TU	Texte und Untersuchungen
TynBul	*Tyndale Bulletin*
WBC	Word Biblical Commentary
WUNT	Wissenschaftliche Untersuchungen zum Neuen Testament
ZAW	*Zeitschrift für die alttestamentaliche Wissenschaft*
ZNW	*Zeitschrift für die neutestamentliche Wissenschaft*

Introduction
Ritual Studies and the New Testament

A man from Jen asked Wu-lu Tzu, "Which is more important, the rites or food?"

"The rites."

"Which is more important, the rites or sex?"

"The rites."

(Mencius 6b: 1; Lau 1970: 171)

In his authoritative study of ancient Greek religion, Walter Burkert begins treatment of archaic and classical Greek religion, the heart of the work, with these words: "An insight which came to be generally acknowledged in the study of religion towards the end of the [nineteenth] century is that rituals are more important and more instructive for the understanding of the ancient religions than are changeable myths" (Burkert 1985: 54). He aligns his analysis with this insight, placing sacrifice at the center of Greek religion and starting his examination of it with a chapter titled "Ritual and Sanctuary" (Burkert 1985: 54–118). Burkert is not alone in recognizing the centrality of ritual in ancient Mediterranean religion and culture. Peregrine Horden and Nicholas Purcell's *The Corrupting Sea: A Study of Mediterranean History* has recently prompted scholars to reconceptualize ancient Mediterranean culture, and that rethinking has placed ritual front and center (Horden and Purcell 2000). If ritual has sometimes been ignored, the neglect has diminished (e.g., Chaniotis 2005). Even the work of the much-criticized Cambridge ritualists – James G. Frazer of *The Golden Bough* fame, Jane Ellen Harrison, and others – is getting a second hearing (Calder 1991).

This realization about the significance of ritual has been slow to dawn on some scholars of the ancient Mediterranean world, however. For various reasons enumerated by scholars both in and outside the field, New Testament scholarship places ritual at the periphery, not the center, of its work (Smith 1990: 34, 43–6, 65–71, 95; Douglas 1966: 19–28; Gorman 1994). Only German history-of-religion (*religionsgeschichtlich*) scholarship from the early part of the twentieth century came close to paying adequate attention to ritual (e.g., Reitzenstein 1978 [1910]; Lietzmann 1979 [1926]). With the field's current interest in recovering the community life behind the writings of the early church, this neglect may come to an end. At this point, however, critical study of its ritual life is only beginning.

This observation does not belittle existing New Testament scholarship on ritual as much as underscore how new and, consequently, how experimental the approach is. To date it is critics of established interpretations or scholars charting the course of social-scientific interpretation who recognize the centrality of rites to communities and propose treating them. A 1996 issue of the journal *Method and Theory in the Study of Religion* is a good case in point. In an article immediately following Ron Cameron's critique of eschatology as an interpretive category for the New Testament (Cameron 1996), Burton Mack calls for a sweeping redescription of the origins of the early church based in part – the fourth of five propositions or theses – on the central importance of ritual to all human communities (Mack 1996: 255–6). Baptism and the common meal or last supper appear four times among the thirty issues he lists as needing attention. For one of those issues, "The rationales and practices of baptism," he identifies someone outside the guild of New Testament scholars, Jonathan Z. Smith, as the scholar best suited to the task (ibid.: 249, 262). This choice speaks volumes about the state of the field and about Mack's unhappiness with it.

Mack's wish list embodies a polemic that is foreign to John Elliott's *What Is Social-Scientific Criticism?* Nevertheless, Elliott shares Mack's thinking vis-à-vis the importance of ritual. In the book's appendices he draws attention both to ritual as a subject of study (Appendix 2) and to ritual studies as an interpretive approach that falls under social-scientific criticism (Appendix 4) (Elliott 1993: 110–21, 124–6).

By comparison, the work already done on New Testament ritual falls short of the programs Mack and Elliott envision. One need only look through the pages of the *Biblical Theology Bulletin* at articles by Mark McVann, Bruce Malina, and Elliott himself to see that the study of ritual is in its pioneering phase (McVann 1988; 1991; Malina 1996; Elliott 1991). Past issues of the journal *Semeia* are also worth mentioning. *Semeia* 41, which treated performative and speech-act theory, and *Semeia* 65, which treated textuality and orality, that is, oral performance, contain articles that bear on ritual (Hancher 1988; Grimes 1988; Ward 1994).

Semeia 67 has ritual and the biblical text as its focus, but the title and content of the issue confirm how exploratory, even unformed, the approach is (Hanson 1994; McVann 1994b). "Transformations, Passages, and Processes: Ritual Approaches to Biblical Texts" not only betrays an indebtedness to Victor Turner but also shows a certain open-endedness. The editor, Mark McVann, is frank about this, likening the issue to a fragile ship venturing into turbulent, murky, and relatively uncharted waters. What unity there is, he notes, is limited: "There is, then, no unity of point of view, except the recognition that ritual is something important and that biblical scholarship will be well-served by an exploration of its meaning for biblical scholarship" (McVann 1994a: 10). *Semeia* 67, it can fairly be said, is experimental, but even more unified studies remain suggestive rather than definitive. The fourth chapter of Jerome Neyrey's *Paul, in Other Words* treats ritual in the apostle Paul's letters under the functional rubrics of making and maintaining (group) boundaries (Neyrey 1990: 75–101). That said, it is more a sketch for a larger work than an exhaustive study.

The last decade has seen more publication on the ritual life of the early church, but the degree to which these studies engage ritual critically varies considerably. The volume edited by Stanley Porter and Anthony Cross, *Dimensions of Baptism: Biblical and Theological Studies*, seems determined to avoid ritual theory altogether (Porter and Cross 2003). Little better is *From Death to Rebirth: Ritual and Conversion in Antiquity*, even though the author, Thomas Finn, is aware of social-scientific studies of conversion as a ritual process (Finn 1997: 34–5). Better grounded in theory are Dennis Smith's study of dining in the early church, *From Symposium to Eucharist: The Banquet in the Early Christian World* (Smith 2003), and Nelson Estrada's *From Followers to Leaders: The Apostles in the Ritual of Status Transformation in Acts 1–2* (Estrada 2004), along with several studies that employ ritual theory to understand Paul's theology (McLean 1996; Davis 2002; Finlan 2004). Nevertheless, these studies are short of being theoretically well-grounded.

More advanced than these studies is one in German by Christian Strecker: *Die liminale Theologie des Paulus: Zugänge zur paulinischen Theologie aus kulturanthropologischer Perspecktive* (Strecker 1999; see DeMaris 2001: 79). In it, Strecker argues persuasively that transformation, which he considers key to Paul's thought, is best illuminated by grounding it in Victor Turner's work on the transformative aspect of ritual rather than apocalyptic theology, which most New Testament scholars would do (Strecker 1999: 82). For example, he makes a strong case for interpreting the so-called Damascus event (Gal 1:11–17; Phil 3:2–21; cf. Acts 9:1–19) as an initiation process rather than a call or conversion (Strecker 1999: 83–157). Also noteworthy is a recent analysis of early church rites by Risto Uro, who draws on models from the cognitive science of religion to suggest why baptism would have enhanced the position of the early church vis-à-vis other religious communities (Uro forthcoming; cf. Whitehouse 2004; McCauley and Lawson 2002).

The studies of Strecker and Uro are comparable in their theoretical sophistication to the work of scholars in Hebrew Bible and the ancient Near East, but these are exceptions rather than the norm. Some recent works on ritual in the Hebrew Bible are theoretically as thin as their New Testament counterparts, such as Saul Olyan's *Biblical Mourning: Ritual and Social Dimensions* (Olyan 2004; DeMaris 2006) and William Gilders's *Blood Ritual in the Hebrew Bible: Meaning and Power* (Gilders 2004). Yet on the whole, the scholarship is becoming well versed in theory. For example, Jonathan

Klawans's *Purity, Sacrifice, and the Temple* goes beyond biblical scholarship on sacrifice to engage the broader academic discourse on the subject (Klawans 2005). Even better is Martin Modéus's study of a specific type of sacrifice, šělāmîm (Modéus 2005). It offers a very well-informed ritual analysis. Also fully engaged with the literature on ritual is David Wright's study of ritual in narrative (Wright 2001), Roy Gane's examination of purification offerings in Leviticus (Gane 2005), Ithamar Gruenwald's *Rituals and Ritual Theory in Ancient Israel* (Gruenwald 2003), and Gerald Klingbeil's *Bridging the Gap*, which integrates ritual studies in the study of biblical ritual texts (Klingbeil 2007). Scholars of the ancient Near East, faced with a relative wealth of legal and cultic texts that prescribe rites and narratives that describe them, understandably turned to theoretical discussions about ritual sooner than their New Testament counterparts. Jacob Milgrom's commentary on Leviticus would be the poorer without such theoretical grounding (Milgrom 1991). By comparison, New Testament scholarship has been slower to study ritual or embrace the field of ritual studies.

The embryonic character of New Testament ritual criticism may not result entirely from the field's slowness to realize the central importance of ritual. A contributing factor may be that the discipline of ritual studies itself has in many ways only recently come of age. In 1984 Ronald Grimes wrote a state-of-the-field essay for *Religious Studies Review* that reappeared one year later as the introductory essay in his book *Research in Ritual Studies* (Grimes 1984: 134–45; 1985: 1–33). The opening sentence of the essay is revealing: "Because ritual studies comprise a newly consolidated field within religious studies, a high degree of methodological and bibliographical self-consciousness is necessary" (Grimes 1985: 1). The field was scattered enough in Grimes's mind that he spoke of it in the plural, and its disciplinary home was not at all clear. Grimes classified it under religious studies, but it could also be legitimately placed under liturgical studies, performance theory, or one of the social sciences.

The next decade brought with it signs of development. Grimes's book of 1990, *Ritual Criticism: Case Studies in Its Practice, Essays on Its Theory*, refused to be definitive about the theory and definition of ritual, but in both cases he was resisting strong trends in the field (Grimes 1990: 4, 9–14). In 1992 Catherine Bell's substantial book, *Ritual Theory, Ritual Practice*, appeared, offering a thorough critique of existing theories of ritual and a new proposal which understood ritual as a kind of practice, not as a special class of action (Bell 1992). Just two years after that, a rival theory of ritual appeared. Caroline Humphrey and James Laidlaw's *The Archetypal Actions of Ritual* presented detailed criticism of Bell and other ritual theorists like Roy Rappaport while at the same time extending and applying the work of ritual theorist Frits Staal to a study of the Jain worship rite (Humphrey and Laidlaw 1994). Another indicator of ritual criticism's coming of age was the changing status of the *Journal of Ritual Studies*, which was in its infancy in the late 1980s but was a well-established, widely circulating publication by the end of the 1990s.

The last decade has seen an explosion of books on ritual, evidencing a field of study coming to maturity. Many of these studies make a case for the centrality of ritual in human societies. Michael Suk-Young Chwe's *Rational Ritual*, uses game theory to explore how ritual is crucial to the formation of common knowledge (Chwe 2001), while Randall Collins develops the notion of interaction rituals as the mechanism cultures use to establish consensus and shared beliefs (Collins 2004). Theoretically challenging works have also come from Don Handelman, who frames an anthropology of public events through the lens of ritual (Handelman 1998), and Roy Rappaport, whose *Ritual and Religion in the Making of Humanity* argues for the primacy of religion and its key component, ritual, in the evolution of humankind (Rappaport 1999). The study of ritual has become so well established in the social sciences and humanities that disciplines like philosophy have begun to realize the utility of ritual studies for their work (Schilbrack 2004). In other words, ritual studies has developed sufficiently that it is a resource for other fields.

This recent blossoming of the field coincides with currents in New Testament studies that focus attention on the communities behind the text and thus necessitate exploration of ritual. If developments within New Testament studies mean that community rites are beginning to move from the periphery to the center of scholarly attention, the field of ritual studies is well prepared to supply models for interpreting them. Simply put, there now exists a great deal more scholarship on ritual than the writings of Arnold van Gennep, Victor Turner, and Mary Douglas. The convergence of the two fields could enhance New Testament studies at a foundational level: interpretation of the early church's rites would be sharpened and expanded, and, once those rites received adequate attention, re-creation of the communities that made up the early church would become more accurate. In addition to the rich theoretical material that New Testament scholars can now tap for illuminating the early church's rites, another resource has appeared that will promote comparative analysis: an encyclopedic collection of ritual in Greek, Etruscan, and Roman religion entitled *Thesaurus cultus et rituum antiquorum* (*ThesCRA* 2004–6).

How should ritual criticism of the New Testament proceed? We are probably several years away from being ready to conduct a comprehensive critical study of rites in the New Testament, but the outline for a program of analysis is suggested by Christian Strecker's remarks about the relationship between ritual and the New Testament. He identifies six ways in which rites and text are interwoven (Strecker 1999: 78–80):

1. A text includes instructions or commands for carrying out a rite. Strecker has in mind imperatival language embedded in a ritual setting, like "Do

this in remembrance of me" (1 Cor 11:24) or texts in which the performance of a rite is ordered (Acts 10:48).

2.   A text reports the execution of a rite. Examples include Jesus's baptism (Mark 1:9–11), the Last Supper narrative (Mark 14:22–5), and the designation or initiation of early church leaders (Acts 6:1–6).

3.   A text concerns itself with the meaning, function, or implementation of a rite. For instance, the synoptic gospels are filled with debate over the significance and value of Sabbath observance, purification, and fasting (Mark 2:23–8; 7:1–23; 2:18–20). Likewise, Paul poses interpretive questions like, "The cup of blessing that we bless, is it not a sharing in the blood of Christ?" (1 Cor 10:16)

4.   A text stems directly from ritual use. Confessional and liturgical formulas have made their way into the New Testament, such as the christological hymns of Philippians 2:6–11 and Colossians 1:15–20.

5.   A text has a ritual function in and of itself, such as the greeting and benediction at the end Paul's letters (e.g., Phil 4:21–3). (Paul's letters were read aloud to the recipients, so the reader would have pronounced the greeting and benediction on Paul's behalf.)

6.   A text is connected synecdochically with a rite. What Strecker means by this is that a text may echo, allude to, or refer to a rite, even though the text may not be about ritual per se. For example, in reflecting about his efforts on behalf of the Philippians, Paul clearly alludes to ritual activity: "But even if I am being poured out as a libation over the sacrifice and the offering of your faith, I am glad and rejoice with all of you – and in the same way you also must be glad and rejoice with me" (Phil 2:17–18).

This is the start at a rite-in-text taxonomy that could be developed into a full-scale study of ritual in the New Testament, if it were coupled with a theoretical framework. It usefully reminds us that the interface between text and rite is varied and complex: a given text may describe, prescribe, or interpret a rite; the verbal elements of rite may appear directly in a text or a text may do no more than hint at or echo a rite. That said, the ritual criticism of the New Testament is early enough in its development that it may be premature to attempt something systematic and comprehensive. With that in mind, the chapters that lie ahead are meant to be introductory and exploratory rather than conclusive and exhaustive.

Investigation of the intersection between ritual and New Testament studies, beyond the first steps that have been taken, might best rely on Ronald Grimes as a guide. The book mentioned earlier, *Research in Ritual Studies*, sets forth goals for ritual studies that remain remarkably relevant two decades later, useful even for those borrowing from the field, like New Testament scholars:

Three major goals of ritual studies are (1) to mediate between normative and descriptive, as well as textual and field-observational, methods; (2) to lay the groundwork for a coherent taxonomy and theory that can account for the full range of symbolic acts . . . ; and (3) to cultivate the study of ritual in a manner that does not automatically assume it to be a dependent variable.

(Grimes 1985: 1)

Consonant with those goals, Grimes describes in a later book how one practically does ritual analysis. Two short quotations from *Ritual Criticism* indicate the best way:

"Ritual studies . . . begins with the act of describing the performance events themselves. . . ."

and (in an analysis of drama as ritual):

"At the very least a ritological approach should describe the whole event, which extends . . . to the cultural occasion and social circumstances in which [the plays] are embedded".

(Grimes 1990: 219, 90)

These quotations put in capsule form broad agreements that ritual theorists have reached. The third quotation reminds us how crucial context is for grasping the significance of a rite, a bit of common sense that New Testament scholars regularly ignore when they treat baptism and eucharist in isolation from other ancient Mediterranean bathing and dining ritual. It is worth reminding ourselves that, "A rite is never conducted in a vacuum, but in the context of other activities" (Tambiah 1985: 48). In the pages ahead, Chapters 2 and 3 give special attention to placing early church rites, specifically baptism, in as complete a circumstance as possible, based on the assumption that a rite's setting is key to determining its effect and significance.

The second quotation from Grimes offers simple advice, but it embodies an important corrective of approaches that move too quickly behind the palpable characteristics of a rite to a perceived meaning. Critiques of functionalism (Penner 1971) and symbolic analysis (Sperber 1975) along with Frits Staal's criticism of linguistic models for understanding rites (Staal 1979; 1989) have raised questions about the widespread notion that ritual is essentially a form of communication. Frank Gorman describes the objections nicely:

Such a referential, symbolic, and linguistic approach fails to take seriously that ritual is activity and embodied enactment. Staal argues that ritual is pure enactment and, as such, is "meaningless." Sperber suggests that ritual is evocative rather than communicative, while Lewis speaks of ritual as stimulative. Grimes points to ritual knowledge as preconscious, implicit, and embodied. These theorists agree that ritual enactment refers to itself and not to a message that exists apart from, outside of, or above the ritual enactment proper.

(Gorman 1994: 23–4)

To counteract the academic impulse to seek meaning *behind* the act, ritual theorist Roy Rappaport stresses what he calls the obvious aspects of ritual (Rappaport 1979: 173–221). Likewise, J. Z. Smith, in a seminal article playfully called "The Bare Facts of Ritual," based his theorizing on the observable features of bear hunting and the rites surrounding it (Smith 1980: 117–21; see critique in Ray 1991). More recently, a revealingly titled book, *Ritual in Its Own Right*, appeared (Handelman and Lindquist 2005). In it, Bruce Kapferer and Don Seeman vigorously contest the assumption that ritual is representative or meaningful (Kapferer 2005; Seeman 2005).

It remains all too common, however, for scholars to "regard rites as enactments of myths, theological ideas, or moral principles" (Grimes 1995: 66). Consequently, this book follows a twofold strategy to counter this persistent disposition. First, it avoids interpretive frameworks that assume the referential or symbolic nature of rites. Chapter 5, for example, steers clear of treating the passion narrative in the gospel of Mark under the rubric of sacrifice and offers several reasons for doing so. One could supplement them with another: sacrifice is so embedded in Christian theology that any analysis of the Marcan passion narrative as sacrifice is bound to diminish what happens in the narrative in pursuit of the "deeper meaning" of the events, i.e., their theological significance. It may surprise the reader that a book on ritual does not treat the passion narrative as a sacrifice, but doing so would ultimately divert attention from the ritual that occurs in it.

For the same reason, Chapter 5 does not engage the work of René Girard, even though it deals with a cultural mechanism that Girard has explored in great depth: scapegoating (e.g., Girard 1977; 1986). (Proponents of Girard's interpretive program have examined the gospels in detail [e.g., Hamerton-Kelly 1994]). As important as Girard's work is, it has drawn heavy fire because of its totalizing, reductionist bent: biblical sacrifice and scapegoating are fitted into a larger theory about the origins of human violence and its mitigation or sublimation (Milgrom 1991: 440–2; Klingbeil 2007: 33; Chilton 1992: 15–25, 163–72). Girard's interpretation also involves psychoanalytical claims about the nature of human desire and aggression that may hold water in the modern, industrialized world but should not be projected back on the ancient world. Theory is essential to the enterprise of ritual criticism but Girard's theorizing moves so quickly behind and beyond ritual activity that it provides little if any assistance in getting at rites in and of themselves.

This book's second strategy for combating the predilection to look past rites to their "real" meaning is to foreground rites (Chapter 1) and to assume their primacy (Part II). A portion of the first quotation from Grimes is worth repeating: a major goal of ritual studies is "to cultivate the study of ritual in a manner that does not automatically assume it to be a dependent variable" (Grimes 1985: 1). More positively put, the strategy will be to regard rites as generative and creative – as having a life of their own – as opposed to how they are often regarded: derivative and ancillary.

Ithamar Gruenwald seems to have this approach in mind when he claims that "rituals are an unmediated mode of expression" (Gruenwald 2003: 2).

How might one give ritual primacy? When Strecker elaborated on the sixth way he thought rite and text were interconnected, he considered the possibility that rites could inspire texts. He quoted Frank Gorman approvingly:

> Ritual structures and ritual processes may serve as the basis for story and narrative. Ritual may serve as the background for narrative construction and development. Indeed, ritual may generate narrative and story in such a way that ritual dynamics will be reflected within a narrative.
>
> (Gorman 1994: 23)

Could ritual do such a thing? Chapter 4 will argue that group purity or holiness and its restoration and maintenance by ritual action were foremost in Paul's mind as he addressed the crises that plagued the house churches in Corinth. In other words, there was a ritual logic at work in the framing of 1 Corinthians. Similarly, Chapter 5 examines the use of curative exit rites in the ancient Mediterranean to account for the distinctive features of Mark's passion narrative.

Rather than focusing on what ancient believers thought or experienced – the latter is the darling of some New Testament scholars (e.g., Johnson 1998) but is practically irrecoverable – this book concentrates on what has been constitutive of every human community: ritual. It is an experiment in making it foundational, by foregrounding it and using it as the avenue for approaching the communities of the early church. Even the book's basic structure follows the lead of ritual. Its specific subject is boundary-crossing rites, which fall into the binary of entry and exit. This pair provides the book's two subdivisions.

Is there any alternative to centering on ritual? If the aim is to get closer to the life of the early church, the choice is clear: not text, not belief, not experience, but ritual.

* * *

We pine and yearn for revelation,
whose fire burns in the New Testament
with dignity and beauty not elsewhere matched.
I feel impelled to open the text on which all rests
and, deeply moved, properly translate
the sacred Greek original
into my own dear native tongue.

It is written, "In the beginning was the *Word*."
How soon I'm stopped! Who'll help me to go on?
I cannot concede that *words* have such high worth

and must, if properly inspired,
translate the term some other way.
It is written: "In the beginning was the *Mind*."
Reflect with care upon this first line,
and do not let your pen be hasty!
Can it be *mind* that makes all operate?
I'd better write: "In the beginning was the *Power*!"
Yet, even as I write this down,
something warns me not to keep it.
My spirit prompts me, now I see a solution
and boldly write: "In the beginning was the *Act*."
    (Goethe, *Faust I*: 1217–37; Atkins 1984: 33)

Part I

Entry Rites

For the last thirty-five years, scholars have directed their attention to the social context of the New Testament in order to sharpen their understanding of the text itself. This interest in finding the *Sitz im Leben*, setting in life, of the New Testament has led scholars to focus more and more on the social features of early Christian communities, and less and less on their theologies or beliefs. This new direction in New Testament studies has fostered interest beyond scholarly circles, for it addresses a question of general import: What was life like among the first Christians?

There are many ways to situate the New Testament documents in their social context and to determine the contours of the early Christian communities that produced them. Close attention to Roman society, particularly in the eastern Mediterranean, has done much to contextualize the text. Likewise, use of the social sciences, especially anthropological studies of Mediterranean culture and cross-cultural studies of advanced agrarian societies, has helped scholars recreate the world in which the church emerged.

Still, the important interpretive task of locating the New Testament in its culture is far from complete. Perhaps the largest and most striking deficiency in contemporary New Testament studies is this: for a field keen on recovering what early Christian communities were like, it has left their ritual life largely unexplored. Studies of baptism and eucharist do exist, but they show limited awareness of the larger ritual world in which the early church found itself. Also, such studies make little or no use of ritual theory. Nor do they make any use of the ancient Mediterranean's archaeological record, a vast source of information about life in that world.

The best remedy to New Testament studies' neglect of ritual is a book that makes ritual its focal point. This study starts from the premise that ritual was central to, and definitive for, early Christian life (as it is for all social orders), and it explores the New Testament through a ritual lens. By grounding the exploration in ritual theory, Greco-Roman ritual life, and the material record of the ancient Mediterranean, it seeks to discover new and insightful perspectives on early Christian communities and their cultural environment. In doing justice to a salient but slighted aspect of community life, it outlines an alternative approach to the New Testament, one that reveals what the lives of the first Christians were actually like.

Situating the New Testament in the ritual world of the ancient Mediterranean could be accomplished in many ways. Since we are after a better understanding of early Christianity and because boundaries are key to defining both individuals and groups, boundaries and the rites that attend them are as good a starting place as any. In the case of individuals, rites of boundary-crossing mark the various stages of social life, whether one is moving from childhood to adulthood, from single to married life, from adulthood to old age, or from life to death. In the case of human communities, boundary-crossing rites are crucial markers of group identity, for they control who is in and who is out and how one gets in and out. They define a community's character and profile. Hence, this study will focus on boundary-crossing and the rites that attended it in the early church.

Boundary-crossing involves either movement into a group or out of it, and both deserve attention. This study falls into two parts, therefore, beginning with entry rites and focusing on a rite of central importance to the early church: baptism. Chapter 1 foregrounds baptism, and in doing so reveals the immense gap between the rite and its depiction in the New Testament. At the same time, Chapter 1 is a non-technical introduction to ritual theory. It explores how scholars, primarily anthropologists, have characterized ritual with a view to filling out the picture of baptism, whose portrait is so incomplete in the New Testament.

As Chapter 1 will show, ritual theorists agree that the circumstances around a rite's performance are crucial to determining the rite's effect and significance. Guided by that insight, Chapters 2 and 3 undertake what anthropologist Clifford Geertz would call a thick description of baptism in a specific location, namely, ancient Corinth. Chapter 2 will look at the many ways that water was used in Roman Corinth as a way of contextualizing its use by the Corinthian Christians for boundary-crossing. As the archaeology of Corinth attests, public baths, fountains, and other water facilities were central to Roman culture, and to understand baptism we need to set it against this backdrop.

Chapter 3 continues the microscopic situating of baptism by examining a peculiarly Corinthian practice, namely, baptism on behalf of the dead. It will consider the Greco-Roman ritual world in general and then concentrate on the cultural dynamics of Roman Corinth, with the goal of accounting for why the Christian community extended the rite of baptism to its dead.

*   *   *

These introductory remarks have used the term Christian freely, but the reader will find it seldom used elsewhere in the book. Why is this? Most scholars of ancient Mediterranean religion have come to the conclusion that

Christianity, along with its sister religion, Judaism, were only forming in the first and second centuries. So to label first-century phenomena Christian or Jewish is historically inaccurate. Unfortunately, alternative terminology is not completely satisfactory. Many scholars refer to early followers of Jesus as the Jesus movement, but some would restrict that label to Jesus groups in Palestine and Syria. Some scholars prefer the word Judean to Jew, but the former could be either an ethnic or geographical designation, so it is not a perfect substitute. With hesitation, this study sticks with the terms Jew and Jewish.

In the case of Corinth, it is probably best to avoid talking about a Jesus movement on Greek soil. I have also avoided referring to Christians at Corinth, and have used the terms early church or Corinthian believers instead. The former is a convenient designation but it could be misunderstood. It is best to picture a loose affiliation of house churches or assemblies rather than a unified, hierarchical institution, which did not emerge until the third and fourth centuries.

1   Perilous Passage

In the New Testament, it is fair to say, Baptism is assumed as the way of entry into the Christian Church. It is taken as a matter of course in (to cite only some of the passages) Acts 2:38, 41; 8:13, 16, 36; 9:18; 10:47; 19:3; Rom. 6:3; I Cor. 6:11 (apparently), 12:13; Gal. 3:27; Eph. 4:5; Col. 2:12; Tit. 3:5; Heb. 6:2 (perhaps), 4 (probably); I Pet. 3:21. And although Matt. 28:19 is the only New Testament reference to an actual command by Christ to perform it, and although the context of this passage and its trinitarian formula raise serious doubts about its authenticity as a literal *verbum Domini* [word of the Lord], yet, even without it, there is little doubt as to the universality of the practice in the Christian Church. In some of the passages just adduced, it is simply assumed that Christians, as such, must have been baptized; and the same is at least implied in others.

(Moule 1961: 47)

Even though C. F. D. Moule made these comments almost fifty years ago, most New Testament scholars today would still agree with him about the universality and self-evident importance of baptism in the early church. Accordingly, two generations later we find the very same perspective expressed in Lars Hartman's important study of baptism, *'Into the Name of the Lord Jesus': Baptism in the Early Church*. As the introduction begins, he observes

Nowhere in the New Testament do we find a text to which could be assigned the title 'On baptism' or the like. Certainly baptism is mentioned occasionally, and in a few cases the author dwells on it for a while. But baptism is taken for granted and apparently writers need not instruct their readers about it. This circumstance, however, enables our authors to adduce baptism, or, rather, ideas concerning its meaning, when they discuss other matters.

(Hartman 1997: 3)

Decades apart, both Moule and Hartman speak of how widely acknowledged and firmly established the rite must have been in order to leave the impression it did on the New Testament.

Yet this longstanding consensus belies the thin evidence and fragile argument it rests on. The one book in the New Testament where baptism appears routinely as the means of entry into the believing community, the Acts of the Apostles, is regarded by most scholars as a highly selective and idealized portrait of the early church, written long after the events it narrates. In other words, few scholars think Acts gives us a historically accurate picture of early church life. If so, baptism's regular appearance in Acts may reveal how one writer pictured early church life but not how it actually was. As for the rest of the New Testament, if baptism really was as universal as Moule, Hartman, and many others claim (e.g., Horrell 1996: 82), references to baptism are surprisingly few. Many New Testament letters do not mention or allude to it at all, and the gospels, if references to John the baptizer's activity are set aside, refer to it sparingly. Hartman seems to concede this very point, even as he claims how taken for granted baptism was.

How does one infer baptism's universality from textual scarcity – its unquestioned acceptance and self-evident centrality despite the New Testament's relative silence about it? While meager attestation could reasonably be taken to indicate the unimportance of a rite, Moule and others read that scarcity as evidence for a rite so widely accepted and well defined that it required neither description nor justification, hence little attention. Crucial to this line of argument is that baptism appears as a given when it is mentioned. In the case of Acts, it appears without fanfare at regular intervals in the narrative, always at points when individuals, families, or groups join the ranks of believers.

The taken-for-granted status of baptism is also clear in the apostle Paul's First Letter to the Corinthians, at least in one passage. When faced with a faith community fragmenting itself in Corinth, he resorts to the analogy of a single body composed of many different parts to argue for unity in the midst of diversity. Then, as he elaborates on the analogy, he reminds his readers of their common experience when they entered the circle of believers:

> For just as the body is one and has many members, and all the members of the body, though many, are one body, so it is with Christ. For in the one Spirit we were all baptized into one body – Jews or Greeks, slaves or free – and we were all made to drink of one Spirit.
>
> (1 Cor 12:12–13)

Paul's claim in these verses that all Christians have undergone baptism and his introduction of it to argue for unity is instructive. Paul does not argue *for* baptism but *from* it. That is, he depends on it as a premise from which to address a problem current among the recipients of his letter.

Baptism was so well established early on, asserts the consensus position, that no one felt obliged to describe the rite or defend its existence. Its practice was so settled and so widely acknowledged that when New Testament writers did refer to it, it served as an incontrovertible basis for addressing disputes. This two-step argument, in the final analysis, asks us to accept baptism's special prominence and permanence by finding it between the lines of the New Testament: baptism enjoyed an unquestioned importance in the early church that the New Testament reveals only at points, and even then usually obliquely.

This interpretation, resting as it does on slim rather than ample evidence, needs the glimpses of baptism we do get to be of a rite so well established that it is beyond controversy. Yet this is hardly the case. In 1 Corinthians, the letter just quoted, baptism also finds itself to be the cause of controversy, not a basis for solving it. Such is the case in the opening verses of that letter, where Paul implies that the conflicting loyalties that threaten group unity stem in part from who baptized whom (1:10–13). Paul's response to the situation is noteworthy:

> I thank God that I baptized none of you except Crispus and Gaius, so that no one can say that you were baptized in my name. (I did baptize also the household of Stephanas; beyond that, I do not know whether I baptized anyone else.)
>
> (1 Cor 1:14–16)

Why has Paul forgotten his hand in baptizing Corinthians? Explanations have typically assumed that baptism was a permanent fixture one could easily overlook. One commentator notes, "It was not a matter that needed close attention on Paul's part" (Barrett 1968: 48). Another calls Paul's faulty recollection an expression of his "relative indifference to baptisms in Corinth" (Orr and Walther 1976: 151). But do we really have here a nonchalance about baptism that reflects how casually it was regarded and administered?

Paul's forgetfulness has another, more obvious explanation. His imprecise memory betrays uneasiness about his involvement in baptism and his unhappiness that the rite has contributed to divisiveness among the Corinthian house churches and within them (1:10–13). Paul's fogginess allows him to disentangle himself from the controversy to some degree. A few verses later, in 1:17, it becomes abundantly clear that he is trying to distance himself from baptism altogether when he makes the surprising claim – unexpected from the lips of an apostle and missionary – that he was sent to proclaim but not to baptize. This distancing reappears in chapter 3 in the division of labor that Paul insists originated with the Lord (3:5–6): "I planted, Apollos watered." This metaphor for the founding of the Corinthian community allows Paul not only to separate himself from any part in "watering," i.e., baptizing, but also to assert priority in the mission to Corinth. More to the point, Paul certainly does not take baptism for granted in the opening chapters of 1 Corinthians, as he seems to do in chapter 12.

Other passages from the New Testament also point to a rite that may have attracted controversy as readily as settling it. Some are puzzling, such as the disclaimer in the gospel of John that pointedly distances Jesus from practicing baptism (4:2) even though we are told earlier in the text that he did (3:22). This is akin to Paul's claim not to have baptized followed by several exceptions. Likewise, just as Paul sought to distance himself from the act of baptism, the narrative of Acts may do the same for another important church leader, Peter. Chapter 10 relates the entry of Gentiles into the early church, a story in which Peter is central. Peter calls for baptism to mark entry to the circle of believers, but does not himself perform the rite: "Then Peter said, 'Can anyone withhold the water for baptizing these people who have received the Holy Spirit just as we have?' So he ordered them to be baptized in the name of Jesus Christ" (Acts 10:46b–48a). Is there some reason why it was best for Peter not to have administered the water?

There are more passages to consider. If we juxtapose two of the references to baptism from the epigraph that begins this chapter, Ephesians 4:5 and Hebrews 6:2, we might conclude that the former's insistence on single baptism – "There is one body and one Spirit, . . . one Lord, one faith, one baptism, one God and Father of all" (4:4–6) – was not simply part of a rhetorical flourish in support of church unity but also a polemic against plural baptism. For Hebrews's mention of instruction about *baptisms* – not the typical Greek term for baptism (Cross 2003: 163–86) – raises the possibility that some circles in the early church practiced multiple baptisms or recognized several types. Hints of such plurality come from Acts. As historically unreliable as it can be, Acts does report some believers knowing and practicing the baptism of John the Baptist (18:25; 19:3), which seems historically plausible. The situation is quickly and smoothly resolved in the narrative – with a second baptism in the latter instance – so we gain no access to the depth of discord that may have existed over differing baptismal practices and understandings in the early church. Nevertheless, the New Testament provides enough hints of actual or potential conflict so that the consensus view of baptism can be seen for what it is: a misleading characterization. What may have been true in later centuries, that baptism was universal and uncontroversial, was not the case in the church's opening decades. Just as Acts smoothes over conflict surrounding baptism, as it does with many other early church crises, the claim (or assumption) that baptism was taken for granted obscures very real conflicts over baptism.

Another common way of characterizing baptism has been to use references to it in the New Testament to determine what role it played in the groups making up the early church. This approach has produced a consensus of its own, one sounded steadily and with growing frequency, as scholars pay increasing attention to the social context of New Testament literature and the social realities of the early church. With a view to how baptism functioned socially, a chorus of scholars has described baptism as a rite of initiation into the movement (Hunter 1961: 66; Beasley-Murray

1962: passim; Fitzmyer 1967: 65; Fuller 1976; Wedderburn 1987: 357; Dunn 1990: 159; Carlson 1993: 256–7; Horrell 1996: 82). This classification has become so commonplace that scholars typically state it without argument, let alone giving an explanation or definition of what a rite of initiation is. Much like the claim about the baptism's universality, its initiatory function is considered obvious and taken as a matter of fact.

Yet on the rare occasion when a scholar makes a case for baptism as a rite of initiation, the conclusion is far from assured. For example, in *The First Urban Christians: The Social World of the Apostle Paul*, at the end of a section entitled "Baptism: Ritual of Initiation," Wayne Meeks fits language about baptism from the Pauline letters into a ritual model originating with Arnold van Gennep and developed by Victor Turner (Meeks 1983: 150–7). Van Gennep coined the term rite of passage (French: *rite de passage*) to describe rites marking the transition of individuals between stages of life. Barbara Myerhoff offers an illustrative definition:

> Rites of passage are a category of rituals that mark the passages of an individual through the life cycle, from one stage to another over time, from one role or social position to another, integrating the human and cultural experiences with biological destiny: birth, reproduction, and death. These ceremonies make the basic distinctions observed in all groups, between young and old, male and female, living and dead.
>
> (Myerhoff 1982: 109)

Such rites have three elements or steps, corresponding to an individual's departure from an existing status, movement between statuses or social categories, and entry into a new status or phase of existence (Van Gennep 1960: 10–11, passim).

Meeks gathered information about baptism gleaned from the Pauline letters and found it fitted this threefold scheme rather well (Meeks 1983: 157). When Paul wrote about baptism in terms of joining in the death and burial of Christ or as a crucifixion of the old self, Meeks found language of the initiates' separation or departure from their former lives (Rom 6:3–4, 6). When Colossians talks of the believer having stripped off the old self and having put on a new self, Meeks detected the movement between statuses and entry into a new status that baptism, as a rite of passage, enabled the believer to make (Col 3:9–10). Thus, the rite of passage model allowed Meeks to integrate the limited data on baptism in the New Testament into a coherent and recognizable ritual pattern and to pinpoint how baptism functioned in the communities of the early church.

The correspondence between Van Gennep's rite-of-passage model and what the Pauline letters say about baptism is not as unambiguous as it might seem, however. Meeks conceded that language for the new status the believer assumed in the final stage of initiation – the new self, a child, an existence beyond ethnicity, gender, or social status (Gal 3:26–8; Col 3:10–11) – most aptly applied to those in the second phase of the rite, in the transitional or liminal stage. There, between the old and new status, one is relatively status-*less*, much like a newborn. To account for this discrepancy, Meeks noted that the passage between life stages *within* a social order was different from a movement *between* social orders, that is, withdrawal from larger society to join the early church. He introduced Victor Turner's work on marginal groups in complex societies, because such groups typically retain transitional or liminal language for their self-description as a way of expressing their ongoing lack of integration in mainstream culture (Turner 1969: 94–130). The early church's marginal status in Greco-Roman society, according to Meeks, explained why baptism departed from a typical rite of passage: liminal language was appropriate for characterizing the newly baptized who did not reenter the established social order but rather entered a marginal, hence ambiguous, status at its edge.

Meeks was quite right to point out how social setting might affect what a rite of passage accomplishes, but his modification of the rite also raises questions about what kind of initiation baptism was and whether it is best understood as a rite of passage at all. First, it is doubtful whether ancient Roman society qualifies as the kind of complex society Turner had in mind when he talked about groups whose identity remains marginal or liminal over time. He mentioned beatniks and hippies in twentieth-century American society, not ancient Christians in Roman society, as examples of more-or-less permanently liminal movements.

Second, Pauline language of participation in Christ's dying and rising does not refer exclusively and unambiguously to the baptismal rite of initiation. For we find Paul characterizing his life in terms of the death and resurrection of Christ at several points without clear reference to baptism (2 Cor 4:10–11; Gal 2:19–20; Phil 3:10–11; see Dunn 1990: 159). Is dying–rising language best understood sequentially, as steps in the initiation process, or existentially, as an expression of the believer's post-baptismal life in Christ? Ambiguity reigns in the very passages Meeks relies on to describe baptism as a rite of passage, which allude to baptism (metaphorically?) but use dying and rising language primarily to characterize the post-baptismal life of the believer (Rom 6:1–14; Col 2:10–12; 3:1–17). A. J. M. Wedderburn's detailed study of baptism and resurrection identified two ways of understanding Paul's death and resurrection language along with the related pairing of dying and living: as "Life through Death" and as "Life in Death" (Wedderburn 1987: 381–90; see also Tannehill 1967). The latter serves as metaphor for the ongoing existence of the believer: "We are treated as impostors, and yet are true; as unknown, and yet are well known; as dying, and see – we are alive" (2 Cor 6:8–9). If so, that is, if dying and death described life after initiation, how accurate is it to characterize baptism as a rite that takes an initiate through and past death into life?

The most devastating blow against classifying baptism as a rite of passage comes from one of the anthropologists Meeks depended on for his analysis: Victor Turner. When Victor and Edith Turner looked for instances of liminality – that transitional state midway through a rite of passage – outside the tribal cultures they had studied, they found little in what they termed historical and salvation religions. Specifically, when they looked at the various rites of the Roman Catholic tradition, including baptism, "though it was possible to discern somewhat truncated liminal phases, we found nothing that replicated the scale and complexity in the major initiation rituals of tribal societies with which we were familiar" (Turner and Turner 1978: 3–4). So they settled on Christian pilgrimage as the phenomenon best matching a rite of passage, and they made it the subject of a detailed study. If the Turners did not find a full-fledged rite of passage in the baptism of the Roman Catholic church, could the model be applicable to baptism in the first century, in its formative stages? New Testament scholars are beginning to answer that question negatively: "The Christian sacrament of baptism, even where it involves total immersion, is clearly no more than a token gesture when placed beside the lengthy 'rites of passage' practiced in other societies" (Ashton 2000: 135).

This critique of understanding baptism as an initiation or rite of passage is not meant to suggest that such an approach has no utility. In fact, a recent study by Christian Strecker proves quite the opposite. Strecker fruitfully employs Turner's work on liminality to illuminate several key features of Paul's theology (Strecker 1999). Nevertheless, classifying baptism in this way can no longer be made without strong supporting argument, which New Testament scholars have rarely offered.

The initiation or rite of passage interpretive paradigm has, in other words, become problematic, a situation biblical scholars would do well to recognize. Scholarly discourse in allied fields, such as classics, has been moving toward this conclusion (see Dodd and Faraone 2003). In light of this, while this book is not averse to considering baptism as a rite of passage, it has opted to explore baptism and other rites in the early church (in Part II) as boundary-crossing rites or, more broadly and simply, as ritual.

So much for the current state of scholarship on baptism. On the one hand, the views that typify scholarly discourse are probably more accurate than older views that resulted from fitting baptism into a theological framework. One standard way to study baptism has been as a sacrament (Bultmann 1951–5: 133–52), and though this approach is patently anachronistic, it still has its advocates (Dunn 1990: xxv). On the other hand, current views may suffer from anachronism, too. To say that baptism was universal and taken for granted in the New Testament, for instance, may amount to projecting a second- or third- or twenty-first-century view back to the first.

Still, if we deem such characterizations – baptism as universal, as taken for granted, as an initiation mimicking a rite of passage – as misleading or inadequate, the considerations leading to such claims may be instructive. For any study of baptism, or any other rite practiced in the early church, faces a scarcity of data. The New Testament rarely speaks directly about ritual practice and reveals only slightly more indirectly, which necessitates a strategy for getting at those rites. Reading between the lines, whatever form that might take, is certainly necessary. To recover the early church's ritual life, an interpretive model will be essential for teasing out a maximum of information from the data we have. Hence, Meeks's move to introduce the rite of passage model to his discussion of baptism, despite the problems with it, was a step in the right direction. His analysis serves as a reminder that we must exercise caution in the approach we take and the model or models we use.

If the reigning characterizations of baptism are off target, is there a better, more accurate way of describing baptism, and, indeed, of gaining access to the whole ritual of life of the early church? Before we claim how common baptism was, before we classify it as a particular kind of ritual, the best course would be to look at baptism for what it most obviously was, a rite or ritual, and, as we do, to inform our examination by considering the nature or character of rites or ritual in general. This may seem to be so obvious and simple a step as to be unnecessary, yet to say that baptism is a kind of ritual and define what that means has, surprisingly, gone undone by the field. A 1996 sociological study of the Corinthian correspondence and community by David Horrell is a case in point. He begins an eight-page treatment of Corinthian ritual with a short paragraph defining ritual, in which he cites a single anthropologist as reference. Is it any wonder that the definition falls short? He claims that "Ritual . . . is an activity in which religious faith is enacted," and that "Rituals . . . express and embody the symbols and stories central to a religion" (Horrell 1996: 80). Yet many rituals make no reference to religion at all, so the definition is too narrow. Ritual theorists would also be unhappy with the derivative status Horrell assigns ritual: that faith, sacred symbol, and sacred story inform or dictate what ritual is about. Ritual is not another word for language, however, contrary to what Horrell's second statement suggests. If we busy ourselves looking for the idea or narrative supposedly behind the rite, we may well miss the rite itself.

Missing from all existing studies of baptism, and of the early church's ritual in general, is attention to the basic features of ritual, which derive from the observation of ritual activities at many times and in many places. Key among them is the general agreement among ritual theorists that rites, especially those marking transition, occur at crisis points in the life of a group or individual. Unfortunately, this agreement sometimes comes to expression in off-putting jargon. In treating ritual formation, for instance, Ronald Grimes offers this statement: "Ritualizing transpires as animated persons enact formative gestures in the face of receptivity during crucial times in founded places" (Grimes 1982: 541). Later in the same study he clarifies what he means by crucial times: "One example of ritual time is associated with transitions – changes in social status, seasonal transitions, and crisis moments in histories and life cycles" (Grimes 1982: 550). Though somewhat obscure, behind this abstract language lie years of field study and potentially useful observations.

One does not have to look too hard to see that society hedges social change, transition, or crisis – birth, coming of age, marriage, retirement, and death – with all manner of rites (Turner 1967: 93–111; Douglas 1966: 94–7; Van Gennep 1960: passim). As Victor Turner notes in the opening of what is perhaps his most significant study of rites, *The Ritual Process*

> As we became increasingly a part of the [Ndembu] village scene, we discovered that very often decisions to perform ritual were connected with crises in the social life of villages. . . . Here I merely indicate that among the Ndembu there is a close connection between social conflict and ritual at the levels of village and "vicinage" (a term I use for discrete clusters of villages), and that a multiplicity of conflict situations is correlated with a high frequency of ritual performance.
>
> (Turner 1969: 10)

Many ritual theorists, including Turner, would define the relationship between social crises and rites in terms of cause and effect. Crises prompt or generate or attract rites, and those rites address, solve, or negotiate crises (Myerhoff 1982: 113, 129; Mead 1973: 89–91; Crocker 1973: 49; Burkert 1996: 34–7). Edmund Leach explains this relationship in terms of boundaries and boundary-crossing. Whether individuals leave or enter a group or shed an old social status or assume a new one, they are crossing or breaking boundaries that constitute the social order. In doing so, they challenge that order and even threaten it with dissolution. Rites arise to facilitate boundary-crossing and thus to reduce the threat such crossing poses the social order (Leach 1976: 34). Victor Turner uses a different framework but characterizes rites the same way. When rules, norms, customs, or laws are breached, society typically resorts to rites to limit the disruption and restore social equilibrium. Hence they are what Turner calls adjustive or redressive social mechanisms (Turner 1980: 151–2).

An instructive example of the relationship between social crisis and rite comes from a study of farm families and towns in the contemporary American midwest. Because land and ownership of it are pivotal to family and community relations, when transfer of land departs from its normal course, the resulting crisis triggers a ritual response. In the conclusion of Sonya Salamon's book, *Prairie Patrimony*, she narrates in some detail the circumstances surrounding a public auction of land: "When cultural guidelines for land transfer break down – no successor is ready, an owner does not write a will, heirs are too numerous or cannot agree on property division – a land auction often results" (Salamon 1992: 249).

As Salamon notes, the auction gives form and expression to the negotiation the community is engaged in to resolve the crisis:

Once the harvest is over, one is likely to see a land-auction notice in any Sunday newspaper in the rural Midwest. The date is announced, the seller's terms are listed, and a reason for the sale is described, such as a retirement or the settlement of an estate. The public announcement only formalizes ongoing community discussions organized by cultural notions about appropriate actions: why the family gave up land, who is expected to buy, what price the land should go for, and how the sale might change the existing social order.

(Salamon 1992: 249–50)

Change in ownership introduces profound uncertainty to the community. It brings a change in status for owner and buyer and thus means the breaking or rearranging of established social boundaries:

An auction is the ultimate gamble, different from typical farm management gambles with weather or markets because it is played out in public by normally restrained and private people. The hope of being able to bid on land may have cost a family years of delayed gratification, yet all is won or lost in only a few moments. This state of standing on the threshold of change is central to the ritual enactment, for it clashes with the routines of daily life; yet it also emphasizes the status quo, which returns when the auction concludes.

(Salamon 1992: 250)

A great deal of anxiety attends the auction for it carries out the change in land ownership that will in turn affect the social order. Yet it also reduces anxiety by allowing change to happen in a way that preserves and affirms the basic community structure:

Enormous tension is evident at an auction. A skillful auctioneer – an outsider, but frequently a community favorite – can knowledgeably manipulate the audience with his banter ("I see many of the fine folks from Heartland are here today to see the sale of this property that was once a showplace farm," one said, looking around the circle of assembled people). As the suspense builds during the competition, the auctioneer jokes to relieve the tension. If bids go higher than expected, he calls a recess to allow the participants to consult with their family or banker. Yet, despite the threat that chaos would ensue if the community social hierarchy were upended, order is typically maintained.

(Salamon 1992: 251)

Even though this example comes from modern rural America, it is useful for understanding ancient Mediterranean rites. First, it suggests when and why rites come into being; it illustrates what kind of crisis generates or attracts rites and how the latter defuse the former. Second, an auction directs our attention to an aspect of rites that is easily overlooked: the ripple effect of ritual activity. One may debate about how much a modern auction is like or unlike ancient baptism; a rite that moves property from one family to another differs from the entry of someone into the early church, even though both carry out a kind of transfer. Yet an auction alerts us to the community-wide repercussions of all rites, including baptism. For rites, past or present, affect not only the subject of the rite but also a broad web of social relations in which the subject is embedded.

It is easy to miss this aspect of baptism in the ancient church because the New Testament omits it. As frequently as Acts reports the occurrence of baptism in its narrative, it provides little detail. The typical account is terribly emaciated, such as the encounter narrated in chapter 8 between the evangelist Philip and a eunuch, a court official of the Ethiopian queen Candace:

> Then Philip began to speak, and . . . he proclaimed to him the good news about Jesus. As they were going along the road, they came to some water; and the eunuch said, "Look, here is water! What is to prevent me from being baptized?" He commanded the chariot to stop, and both of them, Philip and the eunuch, went down into the water, and Philip baptized him. When they came up out of the water, the Spirit of the Lord snatched Philip away; the eunuch saw him no more, and went his way rejoicing.
>
> (Acts 8:35–9)

Besides the historical problems with this account, its very terseness raises questions about its completeness and accuracy. For if baptism marked the entry of a person or persons into the community of believers – no one would deny this basic function – one wonders why this essential feature goes missing in chapter 8 and elsewhere in Acts. The baptismal scene concludes here with Philip and the eunuch going their separate ways, an outcome that ignores, even contradicts, what a rite of entry accomplishes.

As a public auction underscores, rites are not simply two-party transactions, between buyer and seller, between baptizer and baptizand. Property transfer affects the status of the parties immediately involved, which in turn brings change to the whole network of social relations in which those parties are embedded. An auction draws the attention of the whole community, and the whole is caught up in the social change the auction signals. Likewise, baptism reached beyond the one who underwent the rite and the one who administered it; it affected the baptizand's existing social relations and those of the house church the baptizand joined, to say nothing of the altogether new social relations it engendered. The very nature of rites, that they normally take place in communal or public settings and not privately, points to their far-reaching social impact.

How did this reconfiguration of social relations find expression in the early church? Believers frequently invoked the language of family to describe social relations within the house church, so baptism, which brought new members into the group, was in effect a mechanism for crossing the domestic threshold and establishing kinship bonds. The New Testament is replete with the language of sibling relation; addressing a fellow believer as brother or sister was a standard form of greeting. Likewise, the early church understood itself to be a divine household, in which believers were the children of father God. That baptism played a part in this kinship making is manifestly clear in Paul's letter to the Galatians. In chapters 3 and 4, both before and after verses that make obvious reference to baptism (3:27–8), he describes believers as becoming children of God (3:26) and their adoption as God's children (4:6–7).

It is all the more surprising, then, that New Testament baptismal scenes are so brief and simple. For kinship-making, even the fictive sort baptism brought about, was no easy matter. It is complicated enough in modern western societies where, if we take marriage as an example, it involves two individuals forming a new family. Yet it is more complicated in traditional societies, certainly so in the first-century Mediterranean world, where family identity outweighed individual identity. In this case marriage (and the wedding that enacted it) entailed a carefully negotiated alliance between the families of the groom and bride. With regard to the latter, since females were typically under the control of a male head of household, a wedding required removing the bride from her birth household and placing her in the groom's household. Kinship-making, therefore, could require kinship-breaking, too.

If baptism enacted entry into the early church, it coincided with the profound social change that believers underwent in what amounted to joining a new family. By the same token, the household the new believer entered also faced change. Would the believer successfully cut or loosen ties with existing family relations? Gender, age, status, and a host of other factors determined the answer to that question in any given situation, but one must assume that entering the early church sometimes meant the social death of a believer vis-à-vis existing kin relationships. Jesus's sayings in this regard are quite blunt:

> "Whoever comes to me and does not hate father and mother, wife and children, brothers and sisters, yes, and even life itself, cannot be my disciple."
>
> (Luke 14:26)

> Jesus said, "Truly I tell you, there is no one who has left house or brothers or sisters or mother or father or children or fields, for my sake and for the sake of the good news, who will not receive a hundredfold . . ."
>
> (Mark 10:29–30)

Where would the believer fit in the new family? The newly baptized also disrupted the existing fictive kinship network in their new household. As welcome as they might be, their new association with the brothers and sisters or the children of God necessitated the social reordering of that household.

If the New Testament is relatively silent about the complications that attended joining the early church, other ancient Mediterranean sources are more forthcoming about the difficulties inherent in entering a religious community. Two cases are particularly worth noting because the authors, like their New Testament counterparts, resorted to kinship language to describe what religious affiliation entails. Specifically, in both marriage serves as an analogue to conversion.

The first account, *Joseph and Aseneth*, is a Hellenistic romance elaborating on the brief notice in Genesis that pharaoh gave the Israelite Joseph the daughter of an Egyptian priest for his wife (Gen 41:45). Authorship and date of composition are disputed, but most scholars consider it a Jewish text roughly contemporary with the New Testament (see Chesnutt 1995; Kraemer 1998; Humphrey 2000). The book focuses on Aseneth's conversion to the Israelite religion, which is thoroughly intertwined with her marriage to Joseph. It runs longer than the gospel of Mark, takes many turns, and has its share of crises. With marriage and conversion set side by side, the author explores Aseneth's adoption of Joseph's faith as a making and unmaking of familial bonds. Hence, as the prospect of marriage and conversion emerge in the story, Aseneth's father refers to the pair as sister and brother (7:7–8). Later, as Aseneth contemplates departure from her parents' gods, she realizes she will no longer be their daughter (11:5; 12:12). In fact, such a departure causes her family to disown her (11:5). Accordingly, she laments that her religious reaffiliation makes her an orphan (11:16; 12:5). Her only recourse is to embrace God, who becomes a surrogate parent. Hence, Aseneth's lengthy prayer to God includes this appeal: "Have mercy upon me, Lord, and guard me, a virgin (who is) abandoned and an orphan, because you, Lord, are a sweet and good and gentle father" (12:14; Burchard 1985: 222).

The second account from antiquity, *The Metamorphoses*, or more commonly, *The Golden Ass*, tells the story of a young man transformed into a donkey by magic and witchcraft and rescued by the Egyptian goddess Isis, a very popular deity at the time the book was composed, the late second century. Very much like Aseneth, the protagonist Lucius faces no little ordeal in joining the Isis cult; he undergoes a lengthy, costly, and rigorous initiation. In the course of the initiation, the priest that leads him through it becomes a father to him (11:25).

Kinship-making and -breaking figure prominently in the story told midway through *The Golden Ass*, the tale of Psyche and Cupid, which clearly foreshadows Lucius's arduous entry into the Isis cult (4:28–6:24). In this story within the story, the mortal Psyche offends the goddess Venus because of her incredible beauty, and Venus's son, Cupid, sent by Venus to plague Psyche, falls in love with her instead. They marry at the end of the tale, and Psyche joins the divine family, but not without much trial and tribulation, brought on both by her mortal family and prospective divine family. The tale nicely anticipates Lucius's affiliation with the divine household of Isis at the book's conclusion, and it reminds us how seriously kinship relations could be disrupted by shifting one's religious affiliation.

Kinship-breaking and -making constitutes a social crisis that fosters the development of rites around it. Like other rites, baptism arose in response to crisis, in this case to facilitate an alteration in kin relations and thus lessen the disruptive impact of that shift on the social relations involved. The evident effectiveness of baptism as opposed to other rites in settling the kinship crisis accounts for baptism's importance and preeminence in the early church. (If there were other competing or complementary entry rites, they faded or were incorporated in baptism.) In other words, a rite that succeeds at restoring social equilibrium becomes a regular, maybe even standard, part of community life. If we pressed Moule, Hartman, and others, they would probably agree that this is what they meant to say when they described baptism as universal and taken for granted.

Still, this characterization must be set aside because of how misleading it is. Baptism, like countless other rites, was born amidst crisis as a response to it; the very existence of the baptismal rite presupposes a social crisis that summoned forth ritual activity. Baptism may have eased and sped the baptizand's crossing of the group's boundary and dampened the flames of social disruption sparked by that entry, but social crisis was present nevertheless and probably never completely extinguished. Moreover, every time an individual sought to enter the early church, social crisis rose anew. And however successful baptism was at negotiating a community through that crisis, the fact remains that social disruption and baptism went hand in hand.

Other basic features of ritual contribute to making it highly unlikely that baptism could ever have been taken for granted by the early church. Ritual is a complicated rather than simple phenomenon (Grimes 1988: 104–5); ritual theorists agree that rites are not solely adjustive or redressive social mechanisms, as Turner and others stressed. Their complexity means that they can just as readily generate as resolve social conflict – sometimes both simultaneously (Rappaport 1979: 214). Several factors account for this complexity and make ritual as liable to cause social tension as to cure it:

1. **A rite may be defective or misapplied; a rite may have unintended consequences or not work as expected.**

The claim that baptism was taken for granted assumes that it is effortless and automatic, but in fact no rite comes with a guarantee (Grimes 1988). For example, the gospel of Mark describes a healing rite that had to be repeated to produce the desired effect:

> He [Jesus] took the blind man by the hand and led him out of the village; and when he had put saliva on his eyes and laid hands on

him, he asked him, "Can you see anything?" And the man looked up and said, "I can see people, but they look like trees, walking." Then Jesus laid his hands on his eyes again; and he looked intently and his sight was restored, and he saw everything clearly.

(Mark 8:23–5)

Worse, sometimes a rite fails altogether:

Someone from the crowd answered [Jesus], "Teacher, I brought you my son; he has a spirit that makes him unable to speak; and whenever it seizes him, it dashes him down; and he foams and grinds his teeth and becomes rigid; and I asked your disciples to cast it out, but they could not do so."

(9:17–18)

In the scene that follows, Jesus successfully carries out the exorcism, which the disciples had evidently done incorrectly. Because rites may go wrong, anxiety attends each performance of a rite. Hence, they can hardly be taken for granted.

We must also consider the social conflict or disruption that might occur if a rite cannot accomplish what is expected of it or if a rite has consequences that create problems for the group practicing it. Whatever its historical origins, baptism has the pedigree of a purification rite – it eliminates sins – but the early church pressed it into service as a rite of entry, at the group's threshold. Rites of purification are typically preparatory for initiation, but they do not constitute the central rite of entry or initiation (Segal 1998: 85). In the *Golden Ass*, for example, Lucius undergoes a purifying bath (11:23), but it is only one rite among many and certainly not the primary rite in his Isis cult initiation. Were there other ritual activities that joined the baptismal rite, making it the successful rite it evidently was? If so, they are hidden in the New Testament under the vocabulary of baptism.

Having baptism as a rite of entry created a problem for the early church over time. Purification rites are typically repeatable, but baptism in its capacity as a rite of entry was evidently performed only once, at least in most groups. Because of this restriction, the early church soon faced the problem of how to deal with the sins believers committed after their baptism. The purifying action of baptism was no longer available to them. The book of Hebrews warns its readers that "it is impossible to restore again to repentance those who have once been enlightened, and have tasted the heavenly gift, and have shared in the Holy Spirit, . . . and then have fallen away" (6:4, 6). A second-century document, The Shepherd of Hermas, concerned itself with post-baptismal sin and offered a second chance to the baptized that fall (*Vision* 2.2.4; 3.5.5; *Mandate* 4.3.3–5). By the third century an elaborate system of penance – a new means of purification – was coming into being that would solve the problem of post-baptismal sin (Kelly 1960:

216). So it took the church several hundred years to solve a crisis that can be traced back to baptism, or rather, to the pressing of a purification rite into service as a rite of entry.

One can sense the gravity of the problem in the radical solution that some proposed to avoid post-baptismal sin: delay baptism until death was imminent. The fourth-century church leader and writer John Chrysostom repeatedly counsels against such postponement, which confirms how widespread the practice was (*Catecheses ad illuminandos* 1; *Homiliae in Joannem* 18; *Homiliae in Acta apostolorum* 1).

2.   Rites mark difference and determine social hierarchies.

Dining ritual is both a unifying and discriminating activity. Dining together creates solidarity among the diners and therefore eases any social tension that exists between them. It does so in part because the meal distinguishes those at table from those not at table; those invited to the table constitute a group. On the other hand, one's position at table is seldom random, and that position suggests one's relationship to those at table. Moreover, some may get the pick of what is served, others may not. Hence, an order is set up and on display around the dinner table.

This paradoxical aspect of ritual clearly frustrated Paul in his interaction with believers in Corinth. For he hoped that dining together would foster a unity that he found lacking among the Corinthians (1 Cor 1:10–11), and he prescribed a dining protocol with that goal in mind (11:33–4). When dining produced difference instead, he became incensed (1 Cor 11:17–20):

> For when the time comes to eat, each of you goes ahead with your own supper, and one goes hungry and another becomes drunk. What! Do you not have homes to eat and drink in? Or do you show contempt for the church of God and humiliate those who have nothing? What should I say to you? Should I commend you? In this matter I do not commend you!
>
> (1 Cor 11:21–2)

Marking difference and creating social order naturally generate social conflict, because discriminations are seldom to everyone's liking.

Jonathan Z. Smith has alerted us to how readily we tend to think of ritual as a thoughtless habit – shades of baptism as taken for granted! His convincing criticism of this perspective alerts us to the galvanizing, differentiating power of rites, as any reflective diner party invitee realizes:

> Ritual is, first and foremost, a mode of paying attention. It is a process of marking interest.
>   Ritual is, above all, an assertion of difference.
>
> (Smith 1987: 103, 109)

The difference that ritual creates often takes the form of a social hierarchy. Catherine Bell, more than any other ritual theorist, has explored ritual activity's part in the creation of power structures:

> Practice is . . . able to reproduce or reconfigure a vision of the order of power in the world.
>   Ritual practices are themselves the very production and negotiation of power relations.
>
> (Bell 1992: 81, 196)

Bell is not alone in noting the defining role rites play in establishing and reinforcing a social order (Leach 1968: 524; Rappaport 1979: 192–4; Driver 1991: 131–51; Geertz 1973: 118).

How does ritual draw attention to community structure and even create it? The way people conduct themselves in relation to others during ritual activity betokens their social relationship (Bourdieu 1990: 71–2). Eric Reinders, for instance, has explored the ritual expression of social order in the Buddhist rite of bowing. Bowing lowers the junior monk's body in relation to the senior monk and thus represents and embodies the hierarchical relationship between them (Reinders 1997: 245–7). In the early church we have noted already how baptism made and broke kinship ties, which is another way of saying that baptism engendered social structure. Precisely how did the rite of baptism set up a social order? Baptizands did not baptize themselves but rather submitted themselves to baptism at the hand of another, the one who conducted or guided the rite. The contrast between passive (being baptized) and active (baptizing) participation in the rite – who is in charge and who is not – expressed and established a ranking between baptizand and baptizer. Thus, a community structure emerged.

Conflict most obviously results from ritual activity when community members dissent from the distinctions and hierarchy a community rite produces. Hence we see Paul, as we noted earlier, distancing himself from baptism because he found it lending itself to the establishment of competing circles of authority among the believers in Corinth (1 Cor 1:10–16).

3.   Rites engender an idealized situation that may not match – hence may stand in tension with – reality.

What ritual theorists mean by this claim comes to expression in various ways (Wheelock 1982: 65). On his list of ritual's obvious aspects Roy Rappaport includes what he calls their digitizing action or character, that is, their reduction of the continuous and complex to the binary through ritual occurrence (Rappaport 1979: 184–8; cf. Leach 1976: 34). An illustration will show what Rappaport means. The maturation of an individual is a complex and gradual process, involving physiological, psychological, and social development. Hence, it takes many years to move through puberty, as adolescents in modern western societies know only too well. Puberty rites in traditional societies polarize or digitize that process by reinforcing the social distinction between childhood and adulthood and marking unambiguously the transition from one to the other. Instead of allowing a gradual transition through puberty, puberty rites take one sign of the process – menarche for girls, for example – and make it the occasion for their ritual transition from childhood to adulthood. A puberty rite may ease the awkward transition the maturing child faces or the disruption of familial and societal order this transition creates, and it may lessen the ambiguity and concomitant anxiety surrounding what westerners call adolescence. On the other hand, the rite has the potential to generate conflict by imposing a socially prescribed sequence on gradual and continual physiological change.

Another way of expressing this aspect of ritual comes from Jonathan Z. Smith, who writes, "Ritual is a means of performing the way things ought to be in conscious tension to the way things are" (Smith 1987: 109). In the case of baptism, it would have concretized, enacted, and finalized the departure of individuals from their former social identity and their entry into a new identity. In reality, however, breaking with the past and embracing the new is never neat and clean. Believers could not shed their old kinship ties over night; they could not leave their old situation entirely; they did not disappear from the society that formed and defined them. If baptism made the transition from old to new possible, the reality of living simultaneously in both persisted. The tension between ideal and real undoubtedly posed problems for members of the early church.

We get some hint of the problem in 1 Corinthians. What many New Testament scholars consider Paul's criticism of the excessive spiritual enthusiasm of the Corinthians might better be understood as the inevitable tension between ritual ideal and lived reality. Paul's warning not to provoke God in chapter 10 (see vv 5, 11, 22) has frequently been identified as Paul's retort to Corinthian elitism and overconfidence – note his sarcastic response to Corinthian boasts about having become royalty at 4:8. Yet the problem Paul addresses in chapters 8 and 10 may not be Corinthian boastfulness at all. Paul stresses the clean break and new allegiance that ritual signals in his retelling of the Israelites' Exodus and Wilderness experience – a thinly veiled reference to baptism and eucharist (10:1–5). Emphasizing what those rites accomplish positions him to take the Corinthians to task for their inconsistency: some show solidarity with the early church by participating in its common meal – sharing the cup and breaking the bread (10:16–17) – yet continue to dine in pagan temples, thereby acknowledging a second allegiance (8:10; 10:20–1). Quite understandably, some believers found it difficult to sever ties with family and friends and to skirt existing social obligations, such as meeting and dining with friends or family at a local temple. What Paul's comments highlight, then, is not Corinthian elitism as much as the inevitable incongruity and tension between the ideal situation that ritual models and the realities of daily life.

4.   Context is crucial for determining a rite's effects.

The very same rite in different contexts may mirror and confirm the social order or challenge it and enact an alternative to it. Hence, ritual theorists are keen to gather as much information as they can about the setting of a rite. In his analysis of drama as ritual, Ronald Grimes insisted on an approach that "describe[s] the whole event, which extends . . . to the cultural occasion and social circumstance in which [the plays] are embedded" (Grimes 1990: 90). This insistence resonates with the perspective of other social scientists, such as Clifford Geertz, who prize and practice thick ethnographic description. Such microscopic studies are desirable, Geertz says, because of their inherent circumstantiality (Geertz 1973: 23). Likewise, Catherine Bell stresses the situational character of ritual in her book *Ritual Theory, Ritual Practice* (Bell 1992: 81) and devotes a whole section of another book, *Ritual: Perspectives and Dimensions*, to the issue of ritual context. Part I of the book, entitled "Context: The Fabric of Ritual Life," begins

> A ritual never exists alone. It is usually one ceremony among many in the larger ritual life of a person or community, one gesture among a multitude of gestures both sacred and profane, one embodiment among others of traditions of behavior down from one generation to another.
> (Bell 1997: 171)

What Bell and others are getting at is that rites do not have fixed outcomes; what they achieve varies according to their setting. As Stanley Tambiah observes

> It is therefore necessary to bear in mind that festivals, cosmic rituals, and rites of passage, however prescribed they may be, are always linked to status claims and interests of the participants, and therefore are always open to contextual meanings.
> (Tambiah 1985: 125)

The social context of a rite will determine whether it increases or lessens social conflict.

In the case of the early church, it was replete with rites that displaced, overturned, or reversed existing ritual patterns, although few have noticed because they are treated in isolation from their environment. Most obviously, baptism replaced circumcision as the way of marking group affiliation (Col 2:11–12), and eucharistic (symbolic) blood drinking violated Israelite dietary practice (Cahill 2002). Moreover, as noted above, Paul explicitly set the early church's common meal ritual over and against the dining practices that occurred at local Corinthian temples: "You cannot drink the cup of the Lord and the cup of demons. You cannot partake of the table of the Lord and the table of demons" (1 Cor 10:21).

Also in Corinth, Paul evidently wanted to set the worship ritual of the church apart from local polytheistic worship, and he did so by, among other things, issuing stipulations about head coverings: women were to cover their heads (1 Cor 11:5–6, 13), men were not (11:4, 7). Paul may have been introducing gender-based distinctions to worship, but just as important is the ritual context for understanding the significance of these stipulations. Ecstatic worship in the Greco-Roman world was an occasion for women to uncover their hair and let it loose. The early church's worship exhibited ecstatic elements as well (1 Cor 14), but the imposition of female veiling distinguished such worship from that of its neighbors. In the case of men, Cynthia Thompson's study of Corinthian statuary reveals that men covered their heads in religious settings, such as sacrifice (Thompson 1988: 104). Paul's insistence on bareheaded worship for men meant that he effectively reversed existing worship patterns. That such departures from the norm increased social tension – the tension between the early church and its social environment – is quite probable.

What these four factors bearing on rites point to, along with the observation that rites attend social crises, is the inherent complexity of rites – even to the point of messiness. If this is a fair description of rites in general, we must assume that the rites of the early church, baptism and others, had the same character and quality about them. If so, that such complexity or messiness goes unreported or underreported in the New Testament should not be used in an argument from silence to conclude that the early church had little or no ritual (Judge 1980: 212) or that its ritual was taken for granted, as New Testament scholars tend to assume. Rather, such general considerations about rites highlight the gap between what the New Testament reports and what ritual life in the early church was actually like.

Such a realization prompts two questions: (1) what can be done to recover the ritual life of the early church and gauge its significance for and impact on believers; and (2) why does the New Testament give us such limited access to the early church's ritual life? This chapter has already begun the process of recovery by challenging existing characterizations of a key rite, baptism, and by exploring how ritual theorists have described ritual in general. Sensitized to this theoretical discussion – especially to the connection between crisis and ritualizing and to the determinative significance of a rite's context – succeeding chapters will continue an examination of boundary-crossing rites, whether the entry rite of baptism (Chapters 2 and 3) or exit rites (Part II).

As for why we see so little of the early church's ritual life in the New Testament, we begin with ritual itself. Earlier we noted that social crises generate or attract ritual activity and that those rites enabling a community to negotiate and ease the crisis enter the community's ritual repertoire. It is this very property of effective rites, however, that may contribute to their hiddenness – in baptism's case why the New Testament presents it without any fanfare or detail as the standard mechanism for entering the early church. David Wright describes ritual as "a 'traditionalizing instrument,' that is, it makes what is expressed thereby acceptable and common. It hides the novelty and even radicalness of new ideas and acts" (Wright 2001: 10). Entering the family of faith may not appear novel or radical, but what it entailed, the making and breaking of kinship ties, was. In order to make group boundary-crossing possible, baptism diminished the trauma of reconfiguring kinship relations. It camouflaged what must have been a difficult transition and in so doing it deflected attention from that transition and itself.

The second quotation of this chapter suggests another reason that the New Testament is relatively quiet about ritual. Hartman's observation that "Nowhere in the New Testament do we find a text to which could be assigned the title 'On baptism' " holds true for all the early church's rites (Hartman 1997: 3). This lacking becomes rather striking if the New Testament is set alongside the Dead Sea Scrolls, documents collected by a religious community roughly contemporary with the early church. In that collection, texts (mostly fragmentary) on purification practices, liturgy, and ritual abound. Likewise, there exists a very early document of the church in Syria that provided relatively detailed ritual instructions. The *Didache* devotes attention to baptism and eucharist, and gives specific directions as to how to carry out both (7:1–4; 9:1–10:7). This is as close as we get to a ritual instruction manual, but as highly regarded as the *Didache* was, it did not join the circle of writings that became the New Testament.

Even if the New Testament included a manual on ritual practice, however, our picture of the early church's ritual life would be attenuated. For the nature of the New Testament itself, indeed, the very medium of writing generally may not be a good vehicle for conveying what ritual is about. Ronald Grimes contrasts the focus of narrative on sequence and time with ritual's tactile and spatial orientation, and this difference points to the inherent inadequacy of textual descriptions of ritual (Grimes 1990: 168–72).

There is another way of considering the mismatch between text and rite. Writing and reading engage the mind, but ritual engages the body. Most ritual theorists would agree, for instance, with Evan Zuesse's emphasis on ritual's bodiliness: "Even more fundamentally, ritual is intentional bodily engagement in the paradigmatic forms and relationships of reality," and "Ritual centers on the body, and to understand ritual one shall have to take the body seriously as a vehicle for religious experience" (Zuesse 2005: 7834). Because rites focus on the body, on the sensual and sensory, they are incommensurate with texts, even texts whose task is to describe ritual activity. Like the gap between the staging of a play and script for it, much goes missing in trying to put down a rite on paper.

The "disappearance" of rites in the New Testament may not simply reflect the text's – any text's – inability to capture them, however. Earlier in this chapter we looked at literature from the ancient Mediterranean world that describes how complicated it was to join a religious group. In *The Golden Ass* and *Joseph and Aseneth* we encountered narratives that do not hide the monumental change that conversion entails. Why, then, is baptism and entry into the early church such a simple matter in New Testament narratives such as Acts? A strategy for how the early church positioned itself in relation to the larger culture – for apologetic or missionary ends – may have been at work. Presenting affiliation with Isis or Judaism and the ritual activity attending it realistically – as difficult and complicated – may not have been a liability for religions that enjoyed official recognition and relative acceptance in the Roman empire. But quite the opposite may have been so in the case of the early church, which stood in tension with other forms of Judaism and did not enjoy official recognition by the Romans. Given the church's controversial and illegal status, it made sense to make baptism look effortless, thus minimizing the gap between insiders and outsiders and hiding the social disruption that attended affiliation with the early church. Presenting baptism in this fashion probably lessened the possibility that the early church would be perceived as radically – hence dangerously – different. Accordingly, it was not in the best interest of the early church and New Testament writers to be accurate or complete in their description of baptism.

If the New Testament says little about the early church's ritual life, New Testament scholars say even less. They are equally to blame for the disappearance of rites, for the field has historically had a bias against ritual, as has religious studies in general (Smith 1987: 96–103; Smith 1990: passim; Eilberg-Schwartz 1990: 140; Douglas 1966: 19–28). The academic study of the Bible, and the modern study of religion generally, has its roots in Protestantism and the Enlightenment, both of which devalued ritual (Gorman 1994: 14–20). Protestantism privileged faith or inner disposition over ritual or outward expression and identified Roman Catholicism with the latter. Enlightenment thinkers found rites irrational or nonrational, as opposed to rational and efficient, behavior and therefore dismissed them as primitive and obsolete. As a consequence, scholars of religion reached judgments such as these: (1) the great historical faiths, particularly Christianity, are more advanced than, and superior to, tribal religions, which are full of magic and ritual; (2) ancient Christianity's nonritualistic orientation distinguished it from Greco-Roman paganism (temple sacrifice) and ancient Judaism (temple sacrifice and the Pharisees), whose focus was ritual practice and purity; (3) as ancient Christianity developed, the apostolic age of faith (Paul and the gospel writers) degenerated into priestly religion or "early Catholicism" (*Frühkatholismus*). In this last case the polemic against Roman Catholicism, which lay behind all these contrasts, was explicit and blatant. The trouble is, of course, that the early church, like all human organizations, was thick with ritual from its very start.

New Testament scholars have not been alone in minimizing ritual. The academy in general, probably because it is a place of thought and texts, tends to give priority to ideas or beliefs (Douglas 1970b: 1–18; Grimes 1990: 163). In her look at the history of the scholarship on ritual, Catherine Bell notes

> The theories of Max Müller, Edward Tylor, Herbert Spencer, James Frazer, Rudolf Otto, William James, and E. O. James, among others, all stressed the primacy of religious ideas, both of pseudoscientific explanations or emotional experiences, as the basis of religion. Ritual, as exemplary religious behavior, was the necessary but secondary expression of these mental orientations.
>
> (Bell 1992: 14)

This perspective lives on in more recent scholarship. Stanley Tambiah, in his criticism of anthropologists indebted to Tylor, remarks

> We must also clearly realize that cosmological conceptions are not merely – or even importantly – to be understood in terms of the subjects' stated "beliefs," as the neo-Tylorians tend to do, but are most richly embedded in myths, ritual, legal codes, constitutional charters, and other collective representations. Moreover, when beliefs are taken to be prior to ritual action, the latter is considered as derivative and secondary, and is ignored or undervalued in its own right as a medium for transmitting meanings, constructing social reality, or, for that matter, creating and bringing to life the cosmological scheme itself.
>
> (Tambiah 1985: 129)

The best antidote to such bias is to treat ritual as an independent variable, as irreducible, as having its own creative and generative aspect that may trigger innovation (Grimes 1985: 1; 1995: 62, 66, 186–7). This understanding of ritual guides the pages that follow.

2 Contested Waters

Further, the wearing of our dress became a distinction, and the toga came
into fashion, and little by little the Britons were seduced into alluring vices:
to the lounge, the bath, the well-appointed dinner table. The simple natives
gave the name of "culture" to this factor of their slavery.

(Tacitus, *Agricola* 21 [Hutton, LCL])

All major centers (e.g., Corinth, Nikopolis, Athens, Argos) acquired an ample
supply of running water. Nymphaea [fountains] and baths multiplied in
these cities: twenty-four baths, as well as a new, centrally located and highly
decorative nymphaeum, are attested in Athens alone. . . . Yet the gift of
water from afar signals more than a concern for civic health. A more con-
fident control of the physical environment is implied, the harnessing and
channeling of natural resources to serve human needs, as well as the ability
to transgress individual political boundaries by imperial mandate.

(Alcock 1993: 125–6)

This chapter focuses on the context for the ritual activity of the early church,
because, as the previous chapter noted, ritual theorists consider context
crucial for determining the function and significance of a rite. The fuller
and more specific context we can provide, the better the rite in question is
situated, hence understood. In this chapter we focus on a specific place,
namely, Corinth, and for good reason: (1) Paul's Corinthian correspondence
tells us more about the church there than we know about it in any other
location (Osiek 1992: 62–3); and (2) the literary and archaeological record
for Corinth provides considerable information about the city in the early
Roman period, including the time of Paul. Specific to baptism, the architectural record reveals much about how water was used in early Roman
Corinth, so that we can readily locate baptism in a spectrum of water use.
Before we look in detail about water use in Roman Corinth, however, some
attention to the sources we have for the recreation of life in the city and
its environs is needed.

   As much information as we have about Corinth, the sources for it tell
misleading and sometimes conflicting stories about the city in the early Roman

period. Ancient writers considered Roman dominance to be much more pronounced in the west (e.g., Spain, Gaul, Britain) than the east. With regard to Greece, Horace's pithy comment says it all: "Greece, the captive, took her savage victor captive, and brought the arts into rustic Latium" (Horace, *Epistulae* 2.1.156 [Fairclough, LCL]). Hence, scholars have often considered Rome's refounding and colonization of Corinth in the mid-first century BCE a revival and continuation of the Greek city. They were confirmed in this view by a key aspect of the archaeological record: Latin inscriptions that dominated the epigraphical record in the first century CE gave way to Greek inscriptions from the second century on. Understandably, the rest of the archaeological record was fitted into the picture that the literary sources painted.

Foremost among these literary sources is Pausanias, who visited Corinth in the second century and wrote in detail about it. For many scholars – and for many years – Pausanias has been the gold standard for information about Roman Corinth, as one example will illustrate. In his definitive study of travel in the ancient world, classicist Lionel Casson begins a chapter entitled "Baedeker of the Ancient World" with these words:

> Wit, style, a keen and original mind, an eye for the unusual – these are what delight us in the travelogue writer. The compiler of a guidebook, on the other hand, must be a totally different kind of person. His job is to report the location, dimensions, age, and life-history of monuments, and only incidentally, if at all, the emotions or associations they arouse in his breast. Wit and originality have no place in such an assignment; it fact, they might very well get in the way. What he requires above all are the matter-of-fact virtues of thoroughness, diligence, and accuracy.
>
> And these were the virtues *par excellence* of a certain Pausanias who, between roughly A.D. 160 and 180, wrote a *Guidebook of Greece*, the sole guidebook that has survived from ancient times.
>
> (Casson 1974: 292)

There certainly is a difference between what Lawrence Durrell and the Blue Guide say about any given spot in the Mediterranean, but the distinction Casson draws between the writer and the compiler may or may not be relevant for assessing ancient authors. Whether we classify Pausanias as one or the other, is Casson's estimation of him accurate? Casson's own comments reveal the difficulty of making such an assessment: Pausanias's guide to Greece is the lone survivor of its literary type (Bowie 1996: 208). So we have no way of judging it against a class of ancient travel guides. Compared to what other ancient writers reveal about Greece, his is a full and careful text. But does that mean that Pausanias was, to recite Casson's high praise, thorough, diligent, and accurate?

Classicists and ancient historians, with some exceptions (e.g., Habicht 1985), have begun to say "no," which marks a profound shift in scholarly opinion. Generations of classical archaeologists have relied on the *Periegesis* – typically referred to as *Guide to Greece* or *Description of Greece* – as their handbook to the land of ancient Greece, or at least as a starting point, and there is good reason for its preeminence. The paucity of texts treating the realia Pausanias describes gives his text a hegemony that is hard to resist. Moreover, there is something compelling about the text itself: it marches through Greece offering matter-of-fact descriptions at every turn. Historian Susan Alcock characterizes the ruling view of Pausanias, which she opposes, as follows: "Carrying the reader securely with him through space, he reports what he sees in . . . straightforward and truthful fashion" (Alcock 1996: 260).

Increasingly, however, scholars express reservations about Pausanias, concluding that he lacked the very virtues Casson ascribed to him. Like other second-century Greek authors, the writers of the Second Sophistic, Pausanias dwelt on Greece's Classical past. As Ewen Bowie notes, "His focus on the Greek past with minimal attention to Hellenistic monuments and only slightly more to monuments of over two centuries of the Roman empire matches the imaginary world of the sophists and novelists" (Bowie 1996: 229). Whether we see behind this focus an animosity toward Rome or a way of coping with Greece's misfortunes after the glorious Classical Age, Pausanias was selective. He preferred early Greek history and stories about beginnings and foundations, especially the origins of religious cults. Consequently, Pausanias gave his readers a very incomplete and rather biased picture of early Roman Greece.

How would a healthy distrust of Pausanias affect the reconstruction of life in Corinth? Greatly. After lengthy excavation, Corinth has yielded an extensive material record, but it is fragmentary. As a consequence, archaeologists have at times relied greatly – too greatly – on Pausanias's extensive treatment of Corinth and its environs, the Corinthia, for help in piecing those fragments together (e.g., Richardson 1900: 474). As the reassessment of Pausanias gains ground, therefore, many of the Corinth final excavation reports that appeared during the twentieth century will have to undergo review. To the extent our picture of Corinth rests on Pausanias and interpretations of the archaeological record influenced by Pausanias, this new estimate of him will alter that picture significantly.

What form that new estimate will take can be gauged by detecting Pausanias's inaccuracies and the over-reliance of Corinthian archaeologists on Pausanias in their interpretation of the material record. Two examples are illustrative, important for what they reveal about early Roman cultic life in Corinth. A misleading picture of religion in early Roman Corinth has emerged when Pausanias has said too much – and Corinthian archaeologists have made too much of that emphasis – and when he has said too little. One instance of each is worth noting. In both cases, attention to the full archaeological context of Corinth and reference to other comparable contexts, the Roman-period archaeology of other sites, enable us to provide an important corrective to the received picture of Corinth.

First, Pausanias's sin of commission, that is, where he has misled by saying too much. Casson saw real objectivity or detachment in Pausanias, the ideal travelogue compiler: "His job is to report the location, dimensions, age, and life-history of monuments, and only incidentally, if at all, the emotions or associations they arouse in his breast." As counterpoint to this I offer Susan Alcock's observation, which I find the more accurate: "The *Periegesis* is throughout crowded with memories, inspired by the sight of monuments, the reading of inscriptions, or the tales of local guides" (Alcock 1996: 249–50). With regard to Corinth, Pausanias's detachment was not in evidence when he described an important public fountain near Corinth's city center. When he came to the fountain associated with Glauke, he mentioned a cluster of other related monuments he found nearby, immediately northwest of the Roman forum (*Graeciae description* 2.3.6–7). At this point, Pausanias interrupted his travel report to introduce the legends and figures of the rich Greek tradition surrounding Glauke: Jason, Medea, Hera, and others. This aside goes on for thirty-nine lines in the Loeb Classical Library edition (ibid. 2.3.8–11).

This lengthy digression in Pausanias's narrative suggested to excavators that the Glauke Fountain was but one element in an entire precinct of the city devoted to her memory, a devotion with a long Greek heritage that the Romans had preserved or renewed down to Pausanias's day. The precinct boundary (temenos) of the structure designated Temple C abuts Glauke Fountain. Accordingly, Temple C, built by the Romans in the late

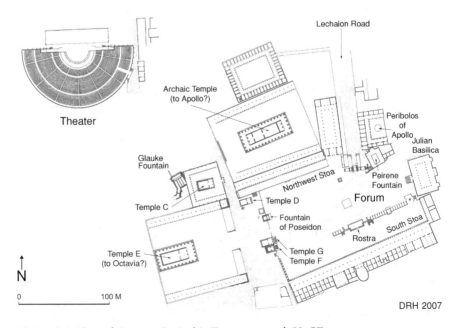

Figure 2.1 Plan of Roman Corinth's Forum around 50 CE

Augustan or Tiberian period, was identified with Hera Akraia, and was thought to be a replacement for an earlier Greek temple also dedicated to her (Stillwell, Scranton, and Freeman 1941: 131–65, esp. 157–65). The final report that reaches this conclusion admits, however, that no data from the site support this identification (Stillwell, Scranton, and Freeman 1941: 149). The identification of the temple and the positing of an earlier Greek-period temple rest solely on Pausanias.

The excavators were evidently carried away by Pausanias's enthusiasm for Medean mythology. He did mention Hera's sanctuary as the place where Medea buried or hid her children by Jason, but he did not pinpoint a Hera Temple near Glauke Fountain. Consequently, the current generation of Corinthian archaeologists distances itself from the final report; they reserve judgment about the identity of the Roman-era temple and dismiss the hypothesis about an earlier Greek temple as, in James Wiseman's judgment, "highly conjectural" (Wiseman 1979: 473 fn. 132).

As for Glauke Fountain, Pausanias is explicit about its identity and location (*Descr.* 2.3.6), and the architectural remains at the site are clearly those of a fountain. Unfortunately, the original excavators of the site were convinced, under Pausanian influence, that the Romans did little more than preserve the Greek legacy that Pausanias described in his travelog. As a result, until recently archaeologists were convinced that Glauke Fountain was originally a Greek structure carved from living rock, which the Romans saved and modified (Hill 1964: 200–28; Robinson 1964: 10). Current opinions include the judgment that the Romans built the fountain from scratch, thoroughly imitating Greek architectural form. Charles Williams, for many years director of the Corinth Excavations, offers this interpretation of the structure:

> With Glauke we have, then, an example of deliberate architectural eclecticism within Laus Julia Corinthiensis. . . . I would suggest that the design was determined by the literary spirit of the educated Roman colonist, who wanted to be able to show a monument of ancient Corinth fitting, as he saw it, the myth of Medea as it was passed down.
>
> (Williams 1987: 35)

Williams saw hellenistic influence at work here in the incredibly close mimicry of Greek architecture by the Roman colonists.

A different motivation may lie behind the construction of the fountain, however. Not to slight Williams's very important correction of how Corinth's material record should be interpreted, but his suggestion about why the Romans built the fountain is too Pausanian. Had the fountain been built under the philhellenic Hadrian, his suggestion would make some sense, but not in the first century CE, when the fountain was constructed.

Glauke Fountain's place in the design of the city suggests a motivation other than literary for building it. The fountain stood beside the route that led to the sole entrance to the Archaic Temple precinct in the Roman era. One former entrance to the temple precinct had been from the south, but that was blocked with the construction of the Northwest Stoa by the Romans. Also, a grand stairway had once given access to the temple precinct from the southeast, but that access was obliterated when the Romans quarried the eastward extension of the ridge on which the temple sat (Williams 1987: 31). The Archaic Temple now had an axial entrance on the west, which meant that the temple and entry to it faced Rome.

The new configuration meant that Glauke Fountain served as a source of water as one approached the Roman forum from the north and west and as one came to the entrance of a prominent temple precinct in Roman Corinth. The arrangement was, therefore, similar to other important sanctuaries in the Greek east that underwent Roman reshaping. The Roman remodeling of the great Demeter Sanctuary at Pergamon, for instance, included construction of a nymphaeum in the sanctuary's forecourt (Bohtz 1981: 15–16). Likewise, the Greater (or Outer) Propylaia at Eleusis, which replaced the older North Pylon and served as the main gate to the walled sanctuary precinct, was flanked by a well (Clinton 1989: 59; Giraud 1989: plate 13, fig. 1; plate 23, fig. 14).

Williams may be right that eclecticism was at work in the construction of Glauke Fountain, and not of a random or unintended sort. By imitating Greek architecture in their reconfiguring of a central Corinthian religious site, the Romans were dressing Romanization in Greek clothing. Anthropologists of colonialism would not call this philhellenism; they would call it cultural imperialism in the form of indigenization: exercising hegemony by the conscious adoption and manipulation of native elements (Stewart and Shaw 1994: 7, 12).

We turn now to Pausanias's second sin, that of omission. Lionel Casson found in him, "the matter-of-fact virtues of thoroughness, diligence, and accuracy." Yet he left a great deal out of his description of Corinth, even though no ancient writer left us more. Pausanias's treatment of the forum, Roman Corinth's massive city center, is relatively brief and not entirely informative. He listed what he regarded as worthy of mention there and quickly moved on: a sanctuary of Ephesian Artemis, two wooden images of Dionysos, a temple of Tyche, a pantheon, a fountain to Poseidon, statues to Clarion Apollo and Aphrodite, two bronzes of Hermes, one housed in a temple, two images of Zeus, and a bronze statue of Athena that Pausanias locates in the middle of the forum. As he led the reader away from the forum, he mentioned a temple to Octavia, sister of Augustus, above (*hyper*) the forum (*Descr.* 2.2.6–8; 2.3.1). This list has been immensely useful to scholars, there is no doubt, but in a forum that ran 200 meters in length and that functioned as the symbolic center of Roman Greece, we would expect to find many other religious objects and monuments. Besides giving us an incomplete list, Pausanias did not describe how the monuments he listed were arranged. Moreover, even in the information he did provide, we do not have full accuracy.

Pausanias's list of "trees" has diverted scholars from looking at the "forest." Archaeologists have devoted so much attention to matching Pausanias to the material record that they have said little about the configuration of cults in Corinth's forum. There might have been other clusters of religious monuments in the civic center, but the forum created by the Romans, as the material record of Corinth shows, featured an impressive row of monuments and temples on a terrace at its western end, which would have attracted the attention of anyone entering the forum. Archaeologists generally agree about a fountain to Poseidon or Neptune in the middle of the row, later replaced by a temple in honor of emperor Commodus (ruled 180–192 CE) (Williams 1987: 29; Williams and Fisher 1975: 25; Scranton 1951: 70). There is little certainty about the rest, however. Opinion on Temple D has shifted from Hermes to Tyche. The current wisdom identifies Temple F with Aphrodite, that is, Venus Genetrix, mother of the Roman people and, of course, the Roman colony of Corinth (Williams 1989: 157; Williams and Fisher 1975: 27; Wiseman 1979: 529). Charles Williams suggests that the other building with strong ties to Rome was Temple G, immediately next to Temple F. He identifies it as dedicated to Clarian Apollo, a nod no doubt to Augustus, who claimed Apollo as progenitor (Williams 1989: 158). (The original excavator connected Clarian Apollo with another temple nearby [Scranton 1951: 71–2]). In the case of Temples G and F, archaeologists are taking Pausanias's mention of a statue as shorthand for a temple.

Temple E would also have drawn the attention of forum visitors to the west end. It seems unlikely that we have a temple to Octavia alone, as Pausanias indicated. Most likely, Temple E was originally dedicated to the imperial family, to Gens Julia, a conclusion supported by numismatic evidence (Williams 1987: 35–6, nn. 6, 7). (Mary Walbank offers a useful survey of the evidence, but few would accept her conclusion that Temple E was a Capitolium [Walbank 1989: 361–94].) An axis projected from Temple E divided the forum temples, left and right (Romano 2005: 35, fig. 2.5). As one approached the west end of the forum, the temple to the imperial cult stood above a set of monumental stairs, elevated by a podium, and flanked by the smaller forum temples below it. If this cluster of forum temples drew the eye to the west end of the forum, they also pointed beyond themselves to the larger, higher temple looking down on the forum (Stillwell, Scranton, and Freeman 1941: 233).

The archaeological record, even though the interpretation of it is far from settled, affords a view of the whole that Pausanias did not give us. At Corinth we have a forum whose cultic focal point lay at the west end. There we find an impressive row of small temples, several having strong associations with the imperial household. And then we raise our eyes to the larger temple that stands above and beyond, which was the architectural center of the imperial cult in Corinth. What Pausanias failed to let us see, therefore, was the dominance of that cult in the civic center of early Roman Corinth.

Because of his own preoccupation with the Greek past, Pausanias left us a distorted picture of Corinth. His text, more than any other, has caused scholars to miss the fact that Corinth in his day was a Roman city and an expression of Roman culture and ideology on Greek soil. As Corinthian archaeologist Mary Walbank has noted

> For long there was an implicit assumption by scholars that *Colonia Laus Iulia Corinthiensis* was not a conventional Roman colony, but rather a re-foundation and continuation of the Greek city destroyed a hundred years earlier. Today most scholars accept that Corinth was a traditional Roman colony.
>
> (Walbank 1997: 95)

Pausanias's tour of Corinth's civic center may have masked the importance of the imperial cult in Corinth, but the architecture and city plan revealed by excavation underscore its centrality. If the Archaic Temple had once dominated the city center because of its elevation and size, the Romans undid its dominance by blocking it off from the forum and turning its face westward, as noted above (Walbank 1989: 365). Now Temple E, a Roman creation, controlled the forum. The imperial cult was, therefore, the new religious focal point of Roman Corinth. In this way, Corinth did indeed conform to what we would expect of a Roman colony. It was not, as Pausanias presented the city, a museum of the glorious Greek past.

A revised estimate of Pausanias and the concomitant revisiting of Corinth's material record gives us a new picture of Corinth, a city of central importance to Paul and the early church. The major Roman shaping of the city means we must regard Roman Corinth, to borrow what Susan Alcock says about Roman Greece generally, not as a "cultural haven, an imaginary world, or a museum locked in spiritual twilight," but rather as, "a society in the process of change, adapting and assimilating itself to a new position within an imperial system – just as countless other subordinate societies have been forced to do throughout the centuries" (Alcock 1993: 230). Alcock and other scholars like her are now articulating what Romanization was like on Greek soil.

As we have already seen, Rome's shaping of the Corinthian cityscape involved the manipulation of water in the case of Glauke Fountain, and such manipulation could take subtle form. Rather than disassembling and reusing the landmark of Greek Corinth, such as the Archiac Temple, they preserved it, but at the same time they reoriented entry to the temple. Similarly, in typical Roman fashion they built a nymphaeum near the entrance to the temple precinct, Glauke Fountain, but they dressed it in Greek clothing and connected it with Greece's mythic past. How else did the

Romans shape the hydraulic systems and facilities of Corinth? This is a vitally important question to answer in order to contextualize baptism. But it is also worth addressing because of how central the control of water was to the expression of Roman culture and hegemony.

We can assemble a great deal of information about the change in water distribution and use patterns between the Greek and Roman periods in the Corinthia, which makes it an informative category. Equally important, it is a significant category for the issue of Romanization because of the meaning Romans attached to the control and distribution of water. Most obviously, the Romans considered the public bath to be a cornerstone and marker of Roman civilization (Fagan 1999). Sure sign, for instance, that Agricola's pacification of the Britons had succeeded came when natives adopted Roman bathing practices. To review the epigraph that began this chapter, I provide a fuller excerpt from Tacitus:

> [Agricola] would exhort individuals, assist communities, to erect temples, market-places, houses: he praised the energetic, rebuked the indolent, and the rivalry for his compliments took the place of coercion. Moreover he began to train the sons of the chieftains in a liberal education, and to give a preference to the native talents of the Briton as against the plodding Gaul. As a result, the nation which used to reject the Latin language began to aspire to rhetoric: further, the wearing of our dress became a distinction, and the toga came into fashion, and little by little the Britons were seduced into alluring vices: to the lounge, the bath, the well-appointed dinner table. The simple natives gave the name of "culture" to this factor of their slavery.
>
> (Tacitus, *Agricola* 21 [Hutton, LCL])

Setting Tacitus's disparagement of bath culture aside, his comments identify the bath not only as cultural marker but also as a Romanizing force (DeLaine 1988: 11). Yet, as the excerpt shows, that force was applied steadily and gently, not heavy-handedly.

Other hydraulic projects also carried great symbolic weight. Nicholas Purcell's study of Roman water management – wetland drainage and reclamation, flood plain control – reveals that the Romans saw in such achievements more than technical expertise or organizational acumen (Purcell 1996). They expressed Roman power in the form of conquest, not of human opponents, but of nature. F. S. Kleiner's study of trophies on Roman bridges documents this perspective well (Kleiner 1991). Likewise, when Pliny wrote Caninius Rufus in 107 CE endorsing the latter's plan to compose an epic poem about Trajan's victories in the Dacian Wars, he appeared as interested in the Roman triumph over nature as the legions' triumphs over mortal enemies. The eighth letter begins "I greatly approve your design of writing a poem upon the Dacian war" but quickly turns to engineering feats: "You will sing of rivers turned into new channels, and rivers bridged for the first time, of camps pitched upon craggy mountains" (*Epistulae* 8.4.1–2 [Melmoth, LCL]).

Similarly, in a poem by Statius that celebrated Domitian's bridging of the Volturnus River, the personified river says to Domitian, "But I give thanks, and my servitude is worth the while, because under your rule and your command I have yielded, and because you will be read of perpetually as supreme lord and conqueror of my bank" (*Silvae* 4.3.81–4 [Mozley, LCL]). Later in the same poem Statius lauds Domitian as "more bountiful than Nature and more powerful" (ibid. 4.3.134–5). Clearly, Romans understood the mastery of water as a key indicator of Roman control and influence, as a form of imperialism, as a means of Romanizing the environment or world.

With this in mind we now approach the record of Roman water projects in the Corinthia. Perhaps the greatest in Roman Corinthia was the aqueduct built during Hadrian's reign that stretched into the Arcadian uplands, bringing water from distant Lake Stymphalus (Pausanias, *Descr.* 8.22.3; Lolos 1997). Another major water project was the renovation and massive expansion of the artificial harbor at Lechaion, Corinth's western port on the Gulf of Corinth (Rothaus 1995). The Romans also built several nymphaea or public fountains in and around Corinth, the most prominent of which was dedicated to Poseidon in the forum (Robinson 2001: 243–381).

As for public baths, Hubertus Manderscheid's and Inge Nielsen's catalogues offer a conservative estimate of three for Corinth: (1) the Great Bath on the Lechaion Road built in the late second or early third century north of the Roman forum on the primary artery connecting Corinth to its western port; (2) the bath at the forum's South Stoa, constructed around 300; and (3) a bath north of the Peribolos of Apollo, which may be the bath Pausanias assigned to Eurykles (*Descr.* 2.3.5), a rich Spartan of the Augustan era (Manderscheid 1988: 130–1; Nielsen 1990: 2.33). Jane Biers's list is longer, for she includes small, unpublished, and probable baths: a small one west of the odeion; a probable bath north of the theater; and another, probable, near the Hadji Mustafa fountain (between the forum and the Sanctuary of Demeter and Kore), as evidenced by the hypocaust construction found there (Biers 1985: 1). Some estimates go as high as a dozen baths (Lolos 1997: 297). The archaeological evidence certainly verifies Pausanias's comment that Corinth had plenty of baths (*Descr.* 2.3.5).

These numerous and impressive water projects were one face of Romanization in the Corinthia and they suggest a real break from the Greek past, but the picture is hardly complete. There was continuity with the past as well. In the Gymnasium area, we have evidence for Roman repair and lavish remodeling of a fifth- or fourth-century BCE Greek bathing facility in the first century CE, perhaps before mid-century (Wiseman 1972: 9–26). At Isthmia, site of a Temple to Poseidon and the Isthmian games, the Romans built a public bath over a large Greek swimming pool in the second century.

Likewise, Corinth's most famous public water source, the (Lower) Peirene Fountain, had a continuous history through the Greek and Roman

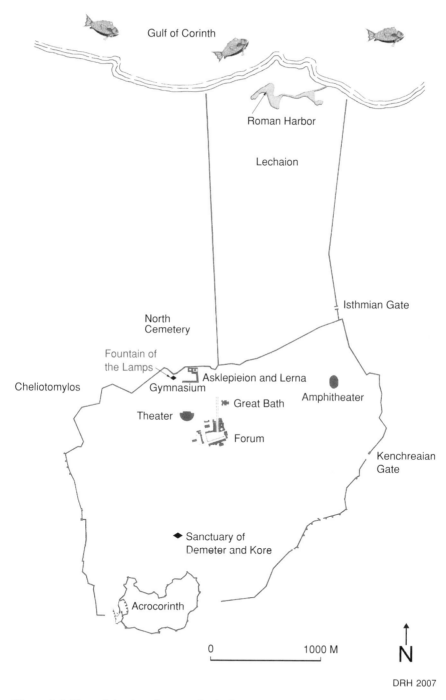

Figure 2.2 Plan of Ancient Roman Corinth

periods. Bert Hodge Hill describes seven phases of Roman use (Hill 1964: 1–115). The Roman remodeling of Peirene, according to Betsey Robinson, was very much according to Roman tastes: they made it into a grotto (Robinson 2005: 116–25). With regard to water control and use, therefore, we see a mix of discontinuity and continuity between Greek and Roman Corinthia. Alcock's observation that the Romans were intrusive but not interventionist is quite apt (Alcock 1989: 124). Put in other words, the Romans were determined to make Corinth a Roman city, but they were practical – that is, they sometimes repaired and modified Greek facilities and sites – in achieving that end.

We will now look at another aspect of water distribution and use as a way of further delineating the character of Romanization in the Corinthia, namely, the availability of water in and around sanctuaries and other cultic sites in the Corinthia, a topic already broached when we considered the Glauke fountain earlier in this chapter. What I present here is a supplement to Alcock's chapter called "The Sacred Landscape" in the book *Graecia capta* (Alcock 1993: 172–214). Alcock describes the displacing, centralizing, and annexing of cult in Roman Greece, and that certainly seems to be the case in Corinth.

With regard to water used for cultic purposes, we have ample evidence of a significant decline in usage between the Greek and Roman periods. The archaeological record suggests that in the Greek period, Corinthian piety was marked by the extensive use of water. The two major religious sites outside the forum that have been excavated, the Temple of Asklepios and the Sanctuary of Demeter and Kore, provide clear evidence of this. Besides its location adjacent to the reservoirs and draw basins of the Lerna Fountain, which suggests a heavy reliance on water, the Asklepieion itself had two important architectural features evidencing water use: (1) a small water basin with supply and waste pipes and covered by a porch, located by the temple altar and entrance; and (2) a lustral room adjacent and connected to the *abaton*, the great hall where those seeking a cure slept. The small basin's location suggests its intended function: to provide water for purification before sacrifice and entry into the temple. The lustral room was tied into a complex water system, and it was equipped with steps and a platform separated from a draw basin by a high parapet. Its location and elaborate design demonstrate how important bathing was to the religious rites that prepared one for incubating in the temple (Roebuck 1951: 26–7, 42–51).

An emphasis on water was just as strong in the Demeter and Kore sanctuary, located between the center of Corinth and Acrocorinth, the fortified heights above the city. Excavators found fragments of over a dozen Greek-era sacral water basins (*perirhantēria*) many of which were recovered in or near the dining rooms located at the sanctuary (Pemberton 1989: 75–8; Iozzo 1987: 355–416). Verifying the connection between ritual cleansing and dining is the architecture of the dining rooms themselves, which are a major feature of the site. Many of those investigated had a small bathing area along with cooking and sitting areas (Bookidis 1990; Bookidis and Stroud 1987: 19–20). Typically these rectangular or square stalls had low walls on three sides, a rim with a low step for entry on one side, a drain, and in some cases a nearby cistern (Bookidis 1969: 301; Bookidis and Fisher 1974: 275–7).

Closer to the heart of the city, excavators have uncovered a sanctuary they call the Sacred Spring. Features identified at the site include a spring-house and a base for a Greek sacral water basin, along with pottery that was typically used to store oil. Combined, these features suggest that bathing was part of the religious practices there (Steiner 1992). All in all, Greek-era archaeological data from in and around Corinth suggest varied and extensive use of water for cultic purposes there.

But such water use came to an abrupt end when Rome sacked Corinth. *None of the features just described was in use in the first century* CE. Corinth's Asklepieion saw activity in the Roman period, but the site changed: early Roman construction covered the water basin in front of the temple; and the lustral room went out of use no later than the Hellenistic period (Roebuck 1951: 27, 50, 79–82). As for the bathing facilities of the Demeter and Kore sanctuary, they did not survive the crisis of 146 BCE, when the Roman general Mummius sacked the city. The numerous dining rooms, many with bathing facilities, that had dominated the site in Greek times fell into disuse. Only one of these buildings saw reuse by the Roman Corinthians, but it was so extensively remodeled that even the tops of the dining couches lay under the earliest Roman floor (Bookidis and Fischer 1972: 299–304). As for the Sacred Spring, it was obliterated when the Romans constructed their new forum. The data provide strong evidence, therefore, of a decline in the religious use of water in the Roman period.

Now with a rather full picture of the hydraulic landscape before us, how would baptism have fit in it? That is, what was its significance in the wider context of water use in early Roman Corinth? Or, as Susan Alcock would put it, what was its role in the process of adaptation and assimilation, as Greece became acculturated to the Roman system (Alcock 1993: 230)?

The answer is a complex one. On the one hand, baptism's obvious importance to the church at Corinth and elsewhere may simply mirror and thus confirm the centrality of bathing in the Roman way of life. As a recent study of early Christian baptism notes, the various use of water and oil – water only, oil followed by water, or water followed by oil – reflected variation in Roman bathing etiquette (Spinks 2006: 35–6).

On other hand, baptism represented departure from the Roman order. Here was a use of water that eluded Roman control and that enabled entry into an alternative society beyond Roman hegemony. This resistance to the Roman way may have been signaled in simple but pointed ways, such as by the church's emphasis on baptism's once-ness, which contrasted starkly with the daily-ness of public bathing (Tertullian, *De baptismo* 15). Similarly, the

Didache calls for baptism in living or flowing rather than "other" water and in cold rather than warm water (7.2). Was this a muted comment about the Roman bath? Any expression of resistance would have taken very subtle form, for indirection is the very the heart of how the dominated resist domination (Scott 1985).

Alcock found in Greece's assimilation to the imperial system evidence of both resistance and accommodation (Alcock 1993: 230), and it is undoubtedly right to see a similar dynamic in baptism. It both mirrored and subverted the dominant order. From this angle, baptism is best understood as a ritual enactment of symbolic inversion. Barbara Babcock's remarks about the two sides of inversion capture the dynamic quite accurately:

> "Symbolic inversion" may be broadly defined as any act of expressive behavior which inverts, contradicts, abrogates, or in some fashion presents an alternative to commonly held cultural codes, values, and norms, be they linguistic, literary or artistic, religious, or social and political.
>
> (Babcock 1978: 14)

Even as inversion contradicts it also confirms: "All symbolic inversions define a culture's lineaments at the same time as they question the usefulness and the absoluteness of this ordering" (Babcock 1978: 29).

Understood as a rite of inversion in the larger context of water use at Corinth, baptism represents an act of creative interaction with the complex cultural situation that typified life there. Properly situated, it becomes much more than a rite of entry significant only to the community that performed it. It was a response to Roman hegemonic control of water, expressed in the proliferation of baths, aqueducts, and nymphaea in Corinth and throughout the Mediterranean world. This contextualization of baptism underscores its political implications, much as scholars have noted the political implications of the New Testament's theological and religious discourse. With regard to Paul and his Corinthian correspondence, several of Richard Horsley's studies of 1 Corinthians are worth noting. In them he insists that we understand Paul as adamantly opposed to the Roman imperial order and his letters to the Corinthians as articulations of an alternative society to that order (Horsley 1997; 2000). If this chapter has situated baptism correctly, then resistance to Rome came to expression not only rhetorically but also ritually.

Who exactly would have expressed resistance to Rome at Corinth? This question naturally arises once Roman Corinth is understood as a thoroughly Roman place and not a revival of Greek Corinth. Plus, unlike most other cities in Greece, Corinth suffered tremendously at the hands of the Romans: it was sacked and its population dispersed. Contemporary literary commentary describes a slate that had been wiped clean:

Where is thy celebrated beauty, Doric Corinth?
Where are the battlements of thy towers and thy ancient possessions?
Where are the temples of the immortals, the houses of the matrons of
  the town of Sisyphus, and her myriads of people?
Not even a trace is left of thee, most unhappy of towns,
but war has seized on and devoured everything.
We alone, the Nereids, Ocean's daughters, remain inviolate,
and lament, like halcyons, thy sorrows.
                    (Antipater of Sidon, *Greek Anthology* 9.151 [Paton, LCL])

Was there a native Greek population that survived Corinth's destruction
and desolation? Apropos baptism as an expression of native resistance, did
these survivors affiliate with the early church at Corinth?

From an elite perspective Corinth was indeed empty, because Corinth's
elite was gone. But it is hyperbole to claim that Corinth was actually
desolate and dormant for a century, between its destruction by Roman
general Mummius in 146 BCE and its resettlement as a colony in 44 BCE
by Julius Caesar. Like Pausanias's description of Corinth, the literary record
regarding Corinth's fall and the aftermath is skewed. While most reports
from antiquity describe a completely devastated and abandoned Corinth,
such as Dio Cassius's (21 [= Zonaras 9.31]), the archaeological record confirms the reports of eyewitnesses like Cicero who encountered inhabitants
among the ruins of Corinth (*Tusculanae disputationes* 3.22.53).

The material record indicates that parts of the city, like the South Stoa,
survived the sack relatively intact. Moreover, ceramic and numismatic data
point to habitation and commercial activity between 146 BCE and the founding of the Roman colony in 44 BCE (Romano 1994; Wiseman 1979: 494–5).
Charles Williams observes that Greek graffiti on early Roman pottery is
evidence for a Greek-speaking element in the early years of the Roman colony
(Williams 1987: 35, n 20; also Wiseman 1978: 12, n 25; Williams 1993: 31,
33). We can be certain, therefore, that devastated Corinth did not lie dormant
and that Greek-speakers were present in Corinth during the interim period.

But was this a residual *indigenous* population that preserved the traditions of the past, such as the pronounced use of water for cultic purposes,
as the archaeology of the Greek period indicates? The answer is not
obvious, for the colonists Rome sent to Corinth may well have included
Greek speakers, and it is possible that Rome authorized Greek-speaking
agents to operate in and around Corinth in the years prior to colonization
(Bookidis 2005: 150).

The question of continuity between the Greek and Roman periods is
complex and unsettled, but the material records provides evidence that is
best accounted for by positing the survival of local inhabitants:

1. The chief excavator at Isthmia, an athletic and cult center near
    Corinth, sees some evidence of continuity between the Greek and Roman

periods in the continuing use of traditional Greek funeral dirges in conjunction with the Palaimon-Melikertes hero cult. Such continuity may have stemmed from Sikyon, a city very near Corinth, which did not suffer Corinth's fate and which took control of the Isthmian festival after 146 BCE (Gebhard 2005: 176–81).

2. The cult of Hoplismene, or Armed Aphrodite, a pre-Roman cult limited in mainland Greece to Corinth, reappeared in the district immediately east of the theater in the Roman period (Williams 2005: 221–47).

3. A diachronic survey of funerary practices in Corinth prompted Mary E. Hoskins Walbank to note "Roman citizens . . . were living side by side with the local population, who may well have maintained their own long-standing religious practices" (Walbank 2005: 249). At the large cemetery immediately north of Corinth, the traditional custom of burial by inhumation continued between the Greek and Roman periods. More to the point, the body orientation remained the same, even though grave markers did not in all probability survive the Greek-to-Roman transition (Blegen, Palmer, and Young 1964: 70; Rife 1999: 222–4).

Some portion of Roman Corinth's Greek-speaking population, therefore, was indigenous. Thus, memory of the customs and practices of the Greek past persisted into Roman times.

It is not hard to picture some of the surviving local population finding its way into the Corinthian church. While we find both Greek and Latin names among those Paul addresses in the Corinthian correspondence, Greek speakers undoubtedly dominated (Sellin 1987: 2997; Theissen 1974: 232–74). As the Roman colonists obliterated or modified Greek religious sites in the city, those proclaiming an alternative to the Roman way may have found a sympathetic local audience. If these surviving residents could no longer engage in the sacred water use their ancestors had – as shown above, water facilities at key Greek religious sites had vanished by Roman times – perhaps they gave expression to their religious disposition in another venue.

Although the evidence for it is indirect, the Corinthian church appears to have emphasized water ritual, specifically, baptism. In Paul's First Letter to the Corinthians the Greek verb baptize (*baptizō*) occurs many more times than in any other New Testament letter, and, comparatively speaking, with greater frequency than in the gospels and Acts, where baptisms are actually narrated. The rite is referred to throughout the letter:

1. Paul's language in the first chapter of the letter indicates the Corinthians based allegiances within the community on it. As he criticizes the factionalism and party divisions at Corinth, Paul asks, "Were you baptized in the name of Paul?" (1 Cor 1:13).

2. Paul makes a thinly veiled reference to baptism in chapter 10 (10:1–2) and mentions it again directly in chapter 12 (12:13).

3. In chapter 15 we learn that the Corinthians regarded baptism as efficacious even for their dead. Paul refers to baptism on behalf of the dead at 15:29 in such a way that it seems to be a Corinthian practice. (More on this in Chapter 3.)

The first and last examples suggest that local believers placed great weight on baptism. Could such an orientation in the church reflect a native Corinthian predilection for sacred water use? If so, the church was providing an outlet for a local Greek religiosity that could no longer come to expression in the sacred landscape that Rome was creating on Greek soil.

Greek resistance to Romanization took place in many different ways and in many arenas, including the sacred landscape. It could be passive. Alcock (Alcock 1993: 259, n. 59) notes the (intentional?) neglect shown the imperial cult at Elis, in the western Peloponnesus: "Adjoining the marketplace is an old temple surrounded by pillars; the roof has fallen down, and I found no image in the temple. It is dedicated to the Roman emperors" (Pausanias, *Descr.* 6.24.10 [Jones, LCL]). More active expression took place in Athens. There a statue of Athena was turned to face west and spattered with blood (Dio Cass. 54.7.2–3). It looked as though the protectress of Athens was spitting blood at Rome (Hoff 1989; Bowersock 1965: 106).

Protest against Roman hegemony naturally took ambivalent form, in order to avoid drawing reprisal. It might also take place at the periphery rather than the center of civic society: "Popular classes also enacted their own rituals and articulated alternative visions of social order, often in the relative safety of 'off-stage' settings – working-class neighborhoods, slave quarters, or rural villages – where elites seldom ventured" (Beezley, Martin, and French 1994: xxv). If we are looking for Greek dissent from the Roman order in Corinth, we might find it in the house churches, which provided safe haven for ancestral sacred water use dressed now as an entry rite.

Because control of water served as a primary marker of Roman culture and expression of Rome's hegemony, dissenters directed their barbs in its direction. A scene from the early third-century *Martyrdom of Saints Perpetua and Felicitas* is a case in point. In the closing scene, as the martyrs face death in the amphitheater, the narrative is keen to point out that it is the martyrs themselves, not imperial power, that ultimately control their fate: Perpetua dies only when she guides the trembling hand of the gladiator to her throat (21.9). At the same time, the narrative introduces the language of the Roman bath:

> At another gate Saturus was earnestly addressing the soldier Pudens. "It is exactly," he said, "as I foretold and predicted. So far not one animal has touched me. So now you may believe me with all your heart: I am going in there and I shall be finished off with one bite of the leopard." And immediately as the contest was coming to a close a

leopard was let loose, and after one bite Saturus was so drenched with blood that as he came away the mob roared in witness to his second baptism: "Well washed! Well washed!" For well washed indeed was one who had been bathed in this manner.

(*Passio sanctarum Perpetuae et Felicitatis* 21.1–3;
Musurillo 1972: 129–31)

The phrase *salve lotus* or *kalōs elousou* – well washed – was a slogan of the Roman bath, so common it was sometimes inscribed or painted at the exits of a public bath (Yegül 1992: 38). So not only does the report display Christian martyrs as masters of the amphitheater – and blood sports were another defining feature of Roman urban life – Roman bathing culture is also being tweaked: the bloodbath is genuine Roman bathing! Here again ritual inversion is at work. (For martyrdom as second baptism, see Tertullian, *Bapt*.16).

Late Roman Corinth provides another example of the cultural contest that surrounded the Roman bath and the use of water. As noted earlier, the Roman reshaping of Corinth's hydraulic systems included modification of a fourth- or fifth-century BCE Greek bath in the mid-first century CE in the Gymnasium district, north and west of the forum. The resulting complex included a subterranean bath chamber, sunken pool, and exterior courtyard, and it continued to be fed by the natural spring the Greeks had originally exploited (Wiseman 1972; Rothaus 2000: 126–34). By 400 CE the site has been so badly damaged by earthquake that it no longer functioned as a bath. The site was not abandoned, however. Access to the courtyard and subterranean chamber was reestablished and it became a cultic site. Until the complex's final collapse in the middle of the sixth century, the site attracted votive offerings. Particularly well represented were terracotta lamps – over 4,000 lamps have been recovered – so that excavators dubbed the site the Fountain of the Lamps.

What kind of cultic activity replaced Roman bathing? Of the four curse tablets found at the site, one invokes the Nymphs, perennially popular minor deities in Greek religiosity. Subterranean places – often caves – and sources of water typically attracted Nymph worship, and the dedication of lamps was common to such piety. So it is no surprise that the sacralizing of a site like a Roman bath would involve the Nymphs.

As the same time, Christian cultic activity is much in evidence. This, too, is not surprising given the time frame for lamp dedication – Late Roman Corinth was largely Christianized. In addition to lamps with crosses and displays of Old Testament stories, there are a handful of inscribed lamps. The graffiti on them is revealing. Along with standard Christian formulas like "Be merciful to your servant" are appeals to angels: "I invoke you by the great god Sabaoth, by Michael, by Gabriel, in order that you do . . ." and "angels who dwell upon these waters" (Wiseman 1972: 28–32; Jordan 1994: 224–5). A small inscribed cross begins this last graffito. These lamps, along with most of the offerings, were recovered from the underground bath chamber, which would have been flooded in the period when the lamps were offered.

Why were Christians invoking angels at the site of a collapsed Roman bath? Christians expressed a wide range of opinions about baths, ranging from tolerance (John Chrysostom, *Homiliae in Joannem* 18) to alarm. The *Acts of Andrews* warns its readers about the dangers that lurked there:

> After some days [Andrew] bade them prepare him a bath; and going there saw an old man with a devil, trembling exceedingly. As he wondered at him, another, a youth, came out of the bath and fell at his feet, saying: "What have we to do with thee, Andrew? Hast thou come here to turn us out of our abodes?" Andrew said to the people: "Fear not," and drove out both the devils. Then, as he bathed, he told them: "The enemy of mankind lies in wait everywhere, in baths and in rivers; therefore we ought always to invoke the Lord's name, that he may have no power over us."
>
> (Gregory of Tours' Epitome 27; Elliott 1993: 281)

The Roman bath was not neutral territory. So perhaps Corinthian Christians were invoking angels to exorcise a former bath of the demons thought to live there – or expelling the Nymphs their neighbors approached there. (We cannot exclude the possibility that certain Corinthians were invoking both angels and Nymphs.)

The Christian writer Tertullian's (ca. 160–ca. 220 CE) lengthy reflection on baptism suggests other possibilities. He describes the danger that unsanctified water posed and offers baptism as an antidote:

> Also, apart from this, without any sacred significance, unclean spirits do settle upon waters, pretending to reproduce that primordial resting of the divine Spirit upon them: as witness shady springs and all sorts of unfrequented streams, pools in bathing-places, and channels or storage-tanks in houses, and those wells called snatching-wells – obviously they snatch by the violent action of a malignant spirit: . . . Why have I referred to such matters? So that no one should think it over-difficult for God's angel to be present to set the waters in motion for man's salvation, when an unholy angel of the evil one often does business with the same element with a view to man's perdition.
>
> (*De baptismo* 5; Evans 1964: 13, 15)

According to Tertullian, God sends an angel to sanctify baptismal water so that it purifies human beings instead of defiling them. He sees such sanctification foreshadowed in a story from the gospel of John (5:3–4), in which an angel periodically stirred a pool of water and brought healing to any who descended into it:

If it is thought strange that an angel should do such things to waters, there has already occurred a precedent of that which was to be. An angel used to do things when he moved the Pool of Bethsaida. Those who complained of ill-health used to watch out for him, for anyone who got down there before the others, after washing had no further reason to complain.

(ibid. 5; Evans 1964: 15)

Because of the paucity of evidence, we will very likely never know exactly what Corinthian Christians were doing at the Fountain of the Lamps when they invoked angels: exorcising a Roman bath of its demons? Competing with Nymph devotees at a site that everyone regarded as sacred? Carrying out baptismal rites? Seeking healing? One thing is certain, however: Corinthian waters did not go uncontested.

3   And the Greatest of These Is Death

Food, reproduction and death are the common factors of humanity, and the greatest of these is death. Human societies are moulded by their dialogue with death: frameworks, by which individuals and communities establish their own world-picture, are stretched and then defined by the need to comprehend and incorporate mortality.

(Kinnes 1981: 83)

It was then that Aisymnos, who was second in reputation to no one in Megara, went to the god at Delphi and asked how they should prosper. During his answer, the god prophesied the Megarians would prosper by making their decisions with the majority. They took this to refer to the dead, and built their council house so that the graves of the heroes were inside it.

(Pausanias, *Graeciae descriptio* 1.43.3; Levi 1971: 119–20)

This chapter continues the work of the previous one, situating baptism in as full as a context as possible. Corinth remains the focal point because of the rich archaeological record we have for the city and its environs in the first century CE and because Paul's Corinthian correspondence tells us much about the early church there relative to other places. The Corinthian church warrants continued attention because it practiced a form of baptism that was little known elsewhere in the early church: baptism on behalf of the dead (1 Cor 15:29). If a ritual critical approach can illuminate this application of baptism, it will go a long way to proving its value for New Testament studies.

   This form of baptism has perplexed New Testament scholars for many, many years. "The phrase *baptizesthai hyper tōn nekrōn* of 1 Cor. 15:29 has always been obscure. It can justly be labeled as a 'crux interpretum.' An all around satisfactory explanation of the words has never ceased to tantalize exegetes" (Foschini 1951: 1). Bernard Foschini wrote these words over a half-century ago to introduce an interpretive puzzle he hoped to solve, but his attempt, like all attempts before and after, has failed to garner broad acceptance from New Testament scholars. To date, no interpretation has swept the field, though not for lack of trying: "Despite dozens of proposed solutions, the reference itself is simply so obscure and our knowledge so limited that we cannot discern just what this rite actually involved or meant" (Carlson 1993: 261).

But is baptism for the dead really so obscure? Is our knowledge so limited? There is, in fact, not much to go in the text itself. Commentators have noted how little the context of the verse prepares us for it and tells us about it. The tone and style of 15:29 change abruptly from that of the preceding section of chapter 15, and while verses 30 to 34 continue the rhetorical questions begun in verse 29, they introduce an entirely different subject matter (Senft 1990: 201–2; Conzelmann 1975: 275–7; Murphy-O'Connor 1979: 144–5). The verse itself is straightforward, but because Paul refers to an evidently known practice at this point, much goes unspoken between writer and audience: "Otherwise, what do people mean by being baptized on behalf of the dead? If the dead are not raised at all, why are people baptized on their behalf?" (1 Cor 15:29; Revised Standard Version). What does this verse reveal? The recipients of Paul's letter very likely knew the point of these questions, so presumably the Corinthian church knew about baptism for the dead. More likely, in light of the rarity of the practice in ancient Christianity (the scant evidence is collected by [Rissi 1962: 6–22]), the Corinthian believers themselves baptized for the dead. In addition to locating the practice in Corinth, most scholars have understood the Greek to describe a vicarious baptism undergone by the living for the benefit of the physically dead (Wedderburn 1987: 287–93; Downey 1985: 23; Conzelmann 1975: 275–6; Barrett 1968: 363; Hurd 1965: 136; Beasley-Murray 1962: 185–7). Beyond these few agreements, however, no unanimity exists.

Even the consensus about the vicarious nature of the rite has not kept scholars from proposing many alternatives to it, encouraged no doubt by the meager textual evidence. Some have proposed altering the accepted punctuation of 1 Cor 15:29 so that baptism and on behalf of the dead belong to different clauses: "Else what will they achieve who are baptised – merely for the benefit of their dead bodies, if dead bodies never rise again? Why then be baptised just for them?" (Thompson 1964: 651, 659; see also Foschini 1951: 92–8). This rendering allows the practice to be understood as baptism for one's own body. Other interpreters take the proposition *hyper* in a final sense – "because of" or "for the sake of" – and argue that baptism *for the sake of* the dead was an act undergone by the living for themselves – that is, by unbaptized family members or relatives – to ensure their reunion with dead Christian relatives or friends in the next world (Raeder 1955: 258–60; Howard 1965: 140). Both interpretations rid the practice of its vicarious action aimed at benefiting the dead and direct it instead to the living.

More recent interpretations have pushed the proposition *hyper* in yet another direction, rendering it as "on account of" instead of "on behalf of." This causal reading of the preposition allows Michael Hull to understand baptism *on account of* the dead as baptism motivated by faith in the resurrection of the dead. Doing so enables him to tie verse 29 to the main theme of 1 Corinthian 15, namely, the resurrection of the dead (Hull 2005). Joel White also understands the preposition causally, and he argues that the dead refer to the suffering and dying apostles and missionaries that motivated their audience to believe and be baptized. Hence, what Paul refers to in 1 Corinthians 15:29 are people who were baptized on account of the (now dead) apostles under whose ministry they were converted (White 1997: 498; see also Patrick 2006).

The isolated character of 1 Corinthians 15:29 in its literary context and the lack of indicators in the verse as to the nature of the rite make it all too easy to propose a range of grammatically possible translations. But the highly speculative interpretations that result only underscore the need to place the text (and practice described therein) in the fullest possible context. Behind all attempts to remove vicarious action from baptism for the dead, one senses uneasiness about Paul or the early church's association with a rite that appears to be "superstitious" or "magical" (Raeder 1955: 258–9; Rissi 1962: 89–92). (Understood vicariously, the practice would affirm that the living can ritually affect the dead.) But who is feeling the discomfort? Paul himself maintained that family members could act vicariously for each other (1 Cor 7:14), and he recognized an efficacy in eucharist that certainly appears to be "magical" (Sellin 1986: 278; M. Smith 1980: 248):

> Examine yourselves, and only then eat of the bread and drink of the cup. For all who eat and drink without discerning the body, eat and drink judgment against themselves. For this reason many of you are weak and ill, and some have died.
>
> (1 Cor 11:28–30)

In the pages that follow, this chapter will describe a culture in which aiding the dead was all-important and which assumed that the world of the living could affect the world of the dead. In such a culture baptism undertaken by the living for the dead would have made perfect sense.

Other interpretations of baptism for the dead have taken a different approach, but the result has not been much better. Instead of restricting himself to a literary or philological interpretive program, Wayne Meeks sought to understand baptism for the dead – and baptism in general – in a broader context. In the fifth chapter of *The First Urban Christians*, entitled "Ritual," he sought to examine baptism as one of many rites among the churches addressed by Paul or associated with his name (Meeks 1983: 140–63). At first glance, this approach is vastly different from earlier studies of baptism in the Pauline churches, such as Rudolf Schnackenburg's *Baptism in the Thought of St. Paul*, for Meeks intentionally avoided theological categories like eschatology and soteriology that anchored Schnackenburg's analysis (Schnackenburg 1964; see also Cullmann 1953, Delling 1962, Hahn 1973).

Yet for all the genuine differences in the two scholars' approaches, striking similarities remain. Despite his intention to do otherwise, Meeks treated baptism apart from other rites practiced by believers. Both it and the Lord's Supper got their own major section in his chapter on ritual. All other rites he consigned to the chapter's opening section on minor rituals or to the closing section on unknown or controverted rituals. The wealth of information in the New Testament about baptism and the Lord's Supper relative to other rites may have justified such compartmentalization and ranking, but it undermined Meeks's professed goal of understanding baptism as one among many rites practiced by the early believers (Meeks 1983: 142). While Meeks wanted to avoid giving baptism a privileged status, as Schnackenburg had done in treating it as a sacrament, his presentation of it slips into such favoritism.

What Meeks and Schnackenburg concluded about baptism on behalf of the dead is also much the same, though again their approaches to it differ widely. Schnackenburg relegated 1 Corinthians 15:29 to a chapter called "Uncertain and Derived Baptismal Statements" (Schnackenburg 1964: 95–102). Meeks placed it under the heading "Unknown and Controverted Rituals" instead of including it in his treatment of baptism (Meeks 1983: 162). True, the text reveals little about this form of baptism, but there may be another reason he excluded it from treatment. As we found in Chapter 1, Meeks drew from the rites-of-passage model originating with Arnold van Gennep and developed by Victor Turner when he analyzed baptism in the Pauline congregations as a rite of initiation or community entry (Meeks 1983: 153–7). Yet once Meeks attached such significance to baptism, what sense could he make of baptism for the dead, that is, baptism for those who were departing or had departed from the living community?

Meeks neglected to note that the common thread Van Gennep detected running through rites that mark birth, coming of age, marriage, and death meant that they could become apt and potent metaphors for one another. This cross-referencing or indexing between rites was common in the ancient Mediterranean world, as evidenced by the juxtaposing and intertwining of funerary and wedding rites in classical Athenian society (Rehm 1994). By the advent of the church, marriage to death was a common means of describing the funeral of a young woman who died before her wedding (Bodel 1995: 456). Within early church circles, too, rites marking transition were cross-referential: baptism became associated with birth (John 3:3–6) and burial (Col 2:12). From the standpoint of Mediterranean transitional or boundary-crossing rites, therefore, connecting baptism with the dead, that is, the funerary, is not an "unknown" application of baptism but a logical extension of it.

We can improve on Meeks's problematic analysis of baptism, including baptism for the dead, by setting it alongside other rites, both inside and outside the early church. Not only would we avoid isolating baptism from other rites, as Meeks did, but we would also not be so quick to join him in assigning a function or meaning to baptism. Rather, the bare facts or obvious features of baptism remain the focus of investigation, and we keep our attention there by comparing them with the features of other rites of the day. In the case of baptism on behalf of the dead what is most conspicuous is the object or beneficiaries of the baptism. Attention to funerary or burial rites is in order, then, as a way of providing a ritual context for this variation of baptism.

Rather than undertaking a general survey of Mediterranean funeral or burial rites at this point, we can restrict our contextualizing of baptism for the dead by looking for types of funerals exhibiting a surrogate or substitutionary aspect, for most scholars think 1 Corinthians 15:29 denotes a vicarious baptism undergone by the living for the benefit of the physically dead, as noted earlier. One of the fullest descriptions of a funeral we have from the Roman world is Dio Cassius's record of the funeral that emperor Severus staged for an earlier emperor, Pertinax:

> His funeral, in spite of the time that had elapsed since his death, was carried out as follows. In the Roman Forum a wooden platform was constructed hard by the marble rostra, upon which was set a shrine, without walls, but surrounded by columns, cunningly wrought of both ivory and gold. In it there was placed a bier of the same materials, surrounded by heads of both land and sea animals and adorned with coverlets of purple and gold. Upon this rested an effigy of Pertinax in wax, laid out in triumphal garb; and a comely youth was keeping the flies away from it with a peacock feather, as though it were really a person sleeping.
>
> (Dio Cass. 75.4.2–3 [Cary, LCL])

Dio's account comes to an end when the bier is ignited: "Then at last the consuls applied fire to the structure, and when this had been done, an eagle flew aloft from it. Thus was Pertinax made immortal" (ibid. 75.5.5 [Cary, LCL]).

Dio's report describes the second funeral held for Pertinax, not the first. This second, honorary funeral was evidently meant to replace the original funeral held for Pertinax, for the latter had been carried out dishonorably by Julianus, emperor between Pertinax and Severus. Dio does not record the first funeral; at least the extant summary of Dio's history does not have it. But another historian, Julius Capitolinus, reports that while Julianus buried Pertinax with all honor, he never mentioned Pertinax's name in public (14.9). Dio verifies the disdain that Julianus had for Pertinax when he reports that the former made fun of the funerary banquet held for the latter (74.13.1–2). In this light, the second, imaginary funeral (*funus imaginarium*; Capitolinus 15.1) substitutes for the first and corrects the injustice done to Pertinax. Of the two funerals, the imaginary was the legitimate and real.

Capturing a similar phenomenon much lower on the social ladder are the rules of a burial club from Lanuvium, a small town in Italy, dating from about 136 CE. Such clubs were popular and numerous in Roman society, reflecting the concern people had to be properly mourned and decently buried (Hopkins 1983: 212–15). Delivery of these services could be complicated in the case of slave club members, as this excerpt from the rules shows:

> It was voted that, when any slave who is a member of the club dies, if his master or mistress would unjustly refuse to hand over his body for burial, and if the slave has left no directions, a token funeral ceremony [*funus imag(ina)rium*] will be held.
>
> (Dessau, *ILS* 2:738 §7212, II, 3–4; Hopkins 1983:215)

In this example we have moved from elite to mass society, yet application of the funerary rite is much the same. The exact funeral arrangements – whether an effigy replaced the corpse, a living club member took the place of the deceased, or some other substitution – go unrecorded. Whatever the arrangements, club members had decided a vicarious rite effectively discharged the duty of the club to deceased members under certain circumstances. An imaginary funeral, with the surrogacy or substitution implied by it, could take the place of a regular one.

As noted above, another salient feature of baptism for the dead is whom it benefits, the dead rather than the living. Like its vicarious aspect, this feature does not appear so unusual in the context of Roman funeral ritual, specifically in comparison with funerals held for the living, another modification Roman funerals underwent. Seneca provides examples of two such funerals, one in the *Essay on the Shortness of Life*, in which he argues against trying to circumvent one's lot in life:

> I cannot pass over an instance which occurs to me. Sextus Turannius was an old man of long tested diligence, who, after his ninetieth year, having received release from the duties of his office by Gaius Caesar's own act, ordered himself to be laid out on his bed and to be mourned by the assembled household as if he were dead. The whole house bemoaned the leisure of its old master, and did not end its sorrow until his accustomed work was restored to him. Is it really such pleasure for a man to die in harness? Yet very many have the same feeling; their desire for their labour lasts longer than their ability.
>
> (*De brevitate vitae* 20.3–4 [Basore, LCL])

A similar theme reappears in Seneca's twelfth epistle to Lucilius which is entitled *On Old Age*. There, he maintains that both young and old should keep death in mind as the fate that everyone faces (12.6). Then he gives another example of a funeral for the living:

> Pacuvius, who by long occupancy made Syria his own, used to hold a regular burial sacrifice in his own honour, with wine and the usual funeral

feasting, and then would have himself carried from the dining-room to his chamber, while eunuchs applauded and sang in Greek to a musical accompaniment: "He has lived his life, he has lived his life!" Thus Pacuvius had himself carried out to burial every day. Let us, however, do from a good motive what he used to do from a debased motive; let us go to our sleep with joy and gladness; let us say: "I have lived; the course which Fortune set for me is finished."

(*Ad Lucilium* 12.8 [Gummere, LCL])

While not happy with the sense of self-importance and ostentation that motivated Pacuvius to stage his own funeral, Seneca finds great value in the reminder that a daily funeral provides (ibid. 12.9).

Staged or imaginary funerals must have had general currency among the elite of Roman society, for the motif occurs in Petronius's *Satyricon*, where all manner of funerary elements appear at the last stages of the banquet Trimalchio puts on for his guests (§§ 71–8). Such usage, like Pacuvius's, may have been a theatrical and ostentatious way to bring an evening of excess to an end.

Further exploration of Mediterranean funeral rites lies beyond the scope of this chapter, but the instances presented are sufficient to document the malleability and adaptability that Roman funerary rites had. Beyond the linkage that they might have to other rites, such as weddings, funerals found creative application to all sorts of separations, from departure for the evening to retirement. They could also mark other transitional moments, as when Pertinax was deified. This is exactly what the use of funerary customs and language in non-funerary situations conveyed in the literature of the time. Seneca, for instance, wrote a letter of consolation to his mother Helvia over the loss of her son when he, Seneca, was sent into exile – when he became socially dead (*Ad Helvium*). Similarly, Cicero resorted to funerary language to describe the consequences of a trial that ends in public disgrace for a defendant, a severe punishment reserved for breach of trust or guardianship. Those so defamed could have their property confiscated and sold at auction, a situation Cicero compares to a funeral, in this case of the bitterest kind. For the defamed are witness to brokers and buyers assembled not to honor them but to squabble over their possessions (*Pro Quinctio* 15 §50).

In addition to what the examples above say about funerary ritual, they also provide an important context for baptism and its variations. At the very least, the adaptability of funerals to non-funerary situations opens the door to finding baptism other than where we might expect to find it, at the threshold of the church. Furthermore, two extraordinary types of funeral are noteworthy for how they elucidate baptism on behalf of the dead: (1) a replacement or substitute rite performed vicariously for the dead; and (2) funerals for the living. Both applications are imaginary rites, whose context indicates whether we further qualify them as honorary or mock. This, then, is the language for baptism on behalf of the dead that is both contextually and ritually sensitive: it was an imaginary rite of the honorary type.

Isolating baptism for the dead, as Meeks did, made it mystifying to him (Meeks 1983: 162), but placing it in context has the opposite effect. Set alongside funerals for the living – those of Turannius and Pacuvius – baptism for the dead does not appear mysterious. In terms of who undergoes them, both rites reverse ordinary practice. Likewise, in light of surrogate or replacement funerals in which a person or community carried out a rite for someone in absentia – for Pertinax and the Lanuvium burial club member whose body could not be recovered – baptism on behalf of the dead falls within the typical range of ritual variation in the Greco-Roman world. In the context of other rites, therefore, baptism for the dead is, contrary to what New Testament scholars claim, not obscure.

Placing a rite in context ultimately draws attention to the rite itself, and this foray into Roman funerary rites gives us fresh eyes for looking at baptism in general. What do we see? If the malleability of rites in the Greco-Roman world as evidenced by Roman funeral rites readies us to expect flexibility in baptism, the examples also indicate that inventive application does not mean haphazard or random use. Funerary rites appeared in new situations not unrelated to their ordinary use: extraordinary funerals like their ordinary counterparts marked separation or transition. If the creative extension of baptism followed a like development, then baptism for the dead continued to serve as a boundary-crossing rite but outside a typical setting. In this new circumstance, where the dead rather than the living benefited from the rite, the movement was not from outside the church in but the reverse, from the inside out. (Or perhaps it is more accurate to think of the boundary-crossing as a movement from the circle of the living to the circle of dead *within the church.*) As an entry rite, baptism on behalf of the dead would have confirmed the departure of deceased community members from the circle of the living and enabled their entry into the community of the dead.

In addition to what this glimpse of the Mediterranean ritual world suggests about the variation that baptism could undergo, it also makes us sensitive to interaction *between* rites. Given the use of funerary rites for enacting separation and transition and given baptism's use to signal separation from one's past and a transformation of those who underwent it, it is not surprising to find funerary elements in baptismal discourse:

> Do you not know that all of us who have been baptized into Christ Jesus were baptized into his death? Therefore *we have been buried with him by baptism into death*, so that, just as Christ was raised from the dead by the glory of the Father, so we too might walk in newness of life.
> (Rom 6:3–4; italics added)

Baptism in Romans 6 is a burial (v. 4) because – in line with the application of funerary rites elsewhere – it marks departure or separation from a previous situation or condition, or in Paul's language, the death of the old self (v. 6). From the standpoint of the Mediterranean ritual world, therefore, baptism according to Romans 6 was an imaginary funeral.

The preceding pages have located baptism in a ritual world that allowed, perhaps even encouraged, both ritual variation and the application of rites to situations where we might not ordinarily expect to find them. As denizens of that world, members of the early church were capable of similar innovation. But why did their ritual innovation take the form it did – baptism for the dead? To answer this question, to find out why baptism became connected with the world of the dead, we return to the funerary and mortuary practices of the ancient Mediterranean.

Both ancient Greek and Roman societies devoted considerable resources to the dead, in part for fear of them but primarily because the living were thought to be obligated to help the deceased become integrated into the realm of the dead. Such help was crucial, for the moment of physical death was thought to mark only the beginning of a long and sometimes difficult transition to the next world (Kurtz and Boardman 1971: 330; Garland 1985: 38–47; Alexiou 1974: 4–23). In Greece this help began with proper mourning and burial rites and continued for some time in the form of periodic commemorations of the deceased, such as festivals. Remembering the dead also involved visiting the grave, a visit that might include sacrifices and feasts held for them. A few Greek graves even had feeding tubes so that blood offerings and libations could be communicated directly to the deceased. Many of these practices appear to reflect a belief that the dead could benefit directly from actions performed on their behalf, particularly at the grave. Acting on this belief, some individuals set up trusts to ensure that they would be adequately commemorated and provided for in death (Garland 1985: 39, 108–18).

Despite some differences in practice, Roman attitudes toward, and beliefs about, death and the dead had much in common with the Greek perspective. Proper burial was so great a concern that clubs, such as the one in Lanuvium, existed to ensure that members were adequately mourned and buried, and these were very popular in imperial Roman society (Hopkins 1983: 212–16). Post-burial commemoration of the dead focused on graveside feasts and annual festivals, much as in Greece (Toynbee 1971: 50–64). Providing for the dead could entail major financial outlays: wealthy Romans established elaborate tombs and even funerary gardens equipped with dining rooms, kitchens, wells, and cisterns (ibid.: 94–100). Obviously, such expenditures reflected well on the living. At the same time, many Romans were convinced that the dead dwelt in the tomb and they needed adequate facilities (Ferguson 1970: 134). In all this, the Romans exhibited the same Greek sense of obligation to, and honor of, the dead.

In broad terms this is how ancient Greeks and Romans related to their dead. Unfortunately, little of the information for this description comes from Corinth. The studies of ancient Greek burial customs by Donna Kurtz and John Boardman and by Robert Garland depended heavily on Attic evidence

(Kurtz and Boardman 1971; Garland 1985), the Roman study by Jocelyn Toynbee on Italian data (Toynbee 1971). Nevertheless, burials in Corinth and its environs, the Corinthia, provide data that support this general picture. At least, the burials there seem to be fairly typical. Corinth's North Cemetery represents the largest excavated burial ground in the Corinthia and it has a broad chronological range of burials. Hazel Palmer's study of the Classical and Hellenistic Greek graves documents a steady interest in supplying the dead with adequate goods, for even the least expensive graves had vases in and by them, sometimes a considerable number (Blegen, Palmer, and Young 1964: 68–86).

Roman-era graves in the North Cemetery contained on average fewer pottery offerings than Greek-era graves, but this fact should not be read as a sign of lessening concern for the dead (Blegen, Palmer, and Young 1964: 82). The continuing strength of this concern found clear expression in impressive Roman chamber tombs dating from the late first century CE, which excavators unearthed in a hillside (Cheliotomylos) near Corinth's North Cemetery. The most elaborate of these had niches for the remains of several individuals, wall paintings, numerous lamps and small finds, and even a well shaft (Shear 1931: 424–41). The size and details of the tomb point to lavish expenditure typical of the Roman era, and underscore how much attention the dead commanded. All in all, the data from Corinthian burials confirm the general picture I have drawn of the deep obligation ancient Greeks and Romans felt toward their dead (Walbank 2005; Rife 1999).

Concern for the dead could find other channels of expression in both Greek and Roman society, and early Roman Corinthia provides ample evidence of an emerging preoccupation with the dead and the world of the dead. The cultic focal point of Isthmia, an athletic and religious center a few kilometers east of Corinth, was the Temple of Poseidon, yet the Panhellenic games celebrated there were dedicated to the dead hero Palaimon or Melikertes and were funerary in nature (Kurtz and Boardman 1971: 202). How early the Palaimon cult emerged at the Poseidon site is uncertain. Walter Burkert sees like development occurring at all the Panhellenic game sites by the seventh century BCE (Burkert 1985: 193), but the evidence for it at Isthmia is thin. Excavations at Isthmia have turned up little evidence for the Palaimon cult before Roman times, and literary evidence comes largely from writers of Roman imperial times (Broneer 1973: 99). As a result, some, such as John Hawthorne, argue that the cult of Palaimon began only after Roman settlement (Hawthorne 1958: 92–8). Others, including the excavators of Isthmia, posit some level of pre-Roman activity but can offer only tentative identification of its location (Gebhard 1993a: 171; Broneer 1973: 99).

No matter when it began at Isthmia, the Palaimon cult became prominent in the Roman period (Koester 1990: 357, 363; Gebhard 1993b: 78–94). Archaeological data – numismatic and architectural – provide evidence of a round temple by the middle of the second century, and predating this are several pits and a high wall enclosing the Palaimon precinct (Gebhard 1993b: 89–93). The pits were evidently used for burning sacrifices, for all showed signs of intense heat and were filled with ash and burnt animal bones (Broneer 1973: 100–12). The earliest of these, pit A, contained pottery that would suggest it was in use from 50 to 80 CE (Geagan 1989: 359; Gebhard 1993b: 79–85). This archaeological evidence accords well with the literary record: Philostratus says that the secret rites of Palaimon (Melikertes) included offerings (*enagismata*) from a slaughtered black bull (*Imagines* 2.16). Excavators also recovered a large number of distinctive lamps from the site, which indicates nocturnal rites, a deduction confirmed by Plutarch's description of the Melikertes rites (*Theseus* 25) (Broneer 1973: 109; 1977: 35–52).

The literary and archaeological evidence not only indicates the prominence of Palaimon in the Roman period, it makes clear the nature of the cult: worship focused on the dead or the underworld (Koester 1990: 365). All the features of the cult and the site – nocturnal rites, the burning of black animals in a sacrificial pit, a round sanctuary – conform to a chthonic rather than Olympic orientation (Burkert 1985: 199–200). And when Philostratus refers to the offerings that go to Palaimon, he calls them *enagismata*, offerings typically associated with the dead or underworld deities (Garland 1985: 110–13; Burkert 1983: 197). Thus, the rise of the Palaimon cult in Roman times indicates that the Corinthia's religious center, Isthmia, hosted not only Poseidon but more and more that side of religion having to do with dead heroes and the world of the dead.

Confirmation of a growing emphasis on the underworld in Roman Isthmia comes from the history of the Demeter cult there. As yet no temple or sanctuary has been found at Isthmia, so the center of cultic practices eludes interpreters. Nevertheless, archaeological evidence points to two places of cultic activity. The first is the ridge spur known as the Rachi, south of and overlooking the Temple of Poseidon site, although the steepness of the slope would have prevented temple construction there. Votive pottery in the form of miniature water jugs (*hydriai*) and baskets (*kalathoi*) unearthed on the Rachi suggest Demeter worship, because miniatures of precisely this type have been recovered in great numbers at the Demeter and Persephone sanctuary in Corinth (Bookidis and Stroud 1987: 13). Moreover, excavators also found many terracotta figurines, some of which reflect distinctively Demeter iconography. The dating of these objects indicates that Demeter worship flourished on the Rachi from the sixth down to the fourth and possibly the third centuries BCE (Anderson-Stojanović 1988: 268–9).

Two chance finds several hundred meters south and west of the Poseidon temple site suggest a second possible center for the Demeter cult. The two items, a statue of a young girl and a large vase (skyphoid krater) with reliefs, were inscribed to Demeter. They both date from some time in the fourth century BCE. Demeter devotion was evidently taking place somewhere in the area, yet excavations in the vicinity of these finds have produced no further evidence (Caskey 1960; Broneer 1959: 323, 326).

There may have been no temple to Demeter at Isthmia in the Greek period, but an inscription verifies the existence of a temple to her in Roman times (*IG* IV, 203, 20–1). Composed to acknowledge the lavish building program of the Isthmian high priest Juventianus, the inscription speaks of constructing the Palaimonion and its place of offering for the dead (*enagistērion*) as well as an enclosure around the temples of the sacred glen, a place yet to be uncovered. In the glen stood temples dedicated to Demeter (Eueteria), Persephone, Dionysos, and Artemis. The first two Juventianus takes credit for having restored, as they had suffered from earthquakes and age. The date of the inscription is disputed; it may be late first, early second, or late second century (West 1931: 54–5; Geagan 1989: 358). Whatever the precise date, the inscription indicates the Demeter temple had been standing for some time.

The Juventianus inscription not only provides evidence of Demeter devotion at Roman Isthmia and locates the center of cultic activity, it also indicates the orientation of that activity. The gods of the underworld were prominent at Isthmia, and Demeter was associated with them. Persephone or Kore, the queen of the dead, had her own temple in the sacred glen. Moreover, the inscription mentions a religious site dedicated to Hades, a Plutoneion (*IG* IV, 203, 20–1). Such sites are very rare in Greece (Garland 1985: 53, 153; Nock 1972: 2.592). That there was a Plutoneion at Isthmia underscores the chthonic disposition of the place. Furthermore, the grouping of Demeter with Persephone and Hades suggests that Demeter devotion in the Roman period had a predominantly underworld orientation.

Roman-era Demeter worship had the same cast in Corinth. The Sanctuary of Demeter and Kore (or Persephone) on the slope below Acrocorinth saw new life in the first century CE after a period of abandonment brought about by Roman general Mummius's sacking of Corinth in 146 BCE. The Roman Corinthians reestablished the sanctuary farther uphill. The three small temples they built there in the latter half of the first century constituted the focal point of cultic activity (Bookidis and Fisher 1972: 313; Bookidis and Stroud 1987: 11, 22). Some time after the temples were constructed, in the late second or early third century, a mosaic went down on the floor of the middle temple. It depicts two baskets and two large snakes wrapped around them (Bookidis and Fisher 1974: 280–1). Given the snake's funerary and underworld affinities (Garland 1985: 158–9), what we have in the mosaic is an iconographical indicator of the Roman sanctuary's chthonic focus, an emphasis that is further confirmed by the dedicatory inscription on the mosaic. A certain Octavios Agathopous recorded the date of his benefaction as the year that Charis served as priestess of Neotera, an appellation the excavators of the Demeter sanctuary believe refers not to Demeter but to Kore or Persephone (Stroud 1993: 73, esp. n. 7). Thus, the central temple of the Roman period sanctuary appears to have been dedicated to the queen of the underworld rather than Demeter.

Other finds at the site further confirm this underworld orientation and prove it went back to the beginning of renewed cultic activity. Curse tablets (*defixiones*) are not unusual finds at a Demeter sanctuary (Jordan 1985: 175–6), but in Corinth they appear for the first time in the Roman era, concentrated at levels dating to an early phase of Roman occupation (Bookidis and Stroud 1987: 30). Their poor condition has made them difficult to decipher, but it is clear that they invoke the underworld gods, often against women (Stroud 1993: 72; Bookidis and Stroud 1997: 281–91).

It would be an exaggeration to conclude from this archaeologically-based reconstruction of Corinth's cultural climate that Corinthian religion in the Roman period differed completely from that of the Greek period. Continuities did exist. The Romans reestablished or refurbished the Temple of Asklepios and the Sanctuary of Demeter and Kore in Corinth and the Temple of Poseidon at Isthmia. They built temples and monuments to the traditional gods of Greece – Apollo and others – at the west end of Corinth's new, impressive forum (Williams 1987: 26). Poseidon and Aphrodite, tradition-ally popular gods of Corinth, maintained their status, if Roman Corinthian coinage is any indicator (Engels 1990: 93, 95–7).

The material record also points to change, however; archaeological data verify the existence of a new and widespread religious perspective. The rise of the Palaimon cult at Isthmia and the orientation of Demeter devotion in the Roman period point unequivocally to a development transcending cult boundaries: the emergence during the middle of the first century CE of a religious outlook focused intensely on the dead and the underworld.

What impact did this orientation have on the church growing in Corinthian soil? Most scholars characterize the church there as largely, if not exclusively, Gentile, so presumably many coming into the church would have brought an underworld orientation with them. Evidence for how pervasive and powerful this orientation was comes from Paul's Corinthian correspondence. First, of course, there is the Corinthian extension of bap-tism to their dead. But this is not the only rite that displays a funerary tone. When Paul writes about the Corinthians' dining ritual, he places the common meal squarely in a mortuary context (1 Cor 11:17–34) (Barrett 1968: 267, 270; Lietzmann 1979: xviii, 182): "For as often as you eat this bread and drink the cup, *you proclaim the Lord's death* until he comes" (1 Cor 11:26; italics added).

Is this Paul's way of tailoring his message to audience expectations? It would seem so, when one considers how he presented Christ to them. What Paul calls a foolish proclamation (1 Cor 1:21–5) may in fact have been carefully crafted presentation. When Paul wrote "I decided to know nothing among you except Jesus Christ, and him crucified" (1 Cor 2:2), stress fell on the tragic death of the movement's hero. Did Paul accent this aspect of the gospel in order to capitalize on the Corinthian devotion to the dead

(Nash 2000; Riley 1997: 69–74)? If so, we can see a correspondence between the archaeological and literary record for Corinth. Also, we see a church whose rites and beliefs have a Corinthian color. (It may be worth adding that Jonathan Z. Smith contends that Corinthian believers were communing with the spirits of the dead in their pneumatically-charged worship services [Smith 2004: 340–61]. Also, Charles Kennedy has argued that the controversy over food offered to idols at Corinth [1 Cor 8 and 10] actually concerned Christian participation in memorial meals for the dead [Kennedy 1987: 229–30].)

Archaeology has given New Testament scholars a clearer picture of the religious environment in which the Corinthian church arose and with which it interacted. This chapter has argued that first-century Corinthians were preoccupied with the world of the dead, so they attached themselves to deities that would allow them to address that concern. Accordingly, the worship of the dead hero Palaimon blossomed at Isthmia, and attention to Persephone and other underworld powers overshadowed other elements within the local Demeter cult. This orientation influenced the Corinthian church as well. While the Greco-Roman ritual world made it conceivable for any circle of believers to imagine applying baptism to its dead, it was the Corinthian believers that acted on the possibility. What triggered this practice at Corinth was a local preoccupation with the underworld, such that the church of first-century Corinth was pushed to innovate. Simply put, had Corinthian religion of the Roman era not been preoccupied with the realm of the dead, the Corinthian church would not have instituted baptism on behalf of the dead.

But maybe it would have anyway. Corinth's archaeological records suggest that there may have been a special urgency behind the church's ritual creativity. Its pronounced concern for the dead, as evidenced by baptism for the dead, may have arisen in part from different, perhaps conflicting, burial practices in first-century Corinth. If the burial data from Corinth's North Cemetery indicate a steady and strong sense of obligation to the dead in ancient Corinth, they also document varying burial practices in the first century CE. Specifically, in the early Roman period the Corinthians were carrying out different burial practices *concurrently* (see also Walbank 2005: 270). In that period – Hazel Palmer contends that the cemetery went out of use at the end of the first century (Blegen, Palmer, and Young 1964: 65, 167) – we have evidence that Corinthians were practicing both cremation and inhumation. Palmer concludes that a residual Greek population inhuming its dead and Roman colonists cremating their dead were using the cemetery, and this conclusion makes sense given the typical burial practice of Romans and Greeks in the first century (Blegen, Palmer, and Young 1964: 70–1; Morris 1992: 52–3). (Recent studies of Roman Corinthian gravesites point to even greater variety in burial practices [Rife 1999; Walbank 2005]).

Did this difference in burial customs draw attention to the dead and the duty the living had to help them in their entry to the underworld? We cannot draw this conclusion for Corinthians in general because we do not know the level of integration between the local Greek population and the Roman colonists. But in the case of the early church, we have an ethnically mixed community. Gerd Theissen's compilation of those known by name attests to a mixture of Romans and Greeks (Theissen 1982: 94–9). If differences in burial practices heightened concern about the disposition of the dead, such a preoccupation would have existed among the believers of Corinth. Perhaps this was the extra push that stimulated the Corinthian church's ritual innovation.

Part II
Exit Rites

The shift from entry to exit rites is not the biggest transition the book makes at this point. Entry and exit are, after all, two sides of the same coin; both are boundary-crossing rites and as such have much in common. They are so alike that the context of a boundary-crossing rite often determines whether the ritual action is primarily that of entry or exit.

The major transition in Part II is from the microscopic analysis of biblical texts and cultural contexts undertaken in Chapters 2 and 3 to a macroscopic perspective. We will no longer restrict ourselves to a relatively small set of verses about baptism in the New Testament. Nor will we be tightly focused on early Roman Corinth and the details of life there. Rather, we will be looking at whole New Testament documents set in a broader theoretical framework.

The previous two chapters illustrated how ritual embodied the early church's engagement with the larger culture, an engagement that entailed ritual innovation. Such innovation lends credibility to theorists' claim that ritual is an independent variable, that it is generative and not derivative (see Introduction).

Yet some ritual theorists have claimed even more for ritual; they assert its primacy in human communities. If ritual is really so foundational, we ought to be able to detect its presence at levels that go beyond a church body's ritual practices, no matter how profound an impact those practices had on the practitioners and the surrounding culture. When the Introduction discussed ritual primacy, it mentioned ritual's influence on texts. A quotation from Frank Gorman bears repeating:

> Ritual structures and ritual processes may serve as the basis for story and narrative. Ritual may serve as the background for narrative construction and development. Indeed, ritual may generate narrative and story in such a way that ritual dynamics will be reflected within a narrative.
> (Gorman 1994: 23)

Part II will try to verify this claim. It will explore representative documents from the New Testament, a letter and a gospel, with a view to discerning a ritual logic in them. Chapter 4 argues that Paul put the problems the Corinthians faced and the solution he proposed (in 1 Corinthians) in the language of group pollution and its removal by ritual action. Likewise, Chapter 5 argues that a particular set of exit rites common in the ancient Mediterranean – what the chapter calls curative exit rites – accounts for the distinguishing features of the Marcan passion narrative (the last third of the gospel of Mark) and may help us better understand the whole document.

Both chapters deal with exit rites, but the focus is on expulsions rather than departures. Moreover, the expulsions treated are more significant than other expulsions we encounter in the Mediterranean world, like exile from imperial Rome or ostracism from classical Athens. The New Testament also records the expulsion – or elimination – of wayward members, such as the sudden death and removal of Ananias and Saphira from the fledging church (Acts 5:1–11). Likewise, the gospel of Matthew provides detailed instructions for dealing with deviant members, including their removal or excommunication from the group (18:15–19). As serious as such removals are, none of these examples presents the expulsion as the ritual restoration of community wholeness or holiness (as 1 Corinthians and Mark do).

Anthropological research on witchcraft beliefs sheds light on the crisis-and-ritual-solution template underlying 1 Corinthians and Mark. The phrase is unfortunate because of the notions, and even images, it evokes, and anthropologists have often found witchcraft so difficult a term to define that some consider it more hindrance than help as an interpretive category (Bond and Ciekawy 2001). Nevertheless, for our purposes it suffices to know that witchcraft and witchcraft accusation are a social diagnosis that emerges in some cultures to account for and interpret misfortune (Moore and Sanders 2001: 3–4). The witchcraft typology developed by Mary Douglas and Leora Nadine Rosen some years ago usefully refines the model. Their typology describes a range of threats a community may face, particularly whether the threat is internal or external. Likewise, they identify a range of mechanisms for eliminating the threat put in terms of where remedial or curative action is directed (Douglas 1970a: xxvi; Rosen 1972: 26–9). These distinctions allow us to articulate a key differ-ence between 1 Corinthians and Mark. Although both documents con-cern themselves with an expulsion rite, in 1 Corinthians the object of expulsion, a group member, is clearly an insider. In Mark, on the other hand, the object of expulsion, Jesus, is an outsider in Jerusalem, the site of his expulsion.

Another way of distinguishing 1 Corinthians from the gospel of Mark is to consider the differing portrayals of who is expelled. It will become clear in the coming pages that Paul pictures the deviate as a Typhoid Mary, a person who embodied contamination and threatened to spread it community wide. In contrast, the gospel of Mark presents Jesus – at least primarily so – as an absorbent able to sponge away the misfortunes that had befallen Roman Palestine. In both documents the ritual action – expulsion – is similar, but the agents undergoing it are strikingly different.

*   *   *

To account for the title of Chapter 4 it might be enough to observe that the logical title, "Paul's Center," is duller than "Paul's Omphalos." In truth, the chosen title is doing more than announcing the chapter's contents. Scholars have been debating about Paul's theological omphalos – literally navel but also central point, hub, focal point – for centuries, without much to show for it. Much of this debate reflects little more than omphaloskepsis, navel-gazing, for modern biblical scholars and theologians consciously or subconsciously picture Paul as someone like themselves – a rational, organized thinker. The realization that Paul is nothing of the sort, that he is very different from a modern westerner, emerged almost a half-century ago (Stendahl 1963), and it is gaining ground. Still, it is difficult to read Paul through first-century Mediterranean lenses, so most readers do not try.

A few years ago, toward the end of a three-day conference on the apostle Paul, I heard the distinguished Dutch-American theologian Franz Jozef van Beeck express his doubts about finding anything approaching systematic thinking in Paul's letters. He concluded, "It's all liturgy." That was overstatement, albeit charming overstatement. Paul is much more than a cobbling together of liturgical fragments. Still, there are more inaccurate characterizations of Paul; liturgy is not too far off target. At least in the case of 1 Corinthians, the inspiration for it more likely came from a ritual mindset than a grand theological program.

4 Paul's Omphalos

> If Paul was not a *systematic* theologian, there seems nevertheless to be a pattern, a center, a commitment, a conviction, a vision, an underlying structure, a core communication, a set of beliefs, a narrative, a coherence – something – in Paul's thoughts or behind them that dispels any abiding sense of mere opportunism or intellectual chaos on the part of the apostle. Yet nowhere, it seems, does this core, center, vision, etc. come to expression in a noncontingent way.
>
> (Bassler 1993: 6)

The study of Paul and the New Testament generally is in the midst of a major transition that began in the late 1970s and early 1980s (Horsley 1994; Schüsssler Fiorenza 1983: 68–95, esp. 70–1). With regard to Paul, one can detect steady erosion in the longstanding scholarly consensus about the centrality of justification in his theology by looking chronologically at chapter and section headings of review literature on Pauline scholarship from the last two decades. "Justification by Faith" is the fourth chapter of Joseph Plevnik's six-chapter look at Pauline scholarship in 1986, *What Are They Saying about Paul?* (Plevnik 1986). A year later Hans Hübner's review of post-war scholarship on Paul appeared in *Aufstieg und Niedergang der römischen Welt*. There, treatment of Pauline justification appears in a section entitled "Rechtfertigung als Mitte paulinischer Theologie?" – "Justification at the Heart of Paul's Theology?" – and what follows is a lengthy presentation of alternative centers (Hübner 1987). More recently, in Veronica Koperski's *What Are They Saying about Paul and the Law?*, we find a chapter entitled "The New Center?" opening with these words: "There is emerging an increasing consensus that justification by faith alone can no longer be considered the center of Paul's theology" (Koperski 2001). The trend is obvious.

Challenges to the centrality of justification in Paul have arisen from many quarters, but perhaps the most serious comes from the so-called New Perspective on Paul, a label that sprang from a 1983 essay of the same name by James D. G. Dunn (Dunn 1983). Taking a seminal essay by Krister

Stendahl about the perils of reading Paul through Luther and E. P. Sanders's groundbreaking reexamination of Judaism at the time of Paul as points of departure (Stendahl 1963; Sanders 1977), Dunn has reexamined justification, particularly in Romans and Galatians, and written extensively about it (e.g., Dunn 1988a; 1988b; 1993; 1998). He holds that justification by faith emerged as a corollary to Paul's mission to the Gentiles, as a way of defending their inclusion in the household of God against Jewish objections. Understood as a rationale rather than a theological universal, justification by faith slips from the center of Paul's thought.

Dunn and other proponents of the New Perspective have drawn heavy scholarly fire. One can cite several titles whose primary goal is to dispute Dunn and his allies, and others will undoubtedly appear (e.g., Stuhlmacher 2001; Kim 2002; Das 2001). A determined rebuttal of Dunn, however, does not mean the field's rejection of the New Perspective. On the contrary, the frequency of such rejoinders, especially from conservative biblical scholars, points to how widely accepted and prominent the New Perspective has become in the field. It is so well established that some scholars now take it as a point of departure for their work (e.g., Byrne 2001; Gathercole 2001).

Even if one discounts the New Perspective, clouds remain on the horizon. There is enough ferment in Pauline scholarship at the moment to suggest that pursuing a center in Paul's thought may be a futile exercise. Besides the position taken by Heikki Räisänen and others that the many contingencies Paul had to address led to incoherence in his thought, there has emerged widespread uncertainty about finding a theological center or centers in Paul (Räisänen 1986). Between 1991 and 1997 there appeared four volumes of papers previously presented and discussed in The Pauline Theology Consultation, a group formed under the auspices of the Society of Biblical Literature in 1985. Its task was to reassess the way Pauline theology should be conceived. The preface to the first volume describes the undertaking as a response both to the collapse of traditional models for understanding Paul and to the claim that Paul's theology lacks coherence (Bassler 1991: ix).

What has resulted from this consultation, undertaken by a distinguished panel of Pauline scholars? In the fourth volume, as he summarizes over a decade of work by the consultation, Paul W. Meyer admits that despite careful and intensive study, "the task of understanding the apostle's theology remains unfinished," and that "there is no consensus at the end of this stage of the inquiry" (Meyer 1997: 140). Accordingly, his contribution to the final volume bears the title "Pauline Theology: A Proposal for a Pause in Its Pursuit."

Such inconclusiveness has opened the door to a host of fundamental reappraisals. A case in point is John Ashton's recent book on the religion of Paul, in which he rejects "conceptualist" interpretations of Paul altogether, turning instead to Paul's religious experience – which Ashton sees matching the career of a shaman – as the best way to get to the heart or center of Paul (Ashton 2000). In this instance we have a scholar casting about for something he regards as more basic and determinative in Paul than theological or doctrinal formulation.

Two characteristics of Paul's letters impede any attempt at finding a coherent center in his writing and thinking (Achtemeier 1996; Beker 1980: 11–19). What prompted Paul to write accounts in part for this hindrance, for his letters were occasional in nature, sent to particular communities, and typically dealt with multiple, often unrelated, crises. Thus, their content depended to a great degree on the problems or issues troubling the communities Paul addressed. Even his letter to the Romans, which scholars judge the least occasional, does not constitute an organized or exhaustive presentation of his thought.

The makeup of a typical letter from Paul also rules against finding a coherent center. A lively debate surrounds some of Paul's letters over the issue of their literary unity. Second Corinthians, for instance, is widely thought to have a letter fragment, what is now chapters 10 to 13, imbedded in it (Meeks 1972: 48–9; Thrall 1994: 3–48, esp. 13, 43; Roetzel 1998: 93, 95). Also, most of Paul's letters contain exhortations and instructions set off from the rest of the letter, such as the final chapters (4 and 5) of 1 Thessalonians (Roetzel 1998: 66, 83). A once-dominant view considered such paraenetical material an appendage to Paul's letters and not well integrated with them (e.g., Dibelius 1966: 239–41). Subsequent scholarship has sought to counteract this view by finding links between the theological and paraenetic sections of Paul's letters. Consequently, much of the scholarly discourse about the coherence and unity of Paul's letters has taken place in the language of theology and ethics (e.g., Bassler 1993; Cousar 1993). A recent contribution to that discourse, an important current in Pauline scholarship, has a subtitle that encapsulates the approach nicely. John Lewis's *Looking for Life: The Role of "Theo-Ethical Reasoning" in Paul's Religion*, reviews two generations' worth of scholarship on the subject and seeks to advance this line of interpretation (Lewis 2005).

Many scholars have come to assume that rooting Paul's ethical prescriptions in his theological formulations will make the case for his coherence. This assumption clearly operates in Richard B. Hays's important study of New Testament ethics, *The Moral Vision of the New Testament: Community, Cross, New Creation*. Quite understandably, Hays devotes a great deal of attention to Paul. When he approaches Paul's ethic, he understands his task to be twofold: once he has identified and characterized Paul's ethical discourse – Paul did not, after all, write a manual of discipline or book of church order – he must demonstrate how it grew out of, and was grounded in, his theology (Hays 1996: 16–19). Accordingly, Hays offers the following remarks:

> The ethical norm, then, is not given in the form of a predetermined rule or set of rules for conduct; rather, the right action must be *discerned*

on the basis of a christological paradigm, with a view to the need of the community.

(Hays 1996: 43)

Hays seeks to join Pauline theology and ethics together under the rubrics of community, cross, and new creation, hence the subtitle of his book. So at this point in his chapter on Paul, Hays tells us that Paul encouraged moral discernment informed by a christological paradigm (i.e., the cross) and community need. He then reflects on the failure of this recommendation among the Corinthians:

> Paul's reluctance to specify narrow behavioral norms was perhaps one of the factors that led to trouble in the Corinthian community. Acting in light of their own spiritual discernment, some of the Corinthians were conducting themselves in ways that Paul found deeply objectionable. In 1 Corinthians 5:1–5, for example, he condemns an incestuous relationship between a man and his mother-in-law as "sexual immorality of a kind that is not found even among the Gentiles." Here he gives no reason for his rejection of this behavior; he merely pronounces condemnation. He formulates his moral indignation in a manner ("not found even among the *Gentiles*") suggesting that this particular normative judgment is rooted in Jewish cultural sensibilities, based ultimately on Leviticus 18:8: "You shall not uncover the nakedness of your father's wife." This background, however, remains implicit.
>
> Even in this disturbing passage, however, the specific directive that Paul gives to the Corinthian church ("Drive out the wicked person from among you" [5:13]) is motivated by a concern for the unitary holiness of the community: "Do you not know that a little yeast leavens the whole batch of dough? Clean out the old yeast so that you [plural] may be a new batch, as you really are unleavened" (5:6b–7a). Thus, concern for the health and purity of the community remains the constant factor in which more specific norms must be grounded.

(Hays 1996: 43)

It is no accident that Hays introduces 1 Corinthians 5:1–5 to his discussion of the unity between theology and ethics. This passage marks a major transition in 1 Corinthians (Sellin 1987: 2942), which some regard as so abrupt that it proves the essential discontinuity between Paul's theological (chaps 1–4) and ethical (5–16) discourses (Conzelmann 1975: 95). Hays seeks to counter this claim in his assessment.

Yet the more Hays says about 1 Corinthians 5, the less appropriate and adequate the category of morality or ethics seems. The way Hays's language shifts over the course of the quotation above is revealing in this regard. "Behavioral norms," "moral indignation," and "normative judgment" give way to Paul's concern for the "unitary *holiness*" and the "health and *purity*" of the community (italics added). What Hays inadvertently shows us is that 1 Corinthians 5 concerns itself most immediately with holiness and purity, not ethics and morality. If morality plays a role here, it derives from and depends on an orientation that is more at home with categories like holiness and unholiness, purity and pollution. The very language Hays resorts to in describing what Paul is about in 1 Corinthians 5, therefore, tells against the priority of ethics in this passage.

The trouble with Hays's analysis and the many like his lies not so much in his characterization of Paul in 1 Corinthians 5 – it is quite accurate in some ways – but in the interpretive frame in which he tries to fit it. Here, at a pivotal point in 1 Corinthians, purity and holiness dominate Paul's thinking, so much so that they define community unity and health. Yet prevailing treatments of Paul miss or obscure this orientation by privileging ethics (e.g., Pascuzzi 1997). While this chapter cannot reexamine all of Paul, it can review chapter 5 along with the rest of 1 Corinthians and offer a different perspective. This alternative interpretation will find that in chapter 5 and at many other important points in the letter, what preoccupies Paul and thus unites the letter is a concern for purity and holiness.

The great problem at Corinth in Paul's thinking was not immorality per se but its effect. The gravest threat was pollution or contamination because of the threat it posed community purity and holiness (Neyrey, 1990: 21–55). In response, Paul, like other inhabitants of the ancient Mediterranean world, turned to ritual as the necessary mechanism for counteracting pollution and restoring holiness, purity, and community health. Read through the filter of theology and ethics, the vital importance of ritual fades from Paul. The alternative interpretation of 1 Corinthians this chapter offers, however, restores ritual to its central place in the letter and in Paul's thought.

In the verses that open 1 Corinthians 5, Paul appears to run the gamut: he speaks of individual morality (or immorality), group disciplinary action (its lack), and ceremonial punishment or banishment. Most scholars read the verses through the lens of personal or group ethics and thus minimize what one scholar calls the "highly unusual" scene that actually dominates the passage (Yarbrough 1995: 129, n. 12). By removing the ethical filter, however, one sees that ritual performance dominates.

> (v. 1) It is actually reported that there is sexual immorality among you, and of a kind that is not found even among pagans; for a man is living with his father's wife [concubine (so de Vos: 1998)]. (2) And you are arrogant! Should you not rather have mourned, so that he who has done this would have been removed from among you? (3) For though absent in body, I am present in spirit; and as if present I have already pronounced judgment (4) in the name of the Lord Jesus on the man who has done such a thing. When you are assembled, and my spirit is

present with the power of our Lord Jesus, (5) you are to hand this man over to Satan for the destruction of the flesh, so that his spirit may be saved in the day of the Lord.

The scene evoked by verses 4 and 5 – the congregational gathering Paul calls for – has generated numerous characterizations. The verses have undergone analysis as a type of prayer (Wiles 1974: 142–50) and a prophetic judgment (Roetzel 1969). What Paul calls for has been variously described as a "charismatic devotion" (Forkman 1972: 12) and "a judicial act of a sacral and pneumatic kind" (Conzelmann 1975: 97; cf. Doskocil 1958: 59–76). That Paul declares *judgment* in verse 3 and that the congregation *assembles* in verse 4 have led some to see a legal or judicial or even legislative process at work, although the procedure there differs markedly from the application of discipline in other communities of the time (1QS 5:24–6:1; Matt 18:15–17) (Bammel 1997; Wiles 1974: 117). In Ernst Käsemann's view, Paul has pronounced holy law against the man and expects the community to go along with his apostolic injunction (Käsemann 1969: 70–1).

Emphasis in interpretations of this sort, however, is misplaced; it falls on Paul rather than where Paul directs it, namely, to the Corinthians. What he writes are instructions to the Corinthians, which is why scholarly analysis of his words as prophetic pronouncement, holy law, or intercessory prayer has limited value. When Paul talks elsewhere in this letter about the Corinthians assembling – it appears insignificant that he uses *synagō* (gather, assemble) in 5:4 but *synerchomai* (come together, meet) everywhere else – the setting is worship, presumably in a household, not administrative council or courtroom (1 Cor 11:17, 18, 20, 33, 34; 14:23, 26). The numerous references in chapter 11 refer to coming together for the eucharistic meal, participation in which, Paul insists, calls for judgment (11:29, 31–2). Hence, a eucharistic setting for the ceremonial punishment seems very likely (Wiles 1974: 147; Johnson 1998: 175). Alternatively, some scholars posit a baptismal setting, since the expulsion will effectively reverse a baptism (Käsemann 1969: 71; Forkman 1972: 146, n. 169; Bohren 1952: 110, n. 131). That suggestion is not as convincing, however. Whatever the case, Paul sets what he expects the Corinthians to do within a cultic ritual setting of some sort, not a deliberative or juridical one.

Confirmation of Paul's ritual orientation in chapter 5 comes in verse 2, which all standard interpretations of that verse miss entirely and many translations obscure. Scholars typically find Paul spelling out his accusation of arrogance against the Corinthians there: their arrogance has led to complacency. They have failed to mourn, that is, to show regret, for the gross misconduct of a community member. Lack of contrition on their part has resulted in a failure to act against that comrade (Rosner 1992). A translation that mirrors this interpretation comes from J. Murphy-O'Connor and runs as follows (Murphy-O'Connor 1979: 41): "Should you not rather have gone into mourning (and shown the sincerity of your sorrow by taking the necessary steps) in order that he who has done this should be removed from among you?" The New International Version puts it more succinctly: "Shouldn't you rather have been filled with grief and have put out of your fellowship the man who did this?" Pitched in this way, verse 2 has everything to do with ethics: a morally outraged Paul is trying to shame the Corinthians into disciplinary action.

This reading makes perfect sense if we assume that ethics is foremost in Paul's mind, but the verse does not fit so readily under that rubric. Paul links mourning with removal, which has puzzled modern interpreters and pushed them to understand mourning figuratively. Yet there is no compelling reason to take the Greek verb for mourning (*pentheō*) as a reference to an inner or psychological disposition – a sense of sadness or regret – rather than ritual practice, that is, the public rite of mourning. While the verb could have an experiential side, it normally meant the mourning connected with a funeral. It clearly has this meaning in the gospels (Matt 5:4; 9:15; Mark 16:10; Luke 6:25) and in Revelation (18:11, 15, 19). Paul's reference to mourning in 1 Corinthians 5:2 should be read, therefore, as a reference to the formal actions connected with a state of mourning, not as a psychological expression of sorrow, as appealing as the latter might be to modern readers (Thiselton 2000: 388).

A metaphorical or figurative reading of mourning also stumbles over the final clause of the verse. The Greek conjunction that opens the clause, *hina* – usually translated "so that" – cannot easily bear the lengthy explanation that such a reading requires of it – recall Murphy-O'Connor's "(and shown the sincerity of your sorrow by taking the necessary steps)." A *hina* clause may also express command (Campbell 1993, 335, n. 19; Moulton, Howard, and Turner 1906–76, 3:94–5; but see Salom 1958: 138). Accordingly, the New International Version renders the last part of the verse as follows: "Shouldn't you rather have been filled with grief and have put out of your fellowship the man who did this?" But reading the clause as a command is troublesome because it departs so much from the Greek, which has the man as the subject of a verb in passive voice: "so that *he* who has done this *would have been removed* from among you?" (1 Cor 5:2; italics added).

A clause beginning with the conjunction *hina* normally has a final sense, expressing the purpose, goal, or aim of the verbal action in the main clause of the sentence. Hence, *hina* is typically translated "in order that" or "so that." Read this way, verse 2 says the expulsion of the deviate is the goal of the Corinthians' mourning. The *hina* clause could even suggest that the expulsion is the result of their mourning (Smyth 1956: 493, §2193). Accordingly, the New Revised Standard Version translates the latter part of 1 Corinthians 5:2, "Should you not rather have mourned, so that he who has done this would have been removed from among you?"

The unexpected cause and effect indicated by the likeliest syntax of verse 2 along with the assumption that Paul framed his response in ethical terms lie behind the tendency to read mourning figuratively. Yet from the standpoint of ancient Mediterranean ritual, the linkage of funerary rite to expulsion is not odd at all. A case in point comes from the Babylonian Talmud, which describes the excommunication or execration of Eliezer b. Hyrcanus from the circle of rabbis (*b. Bava Metzi'a* 59b). To report the excommunication to Eliezer, R. Akiba dressed in black – in mourning garb – and once R. Eliezer was informed of his excommunication, he rent his garment, put off his shoes, and sat in the dirt, as Job did when he lost his children. Funerals marked exit from community, so they are functionally like expulsions. Accordingly, funerary ritual could signal execration or excommunication.

More to the point, mourning could enact expulsion, which is what 1 Corinthians 5:2 indicates. Evidence for this ritual effect comes from the Roman historian Tacitus, who recorded what befell a Roman senator visiting a colony in Italy:

> A senator, Manlius Patruitus, complained that he had been beaten by a mob in the colony of Sena [modern Siena], and that too by order of the local magistrates; moreover, he said that the injury had not stopped there: the mob had surrounded him and before his face had wailed, lamented, and conducted a mock funeral, accompanying it with insults and outrageous expressions directed against the whole senate.
>
> (Tacitus, *Annales* 4.45 [Jackson, LCL])

Along with the expected ways of throwing the senator out of town, the colonists of Sena included a funeral; they mourned as a way of expelling him.

This report from Tacitus portrays what the Greek in 1 Corinthians 5:2 describes: a funerary exit rite. Such a rite was evidently part of the ritual repertoire of the believers at Corinth, and it represents one of several rites connected with Paul and Pauline communities that show funerary elements or orientation. The Corinthians themselves evidently practiced baptism in a mortuary setting – baptism on behalf of the dead – as we saw in Chapter 3 (1 Cor 15:29). And two key rites, the common meal and baptism, had a funerary cast in Paul's thinking. As noted in the previous chapter, what Paul writes about the Corinthians' dining ritual places the common meal squarely in a mortuary context (11:17–34): "For as often as you eat this bread and drink the cup, you proclaim the Lord's death until he comes" (v. 26). Likewise, he viewed baptism as participating in Jesus's death and burial (Rom 6:3–4). If a rite of entry – baptism – could have a funerary aspect, it is understandable that an exit rite would too.

A look at 1 Corinthians 5:1–5 attuned to the ritual world of the ancient Mediterranean reveals that Paul spoke not of one rite of expulsion but two. At the center of those verses, therefore, is a ritual crisis: the Corinthians' failure to act ritually and Paul's ritual intervention in response. If Paul already turned to ritual matters in 5:2, how central are ethics or discipline to chapter 5? They appear to be secondary to ritual. Paul may well have been unhappy about Corinthian moral laxity or lack of discipline, but the primary disappointment in 5:2 is over their failure to carry out a rite. In response, Paul intervenes with an alternative rite. Verse 3, therefore, does not broach the subject of ritual but rather continues a ritual discourse, one that controls the opening of the chapter.

The ritual Paul prescribes in verses 4 and 5 was not merely an alternative exit rite, however. The substitute Paul orders comes with a rationale in verses 6 through 8 rooted in pollution and purity concerns. This is not the language of burial society or religious association (*collegium, thiasos*) expelling a delinquent member. Purity was a central concern of the Qumran community, yet the grounds for expulsion from it did not necessarily revolve around the elimination of pollution (e.g., 1QS 7:18–19, 25–7). For Paul they evidently did, at least in this case.

To justify his introduction of a new rite, Paul likens the Corinthian situation to a community that must rid itself of a contaminant. It becomes clear in those verses that we no longer have a simple expulsion rite; we have a rite that will purify the community. The three verses that follow 1 Corinthians 5:1–5 make that clear:

> (v. 6) Your boasting is not a good thing. Do you not know that a little yeast leavens the whole batch of dough? (7) Clean out the old yeast so that you may be a new batch, as you really are unleavened. For our paschal lamb, Christ, has been sacrificed. (8) Therefore, let us celebrate the festival, not with the old yeast, the yeast of malice and evil, but with the unleavened bread of sincerity and truth.

Yeast proved to be a useful metaphor for Paul's articulation of the dangers to the community posed by the presence of the immoral man in it. He began with a common proverb based on the leavening action of yeast. Set in the context of chapter 5, Paul is saying, "even a single individual can affect the whole community." Perhaps it was also common knowledge that yeast was a product of corruption and infected whatever it was in. This, at any rate, is how the ancient Greek writer Plutarch explains why priests of Jupiter cannot touch it (*Quaestiones romanae et graecae* 109 [289E–F]). But even if Paul's audience did not share Plutarch's view of yeast, Paul's allusion to its infectious or contagious nature would have sufficed to support his point in the passage: removal of the "old yeast," i.e., the immoral man, was imperative because even a little impurity tainted the whole community.

The shift from old yeast versus new batch to old yeast versus unleavened bread in verse 7 allows Paul to restate the rationale for acting against the immoral man in the language of purity and impurity. Israelite cultic traditions come into play, as Paul places his readers at Passover time. While it is a novel Passover that has Christ as the paschal lamb, the demand for purification associated with traditional Passover remains in force. Just as Israelite households have to purify themselves by getting rid of all leaven, so too must the Corinthian assembly (Exod 12:8, 15–20). Since one could not celebrate Passover with the old yeast – Paul adds – "of malice and evil," the embodiment of those vices among the Corinthians, the immoral man, has to go. In these verses Paul invokes the requirements of cultic preparation to convince the Corinthian community to cleanse itself.

If Paul called for ritual purification rather than mere expulsion in 1 Corinthians 5:3–5, the question arises, "who or what would have to undergo purification?" A great many interpreters have answered "the immoral man," and concomitantly understood the action that Paul called for as revocable and remedial (South 1992: 23–88; Joy 1988; Thornton 1972; Cambier 1968–9). As biblical commentator J. Murphy-O'Connor states

> If read carelessly Paul's decision appears brutal, but there is no doubt that he conceived such excommunication, not as a punishment, but as a remedy. The ultimate goal is the salvation of the individual. . . . Paul's hope was that the sinner would change his pattern of behaviour, and conceived excommunication as the stimulus that would produce this effect.
>
> (Murphy-O'Connor 1979: 41–2)

This interpretation's emphasis on the individual, however, flies in the face of Paul's consistent emphasis on *community* purity or holiness throughout chapter 5 (1 Cor 5:7, 9, 11).

So strong is the pull to focus on the individual and his fate that scholars have sought resolution to the situation – often a positive resolution – in various places. The temptation to find an outcome in 2 Corinthians to the crisis of 1 Corinthians 5 has attracted some. Scholars have found evidence for his expulsion and the aftermath in the second chapter of that later letter (Lampe 1967: 342–55; Hughes 1962: 59–72):

> This punishment by the majority is enough for such a person; so now instead you should forgive and console him, so that he may not be overwhelmed by excessive sorrow. So I urge you to reaffirm your love for him. . . . Anyone whom you forgive, I also forgive.
>
> (2 Cor 2:6–8, 10a)

Very few scholars go along with this proposal, however, and the reasons for their hesitation are clear. First, the expulsion from the community Paul called for in 1 Corinthians 5 sounds permanent and irrevocable, quite unlike the limited punishment Paul calls for here (Thrall 1994: 174). Second, the context of this consolatory language indicates that Paul was recommending reconciliation in an entirely different situation (Furnish 1984: 164–8). The verse that precedes this quotation, points to an offense against Paul himself that he hoped would be treated as a community matter: "But if anyone has caused pain, he has caused it not to me, but to some extent – not to exaggerate it – to all of you" (2 Corinthians 2:5). If Paul's primary focus in 1 Corinthians 5 had been on the immoral individual and the disciplining of him, we might expect Paul to have expressed concern for his fate. But Paul's concern lay with the community, not the individual, and with purifying, not remedial or rehabilitating, action.

Relatively few scholars turn to 2 Corinthians to learn the fate of the sexual deviate, but the pronounced individualism of modern westerners is so powerful that many have found his destiny spelled out in 1 Corinthians 5:5. Contemporary translations reflect this perspective; over time English translations have made verse 5 explicitly about the immoral individual. A premodern (1560) translation renders the verse as follows: ". . . be delivered unto Satan, for the destruction of the flesh, that the spirit may be saved in the day of the Lord Jesus" (Geneva Bible). Modern translations specify whose flesh and spirit the verse is referring to. Here is a contemporary dynamic-equivalence translation: "You must then hand that man over to Satan. His body will be destroyed, but his spirit will be saved when the Lord Jesus returns" (Contemporary English Version, 1991).

In a culture that values individualism, it is almost inevitable that translations made for that culture will reflect a concern for the individual. But this is a modern, western sensibility, one not shared by most of the world and certainly not by ancient Mediterranean culture. Social scientists engaged in cross-cultural research place human cultures on a continuum whose end points are collectivism and individualism. In individualist cultures, values are expressed in personal terms and personal fate is foremost. In contrast, collectivist cultures define the self in terms of the group and stress common fate (Triandis 1990: 59–60). Because such cultures recognize that the basic unit of survival is the whole rather than the part, the collectivist psyche focuses on the ramifications of an individual's actions for the group:

> Not only do collectivists *believe* that the human race is so intricately woven together that one person's misbehavior may harm many, they also *feel* and *experience* this interdependence. Hence, in a collectivist culture a person's misbehavior or failure is a disgrace to the family, or even the entire clan.
>
> (Hui and Triandis 1986: 231)

As a denizen of a collectivist culture, when Paul expressed his concern about the sexual deviate, we would expect to find him focused more on the Corinthian assembly than any single member of it. Hence, we should be wary of translations and interpretations that direct us to the individual.

When Paul called for purification, we should assume that he had the Corinthian church in mind. Resistance to this understanding has resulted in translations and interpretations of verse 5 that make the immoral man the focal point of the rite: "consign this man to Satan for the destruction of his flesh, so that his spirit may be saved on the day of the Lord" (so Conzelmann 1975: 94; cf. Barrett 1968: 125). Yet this reading does not square with Paul's anthropology: flesh and spirit were not distinct parts of the human being; they were orientations that human beings could embrace, or realms or theaters in which they could operate (Gal 3:3; 5:16–26; Rom 8:1–17) (Collins 1980: 257–8). More important, the Greek at the end of verse 5 does not actually say *his* (the man's) flesh and *his* spirit but *the* flesh and *the* spirit, as reflected in the Geneva Bible translation above.

If the group's survival is foremost in Paul's thinking, then we need to consider verse 5 not as a statement about the fate of the offender but about the consequences of the expulsion for the group: their action will purge the community of defilement – the works of flesh embodied in the deviate – and thus preserve the community – God's spirit will continue to dwell there (cf. 1 Cor 3:16–17). As one scholar in tune with Paul's communal orientation concludes, "The more or less explicit reason for expelling the incestuous man in 1 Corinthians 5 was to guard the holiness of the community and to avoid offense to the presence of the Holy Spirit" (Collins 1980: 263). This community-focused reading of verse 5 is particularly attractive because it resonates with several points in the remainder of chapter 5, where Paul's concern is not individual but corporate purity or holiness (1 Cor 5:7, 9, 11) (Martin 1995: 168–74; Donfried 1976: 150–1; Campbell 1993).

How, then, were the Corinthians to undertake their own purification? The German scholar Adolf Deissmann suggested almost a century ago that the closest parallel in language to the handing over of someone to a supernatural power came from the magical papyri (Deissmann 1927: 302–3; cf. Preisendanz 1973–4: 1.192–3, pap. V.334–6; fully explored as an act of cultic devotion by Brun 1932: 106–11). He has been joined in recent years by several other scholars exploring magical execrations and curses that deliver a victim to supernatural wrath (Conzelmann 1975: 97; Aune 1980: 1551–3; Collins 1980).

As convincing as the correspondence in language is, however, reference to the magical papyri does not adequately account for the execration's setting. The background in Greco-Roman magic explains the procedural but not the communal aspect of the expulsion, as New Testament scholar Adela Yarbro Collins notes (Collins 1980: 256). The execration of 1 Corinthians 5:5 was not a personal vendetta, as was evidently the case with the execrations of the magical papyri. In the instance cited above, an individual was to prepare a *defixio*, a curse tablet, and bury it at the grave of someone whose death had been untimely (Betz 1986: 106). The Corinthian execration, in contrast, was to be neither private nor personal but public and communal. Paul did prescribe it but expected the community to carry it out. Once the community was gathered, presumably for worship, a group leader or leaders would pronounce the curse and thus enact the community execration. (In a Mediterranean civic setting, a city magistrate would pronounce a public curse against behavior that threatened public welfare, in a household, the father [Parker 1983: 193–8].)

The alternative reading of 1 Corinthians 5 just presented becomes more convincing once one sees how it accords with the logic and flow of the entire letter. Anthropologist Mary Douglas has written extensively on purity and pollution issues and her insights will guide the final portion of this chapter, as we try to understand the place of that chapter in the whole letter. She has argued that matters of purity, pollution, and purification give voice to a group's or culture's ordering of reality, challenges to that order, and the maintenance or reestablishment of that order (Douglas 1966). In ancient Mediterranean society, for example, death was polluting and those affiliated with the deceased, typically family members, had to undergo purification. What such beliefs and practices reflected, Douglas would say, was the disruptive force of death on familial and other social structures. Death left existing family patterns in disarray, but ritual purification enabled and signaled the reorganization of the family and its reintegration in society. Funeral, burial, and mourning rites brought order out of disorder.

In this light we can understand how Paul's attention to purity and purification ritual in chapter 5 served as his answer to the problem he articulated in the opening chapters of 1 Corinthians. As noted at the beginning of this chapter, 1 Corinthians 5 marks a significant transition in the letter, which has prompted much debate about the continuity between chapters 1 to 4 and the rest of the letter. Those opening chapters focused on what Paul identified as the major crisis the community faces, namely, factionalism or divisiveness. Almost all scholars would agree with Margaret Mitchell that 1 Corinthians is an argument for ecclesial unity, introduced at the very start of the letter (Mitchell 1991: 1; cf. Kennedy 1984: 24–5):

> Now I appeal to you, brothers and sisters, by the name of our Lord Jesus Christ, that all of you be in agreement and that there be no divisions among you, but that you be united in the same mind and the same purpose.
>
> (1 Cor 1:10)

If Paul was arguing for group harmony in the letter, how was he doing it in chapter 5? What follows is an interpretation informed by Douglas. When Paul's discussion of divisions concluded at the end of chapter 4, he framed the problem in terms of purity and pollution and prescribed a solution in chapter 5. Paul understood the Corinthian church's disorder as a symptom of pollution or defilement compromising community purity. Accordingly, he insisted on a ritual of community purification: expulsion of the group member who embodied defilement and epitomized disorder in his flagrant departure from cultural norms. So, while Paul changed his vocabulary between chapters 4 and 5, he still had the unity and health of the community in mind.

The linkage Douglas makes among order, purity, and ritual suggests that the disjunction that most scholars detect between 1 Corinthians 1 through 4 and what follows is actually a misperception. That Paul assumed a connection between order and purity is evident in chapter 3, where he moves effortlessly from picturing the Corinthian community as a structure being assembled to the church as a holy temple:

> (v. 14) If what has been built on the foundation survives, the builder will receive a reward. (15) If the work is burned up, the builder will suffer loss; the builder will be saved, but only as through fire. (16) Do you [plural throughout] not know that you are God's temple and that God's spirit dwells in you? (17) If anyone destroys God's temple, God will destroy that person. For God's temple is holy, and you are that temple.

Moreover, the language there about the temple as a holy place, as God's dwelling place, and about the fate of anyone who threatens to defile the temple fully anticipates the discussion of chapter 5, where Paul stresses purity and the eliminatory rite that will achieve it (Rosner 1991): "Clean out the old yeast so that you may be a new batch, as you really are unleavened" (5:7); "You are to hand this man over to Satan for the destruction of the flesh" (5:5). Modern readers may perceive a shift from the theological to the ethical or from the theoretical to the practical as chapter 5 opens, but the unity in Paul's mind between order and purity made the transition effortless.

Douglas can help us in another way to see the coherence of 1 Corinthians and chapter 5's place in the whole letter. Her study of purity and pollution led her to realize that human societies typically draw an analogy between society and the individual, between the corporate body and the physical body: "the human body is always treated as an image of society" (1970b: 70). The New Testament scholar Jerome Neyrey has applied this insight to 1 Corinthians with fruitful results (Neyrey 1990: 102–46). Paul's worry about the integrity of the body of believers (1 Cor 1–4), Neyrey argues, corresponds to his concern for bodily matters in the remainder of the letter. Thus, from chapter 5 on, Paul is steadily occupied with the physical body and bodily actions: illicit sexual union (5:1–8); fornication (6:12–20); the joining of bodies in marriage (7:1–9, 25–40); the separating of bodies in divorce (7:10–16); proper eating, be it of idol food (8 and 10) or during eucharistic dining (11:17–34); proper dressing (11:2–16); proper speaking, be it in tongues, prophecy, or otherwise (12–14); and the nature of the resurrection body (15:35–58). Paul's anxiety about bodily disposition and behavior, which begins in chapter 5, mirrored Paul's fears about the corporate body of believers in Corinth, which came to expression in the letter's opening chapters. These concerns are two sides of the same coin, and their interconnection gives the letter its unity.

From the standpoint of purity and bodily matters, it is not coincidental that the item foremost on Paul's agenda was ritual when he turned to practical matters in 1 Corinthians 5. Ritual is the way, after all, traditional human communities achieve and maintain purity; it is also how they negotiate bodily matters. For his part, Paul counted on community dining and worship ritual to control bodies: to maintain proper eating, dressing, and speaking. Likewise, when it came to unifying the splintered corporate body at Corinth, Paul turned to ritual purification to bring it back to health, order, and wholeness.

5 Jesus Jettisoned

Gibson also said in the interview that he was nearly suicidal before he made his controversial film. "I got to a very desperate place. Very desperate. Kind of jump-out-of-a-window kind of desperate," he said in the interview. "And I didn't want to hang around here, but I didn't want to check out. The other side was kind of scary. And I don't like heights, anyway. But when you get to that point where you don't want to live, and you don't want to die, it's a desperate, horrible place to be. And I just hit my knees. And I had to use 'The Passion of the Christ' to heal my wounds."

(Walls with Pearson 2005)

Gibson, of course, is free to skip over the incomparable glories of Jesus' temperament and to devote himself, as he does, to Jesus' pain and martyrdom in the last twelve hours of his life. As a viewer, I am equally free to say that the movie Gibson has made from his personal obsessions is a sickening death trip, a grimly unilluminating procession of treachery, beatings, blood, and agony. . . . Gibson is so thoroughly fixated on the scourging and crushing of Christ, and so meagerly involved in the spiritual meanings of the final hours, that he falls in danger of altering Jesus' message of love into one of hate.

(Denby 2004: 84)

Mel Gibson and the many critics of his film, *The Passion of the Christ*, have generated fresh public interest in what are actually age old questions, ones that have occupied western culture for two millennia: why was Jesus put to death? What is the significance of his death? What stands out about the circumstances around his death? For Gibson, the answer to the last question is clear. He underscores the brutality and violence surrounding it. Critics, such as the *New Yorker*'s film critic David Denby, find this focus dangerously misguided. He emphasizes instead what he calls Jesus's personal radiance, which shines especially brightly in the face of authority and death (Denby 2004: 84).

However we may answer questions like "Who killed Jesus and why?" and whatever we make of Gibson and his critics, one thing is clear: a considerable portion of all four gospels in the New Testament – the percentage of Mark is especially high – is devoted to narrating Jesus's final days. We may fault Gibson for obsessing on one aspect of Jesus's final hours, but that should not obscure the fact that the gospel writers themselves laid their emphasis on Jesus's final week, and especially the final hours of his life.

Why the passion narrative – the story about Jesus's last days in Jerusalem – should be so prominent in the canonical gospels and why it took the form it did has been explained by scholars in various ways. Scholars in the early and middle decades of the twentieth century tended to view the gospel writers more as compilers and editors than as genuine authors. They posited that the gospel writers inherited many stories about Jesus that they fitted into a narrative framework they supplied. In the case of the passion narrative, the stories in it, it was thought, had already evolved into a coherent narrative before they reached the gospel writers. Some scholars considered the passion narrative a dramatized but somewhat historical report about Jesus's final chapter. Others detected so many fictional elements that they regarded it as historicized drama. But they agreed for the most part that a sizable and complex narrative about Jesus's final days had formed prior to the writing of the gospels and had been adopted by the evangelists without massive alteration. Hence, the prominence of Jesus's final days in the canonical gospels simply reproduced an emphasis that was already in the traditions about Jesus they received.

In the second half of the twentieth century, scholarly opinion about gospel composition shifted. Scholars began to consider the evangelists less as passive compilers and arrangers and more as active and creative authors. Consequently, they reexamined the gospels for evidence of authorial intent, i.e., for the theological perspectives and agendas that motivated the gospel writers to arrange and edit sources in order to create their distinctive stories. As this reexamination proceeded, many scholars become convinced that the gospel writers not only heavily edited received stories about Jesus but also freely composed them. For example, a 1976 study of Mark's passion narrative found the evangelist more often composing the narrative than editing received tradition (Kelber 1976b; cf. Donahue 1973: 237–40). The study concludes, "The understanding of Mk 14–16 as a theologically integral part of the M[ar]kan Gospel calls into question the classic form critical thesis concerning an independent and coherent Passion Narrative prior to M[ar]k" (Kelber 1976a: 157).

Once the gospel writers came to be regarded as genuine authors, the hunt was on for their theological or ideological commitments and the literary influences on them. The hunt has produced widely varying results, as a few examples will demonstrate. Ched Myers's *Binding the Strong Man* reads the gospel of Mark through a political lens and finds that the evangelist gives voice to an "alienative, confrontative, and nonaligned" ideology through his story of Jesus (Myers 1988: 85–7). A critic of Myers's offers this summary of what motivated the evangelist according to Myers:

Mark wrote his Gospel to encourage [the Marcan community] to chart a political middle course for themselves – to say "no" to Roman imperialism, and to say "no" to the hegemony and human-oppressing political economy of the elitist temple establishment.

(Peterson 2000: 127)

Accordingly, Mark presents a Jesus who confronts the powers that be and offers an alternative political vision – a discipleship that runs contrary to the way the world operates. Alienation, confrontation, and nonalignment come to full expression in the climax of the story, in the passion narrative, where Jesus meets both temple and Rome head on.

Those who stress the evangelists' sophistication as writers have looked for the literary models that influenced them. George Nickelsburg, for instance, turned to ancient Near Eastern stories – most of them in the Hebrew Bible – of the rescue and vindication of a persecuted innocent person or persons (Nickelsburg 1980; adopted and elaborated by Crossan 1988: 297–334; also see Mack 1988: 266–8). He found a common thread running through stories like that of Joseph in the closing chapters of Genesis, Daniel in the fiery furnace and the lion's den, and the martyrdoms narrated in the books of Maccabees. By the time of Mark, a well-defined genre had emerged, elements of which Nickelsburg detects in that gospel, especially its passion narrative. Alternatively, scholars versed in classical literature have found striking correspondences between Mark and Greek and Latin texts. Dennis MacDonald, for instance, claims that Mark "used the *Odyssey* as his primary literary inspiration but also imitated Books 22 and 24 of the *Iliad* for narrating Jesus' death and burial" (MacDonald 2000: 3; critiqued by Sandes 2005).

Many, if not all, contemporary scholarly studies of Mark and its passion narrative have something to offer; they shed light on and make sense of certain aspects of the gospel and its ending. Confrontation, à la Myers, is certainly a prominent feature of the passion narrative, as are elements expressive of the oppressed-but-vindicated-innocent story line, à la Nickelsburg: conspiracy, accusation, trial, condemnation, ordeal, and vindication. (Vindication is more explicit in the gospels with resurrection appearances, and stress on Jesus's innocence is more a concern of Luke's than Mark's [compare Mark 15:39 to Luke 23:47].) Even Mel Gibson is on target in alerting us to the cruel and brutal nature of Jesus's martyrdom. Yet there is more to the passion narrative than these interpretations can capture.

Denby criticizes Gibson for fixating on the "grimly unilluminating procession of treachery, beatings, blood, and agony" in his portrayal of Jesus's final hours, but there is in fact a long process narrated by Mark that culminates in the crucifixion. Bruce Malina and Jerome Neyrey usefully characterize this elaborate process as status-degradation rituals, and their repeated occurrence makes them a prominent feature of the passion narrative (Malina and Neyrey 1988: 51, 88–91). This is not an unilluminating procession. Rather, as Malina and Neyrey show, status-degradation ritual is the mechanism a society typically employs to stigmatize society members as deviant so that the society acts to eliminate them. Ritual destruction anticipates and facilitates physical elimination.

Taking our lead from Malina and Neyrey's treatment of the passion narrative in Matthew, we can readily identify the status-degradation rituals in Mark. There are at least four: (1) a sham trial before the ruling Jerusalemite elite at which Jesus is spat on, blindfolded, and beaten (14:53–65); (2) a sham trial before Pilate that results in Barabbas, a murderer and insurrectionist, being acclaimed worthier than Jesus (15:1–15); (3) a mock investiture of Jesus as king during which he is struck and spat on (15:16–20); and (4) Jesus's crucifixion, a very demeaning form of execution, at which he is publicly derided by all parties present, even those crucified with him (15:25–32).

Yet the narrative does not simply record the status-degradation rituals. Complicating the story line is the gospel's ingenious way of reminding the listener or reader of Jesus's status prior to degradation (and ultimate status in the eyes of believers). Literary irony is in full swing when the mocking words and actions of Jesus's antagonists enunciate and act out his high status. At the first trial Jesus is asked, "Are you the Messiah, the Son of the Blessed One?" At the second trial Pilate asks, "Are you the King of the Jews?" Those coronating him kneel before him, salute him, and hail him as King of the Jews. Likewise, the charge at his crucifixion reads "The King of the Jews." Mark clearly wants us to read between the lines and to think back to the rising status of Jesus in the course of the gospel – from the baptismal scene (1:9–11) to his transfiguration (9:2–8) – which culminates with Jesus's royal entry into Jerusalem:

> Many people spread their cloaks on the road, and others spread leafy branches that they had cut in the fields. Then those who went ahead and those who followed were shouting, "Hosanna! Blessed is the one who comes in the name of the Lord!"
>
> (Mark 11:8–9)

If Jesus suffers ritual degradation at the end of his brief days in Jerusalem, Mark does not want us to forget that he enjoyed a ritual of status elevation at the start, when he entered the city.

The complex narrative that Mark has created highlights the profound status transformation that Jesus undergoes in Jerusalem, which is what successful degradation rituals achieve (Garfinkel 1956: 421). The end result is Jesus's elimination – his expulsion from the city and execution. At first glance, it is puzzling that Mark would dwell on events that reflect so negatively on Jesus. We return to the question that opened this chapter: Why is the passion narrative so prominent in the gospel and why did it take the form it did? More sharply put, why would a partisan of the early church have emphasized the shameful humiliation and dishonorable death of the movement's founder? (There are mitigating features in the narrative that point to an honorable death [see Pilch 1995; Neyrey 1998: 139–62], but they confirm how dishonoring degradation and crucifixion were. What this chapter sketches is the larger, programmatic step Mark took to put a positive spin on Jesus's humiliation.)

Mark would not have dwelt on Jesus's humiliating death had he not seen something positive about it that overshadowed its negative aspects. Denby finds something positive, too, or he would not decry *The Passion of the Christ* for its lack of "spiritual meanings." The reported impetus for the film seems to provide Gibson's rebuttal to Denby: "I had to use 'The Passion of the Christ' to heal my wounds." Both critic and director point to the positive aspect of Jesus's end, and there can be no doubt that Mark views what befalls Jesus as profoundly redeeming. He says so through Jesus at the Last Supper. In what amounts to a commentary about Jesus's impending degradation and death, which he has Jesus announce at several points in the gospel (8:31; 9:31; 10:33–4), Mark offers the following interpretation: " 'This is my blood of the covenant, which is poured out for many' " (14:24). But *how* does Jesus's horrendous ending constitute a beneficial action for many?

The logic for understanding how it does, this chapter proposes, came from the ritual world of the ancient Mediterranean. Running like a red thread through the passion narrative is the depiction of a rite that carries out the dramatic status transformation of a designated individual and his concomitant exit from the community. It resembles a rite widely practiced and well known in the ancient Mediterranean world, one carried out to rescue communities from threatening situations. This ritual mechanism, more than any literary model or ideological agenda, is what best accounts for the prominence and profile of the Marcan passion narrative.

At this point the reader may interject that there is indeed a ritual operating behind the lines of the Marcan passion narrative, namely, sacrifice. The Christian tradition certainly found what happened to Jesus to be atoning, and even specified the nature of the sacrifice as expiatory, freeing humankind from its sin. There is good reason, however, not to consider what we find narrated in Mark as a sacrifice. Scholars have labored hard to define sacrifice for over a century, but no consensus has emerged about what is essential to it (Chilton 1995: 136; Henninger 1987a). It makes little sense, therefore, to introduce a term whose meaning remains hotly debated.

Even if there were a consensus about sacrifice, employing it would not do justice to the Marcan passion narrative. Bruce Malina offers a definition of sacrifice from an ancient Mediterranean viewpoint that is as good as any: "sacrifice is a ritual in which a deity or deities is/are offered some form of inducement, rendered humanly irretrievable, with a view to some life-effect for the offerer(s)" (Malina 1996: 37). If we go with that definition, we would reasonably ask whether Jesus was offered to a deity – to God – in the Marcan narrative. In medieval Christian thinking about how

Jesus saved humankind, atonement became understood as the sacrifice of Jesus to God to satisfy God's offended honor or to meet the demands of divine justice. But Mark does not so much as hint at such an understanding. Moreover, a focus on sacrifice diverts us from the elaborate status-transformation rites that crowd the narrative.

Since Mark placed Jesus's death at Passover time, it is not unreasonable to think that the gospel writer meant to link Jesus's death with the sacrificial cult of ancient Israel. Certainly, some New Testament documents made that connection. For instance, when 1 Peter refers to the rescue effected by Jesus's blood, it clearly alludes to the Passover lamb (1:18–19; cf. Exod 12:5). More broadly, the letter to the Hebrews describes Jesus both as a great high priest (4:14–5:10) and as a sacrifice (9:23–10:18). Yet while Mark does talk about Jesus's blood poured out for many (14:24), it is difficult to see how all the abuse that Jesus undergoes reflects Israelite cultic ritual.

An Israelite rite closer to what is described in the Marcan passion narrative is the so-called scapegoat rite in Leviticus 16, one of the rites prescribed for ancient Israel's annual day of atonement (16:34). It is worth reproducing the whole passage:

> [Aaron] shall take from the congregation of the people of Israel two male goats for a sin offering, and one ram for a burnt offering. Aaron shall offer the bull as a sin offering for himself, and shall make atonement for himself and for his house. He shall take the two goats and set them before the Lord at the entrance of the tent of meeting; and Aaron shall cast lots on the two goats, one lot for the Lord and the other lot for Azazel. Aaron shall present the goat on which the lot fell for the Lord, and offer it as a sin offering; but the goat on which the lot fell for Azazel shall be presented alive before the Lord to make atonement over it, that it may be sent away into the wilderness to Azazel.
> (Lev 16:5–10)

In the verses that follow, Aaron is instructed to sprinkle the blood of the goat offered for sin around the sanctuary. Then attention turns to the second goat:

> Then Aaron shall lay both his hands on the head of the live goat, and confess over it all the iniquities of the people of Israel, and all their transgressions, all their sins, putting them on the head of the goat, and sending it away into the wilderness by means of someone designated for the task. The goat shall bear on itself all their iniquities to a barren region; and the goat shall be set free in the wilderness.
> (Lev 16:21–2)

Scholarly commentators on this passage are quick to point out that though the setting is one of sacrifice and the atonement of the people, the rite involving the second goat is not sacrificial. Rather, it is eliminatory (Henninger 1987b: 92–3; Milgrom 1991: 1009–84; Gorman 1997: 93–9: "rite of banishment"; Levine 1989: 99–110: "rite of riddance"). The first goat is sacrificed, but the second serves as the vehicle for the transfer and disposal of sins.

Early Christian writers saw a foreshadowing of Jesus's passion and death in the scapegoat, and they freely supplemented the Leviticus account to make the connection obvious. Tertullian reports, "One of these goats was bound with scarlet, and driven by the people out of the camp into the wilderness, amid cursing, spitting, and pulling, and piercing, being thus marked with all the signs of the Lord's own passion" (*Adversus Marcionem* 3.7.7; Tertullian, trans. Roberts and Donaldson 1951: 327; cf. *Adversus Judaeos* 14.9). Likewise, the anonymous *Epistle of Barnabas* (late first–early second century) says

> But what are they to do with the other [goat]? "The other," he says, "is accursed." Notice how the type of Jesus is manifested: "And do ye all spit on it, and goad it, and bind the scarlet wool about its head, and so let it be cast into the desert."
>
> (*Barn.* 7.7–8; Lake 1912: 1.364–7)

Even before such heavy-handed embellishment, however, a correspondence between the ritual action of the passion narrative and the scapegoat is evident: a community member is specially designated and driven out of the community.

Does this mean that the atonement rite of Leviticus 16 served as a template for the Marcan passion narrative, as John Dominic Crossan has argued (Crossan 1991: 376–83)? Despite some similarities, there are enough differences between the two accounts that direct borrowing is unlikely. We should think instead of the two stories – also the versions created by early Christian writers – as tributaries of a larger stream; they both participate in a broader pattern that came to expression in many different ways. This broader ritual action or pattern has frequently been labeled the scapegoat rite, but it seems unwise to use a term derived from one instance of it for the whole (McLean 1990). Rather, we designate the ritual pattern remedial or curative exit rites.

To situate this model properly, we should consider its place in the larger context of ritual action in the ancient Mediterranean world. To the left of this chart we would place other forced-exit rites expressed in more juridical or political terms. Thus, ancient Athens tried and executed Socrates for corrupting young boys as a way of protecting or preserving the status quo. Similarly, the male elite of Athens occasionally carried out the rite of ostracism, banishing one of their fellow elites from the city for a period of time. While these actions entailed the designation and expulsion of a community member, they were not perceived as purifying and cathartic in the way that curative exit rites were.

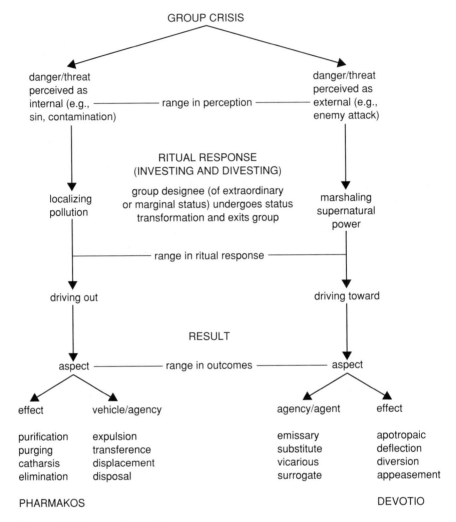

Figure 5.1 Curative Exit Rites

To the right of the chart would appear military action, beginning with strategies that achieve the defeat of the enemy by ruse and ending with brute force. Some of the best examples of trickery come from an anthology of military strategies that the rhetorician Polyaenus composed and dedicated to the co-emperors Marcus Aurelius and Lucius Verus at the time of Rome's war with the Parthians in the mid-second century CE. Here is one:

> When the Ionians colonized Asia, Cnopus of the family of the Codridae, began to wage war on the Ionians who held Erythrae. The god declared

to him to take a general from the Thessalians – the priestess of Enodia (Hecate). He dispatched a representative to the Thessalians, disclosed the oracle of the god, and the Thessalians sent him the priestess of the goddess – Chrysame. Experienced with drugs, she took the largest and handsomest bull from the herd, gilded his horns and dressed his body with garlands and purple robes sprinkled with gold. She mixed up with his food a drug inducing madness and gave it to him to eat. The drug both drove the bull wild and was going to drive mad all who tasted it. Indeed the enemy was encamping opposite them, and Chrysame, having set up in view of the enemy an altar and all requirements for sacrifice, ordered to bring the bull which, crazy from the drug's influence and in a frenzy, leaped away and escaped bellowing loudly. When the enemy saw the garlanded bull with gilded horns charging from the enemy's sacrifice into their own camp, they welcomed it as a good sign and an auspicious omen. They captured the bull, sacrificed it with good omens to the gods, and each feasted eagerly on the meat as though having a part of miraculous and divine worship. In an instant the whole camp was disordered by madness and derangement. Everyone began to jump up and down, to run in different directions, to skip with joy, and to abandon their guard posts. After Chrysame saw this, she ordered Cnopus to equip his army speedily and to attack the defenseless enemy.

(Polyaenus, *Strategemata* 43; Krentz and Wheeler 1994: 2.809–11)

In this instance we see a familiar pattern: designation followed by forced exit. Yet there are differences between this military stratagem and curative exit rites: the designee acts as a kind of bait rather than rallying supernatural force. Also, the example depicts aggressive military action, not defensive action taken to ward off an enemy.

Curative exit rites overlap to some degree with purification rites, and their ends are much the same: the restoration or preservation of community wholeness or holiness. Differences remain, however. Purification rites could and often did use inanimate instruments like fire or water to achieve or restore purity, while curative exit rites always employed an animate – animal or human – instrument. Traditional communities can drive out impurity without parting with a community member, such as the exorcism of demons as part of new year's rites (Katz 2005), but curative exit rites necessarily involved the designation and departure – the investment and divestment – of a community member. The more a curative exit rite was understood to counteract an external, as opposed to internal, threat, the less it looked like a purification rite.

Returning to the go-away goat rite – Mary Douglas prefers this phrase to scapegoat (Douglas 2003) – will help us understand the variation that can exist among curative exit rites. On the one hand, the go-away goat rite falls toward the left side of our model. The Israelites perceived a threat among themselves, the accumulation of sins and iniquities, which a priest transferred to the he-goat, which then departed the community, taking the sins with him. (The end of Leviticus 16 commands that the rite should take place periodically – yearly as part of Yom Kippur, the day of atonement [16:34], but the stress on sanctuary purification in the passage hints that the rite may have been used in the emergency removal of sanctuary pollution.)

On the other hand, mention of Azazel may push us to the other side of the chart. Leviticus reads, "but the goat on which the lot fell for Azazel shall be presented alive before the Lord to make atonement over it, that it may be sent away into the wilderness to Azazel" (16:10). Who or what is Azazel (*'aza'zel*)? Scholars are not positive, but two possibilities are worth noting. First, some scholars argue that Azazel refers to an evil supernatural power. They base their argument on the following observations: (1) if one goat is for God, the other logically goes to a supernatural being as well; (2) the wilderness, the go-away goat's destination, is the stereotypical abode of demons (e.g., Isa 34:8–15); and (3) Israelite tradition subsequent to Leviticus identifies Azazel as a demon or fallen angel (e.g., 1 *Enoch* 9:6). Second, the "el" in Azazel may refer to a deity, and the word might properly be rendered "divine anger" (Roo 2000: 234; Janowski and Wilhelm 1993). In both cases, the ritual action of the rite shifts to, or broadens to include, empowering the goat as an emissary that will meet an external threat, placating an evil demon or appeasing an angry god.

A single curative exit rite may exhibit elements from both sides of the chart. Corresponding Hittite rites from an earlier period, for instance, often took action against a twofold threat, both within the community and without (Gurney 1977: 47–58). Typical of these is the following, in which ritual action is directed to a plague, which has entered the country, and to the remote enemy god who sent it:

> These are the words of Uhha-muwas, the Arzawa man. If people are dying in the country and if some enemy god has caused that, I act as follows:
>
> They drive up one ram. They twine together blue wool, red wool, yellow wool, black wool and white wool, make it into a crown and crown the ram with it. They drive the ram on the road leading to the enemy and while doing so they speak as follows: "Whatever god of the enemy land has caused this plague – see! We have now driven up this ram to pacify thee, O god! Just as the herd is strong, but keeps peace with the ram, do thou, the god who has caused this plague, keep peace with the Hatti land! In favor turn again toward the Hatti land!" They drive that one crowned ram toward the enemy.
>
> (Goetze 1955: 347)

The Israelite go-away goat rite grew more elaborate over time, if the prescriptions of the Mishnah, a Jewish legal writing from about 200 CE, are any indication. Among other things, the Mishnah mentions a thread of crimson wool on the go-away goat's head – crowning it? – and the duty that the goat's escort had to ensure its death by pushing it down a hill (*m. Yoma* 4:2; 6.5–6). Interestingly, the Mishnah knows of a similar rite carried out by the "Babylonians" – evidently a euphemism for Alexandrians (Danby 1933: 509, n. 2) – which involved mistreating the goat (6.4). These additional elements only sharpen what the Leviticus rite already carries out: the investment and divestment of a community member.

The Mishnah provides no further insight into the significance of the term Azazel, but ancient translations of Leviticus are worth noting, for they indicate how the rite would have been understood in the two principal cultures of the first-century Mediterranean world. The Septuagint, a Greek translation of the Hebrew Bible, describes the goat as *apopompaios*, a word having to do with processions – related to the English word pomp – and understood as bearing something, usually evil, away or averting or driving off something undesirable (Liddell and Scott 1996: 213). The Vulgate, a Latin translation of the Hebrew Bible, renders the goat to Azazel as *emissarius*, an agent with a specific mission, like a scout or spy (Lewis and Short 1897: 643; Glare 1968 [1982]: 604). What kind of rite would such language have evoked among Greek and Latin speakers? In both cases the designee of the curative exit rite that would have come to mind was human, not animal, which brings us closer to what happens in the Marcan passion narrative.

The Greek-speaking world would have identified a procession that bore evil away with a *pharmakos* rite, and the Latin-speaking world would have associated an emissary that diverted evil or averted disaster with an act of *devotio*. (Examples of both are usefully collected and presented by Bremmer 2000 and Burkert 1979.) The latter took two forms, some scholars have argued, both of which are worth exploring for the refinement it brings to our curative exit rites model (Versnel 1976).

One type of *devotio* occurred in the context of aggressive military action, as Rome besieged a city, a rather frequent event in Roman history. First, the gods of the besieged city were invited to abandon it and take up residence in Rome, where they would be welcomed with public games and new temples (Macrobius, *Saturnalia* 3.9.7–8). (The gospel of Mark may allude to such a rite at 13:2 [Kloppenborg 2005]). This invocation of the gods (*evocatio deorum*) would then be followed by a *devotio*, in which the city and its defenders would be devoted to destruction. The supreme commander of the Roman forces would ask underworld deities like Dis Pater to fill the besieged city with terror and to doom its inhabitants, adding

> By my honor and in virtue of my office, on behalf of the Roman people, our armies and legions, give and devote [our enemy] *in our place*; so that ye allow me, and my honor and authority, our legions and army, who are herein engaged, to be well and safe.
>
> (Macrob., *Sat.* 3.9.11; Davies 1969: 219; italics added)

Macrobius claimed that the Romans treated many enemy cities and armies in this way. While we cannot be sure how often and exactly in what way the *evocatio* and *devotio* were carried out – Macrobius wrote very late in antiquity (ca. 400 CE) – there can be little doubt that this was a well known Roman military practice (Kloppenborg 2005: 434–41).

One can see in this version of *devotio* several features of a curative exit rite: a designee of extraordinary status marshals divine power against an enemy. Plus, surrogacy or substitution is an aspect of the ritual action, as the italicized text above suggests (Versnel 1981: 143–63). Still, the ritual action and the context for it are different from, in fact the very the opposite of, our model (but not totally different, contra Janssen 1981: 359). This is not an exit rite as defensive measure but rather a summoning of the gods to facilitate invasion.

Falling firmly under the rubric of curative exit rite is a second type of *devotio*, examples of which were recorded by Livy, a Roman historian of the late first century BCE. The Decii, an old and elite Roman family, produced many military leaders over the generations, and the family's dedication to the Roman people and its armies was well known (e.g., Cicero, *Tusculanae disputationes* 1.37.89; *De finibus* 2.19 §61). Livy's history of Rome includes not one but two *devotiones* by the Decii, a rite by which a family member sacrificed himself for his troops in order to reverse a dire battlefield situation (8.9; 10.28). One of Livy's accounts is worth quoting extensively, even though many of its details are undoubtedly legendary:

> In the confusion of this movement [Publius] Decius the consul called out to Marcus Valerius in a loud voice: "We have need of Heaven's help, Marcus Valerius. Come therefore, state pontiff of the Roman People, dictate the words, that I may devote myself to save the legions." The pontiff bade him don the purple-bordered toga . . . and say as follows, ". . . I invoke you and worship you [various gods], I beseech and crave your favour, that you prosper the might and the victory of the Roman People of the Quirites, and visit the foes of the Roman People of the Quirites with fear, shuddering, and death. As I have pronounced the words, even so in behalf of the republic of the Roman People of the Quirites, and of the army, the legions, the auxiliaries of the Roman People of the Quirites, do I devote the legions and auxiliaries of the enemy, together with myself, to the divine Manes and to Earth." . . . He then girded himself with the Gabinian cincture, and vaulting, armed, upon his horse, plunged into the thick of the enemy, a conspicuous object from either army and of an aspect more august than a man's, as though sent from heaven to expiate all the anger of the gods, and to turn aside destruction from his people and bring it on their adversaries. Thus every terror and dread attended him, and throwing the [enemy] Latin front into disarray, spread afterwards throughout their entire host. This was most clearly seen in that, wherever he rode, men cowered as though

blasted by some baleful star; but when he fell beneath a rain of missiles, from that instant there was no more doubt of the consternation of the Latin cohorts, which everywhere abandoned the field in flight.

(Livy 8.9.4–12 [Foster, LCL])

All the elements of a curative exit rite are here: (1) a threat to the community, in this case an external one; (2) the designation of a community member in response, who undergoes status transformation over the course of the rite; (3) ritual action that concentrates and directs divine power and (4) entails the exit of the designee from the community toward the enemy; and (5) the designee's vicarious action that diverts disaster away from his community and toward the enemy.

The Greek world did not practice *devotio*, yet the stories it told about its heroes could come very close to this ritual pattern. The story of Athens's legendary last king, Codrus, is a case in point. The fullest version comes from the Athenian orator Lycurgus, who narrates the story in a fourth-century BCE court case against Leocrates.

> Remember the reign of Codrus. The Peloponnesians, whose crops had failed at home, decided to march against our city and, expelling our ancestors, to divide the land amongst themselves. They first sent to Delphi and asked the god if they were going to capture Athens, and when he replied that they would take the city so long as they did not kill Codrus, the king of the Athenians, they marched out against Athens. But a Delphian Cleomantis, learning of the oracle, secretly told the Athenians. Such, it seems, was the goodwill which our ancestors always inspired even among aliens. And when the Peloponnesians invaded Attica, what did our ancestors do, gentlemen of the jury? They did not desert their country and retire as Leocrates did, nor surrender to the enemy the land that reared them and its temples. No. Though they were few in number, shut inside the walls, they endured the hardships of a siege to preserve their country. And such was the nobility, gentlemen, of those kings of old that they preferred to die for the safety of their subjects rather than to purchase life by the adoption of another country. That at least is true of Codrus, who, they say, told the Athenians to note the time of his death and, taking a beggar's clothes to deceive the enemy, slipped out by the gates and began to collect firewood in front of the town. When two men from the camp approached him and inquired about conditions in the city he killed one of them with a blow of his sickle. The survivor, it is said, enraged with Codrus and thinking him a beggar drew his sword and killed him. Then the Athenians sent a herald and asked to have their king given over for burial, telling the enemy the whole truth; and the Peloponnesians restored the body but retreated, aware that it was no longer open to them to secure that country.

(Lycurgus, *Against Leocrates* 84–7; Burtt 1954: 75–7)

Earlier and later Greek authors cited the story, too, and it also made its way into Latin literature, with some variation. Fifth-century BCE chronicler Hellanicus of Lesbos clothed Codrus in the worthless garb of a woodcutter and equipped him with a pruning hook (*FGrH* 323a F23; cf. Polyaenus, *Strat.* 1.18). First-century CE Roman historian C. Velleius Paterculus reported that the king shed his royal robes for shepherd's garb (1.2.1). Details varied, but the accounts agree about the change of clothing, a switch that enables Codrus to save his people.

Many components typical of a curative exit rite are present in the Codrus story: in the face of an external threat, Codrus departs Athens to defeat the enemy via deception. Moreover, Codrus acts vicariously; his death saves his people from death. Notably absent is any ritual action that marks Codrus's exceptional status or status transformation. Yet the change of clothing, understood metaphorically, is the perfect signal of Codrus's profound status change.

A better-known curative exit rite in the Greek world was the *pharmakos* rite. The best known took place yearly in Athens as part of a festival to Apollo called the Thargelia, falling as it did in the Greek month of Thargelion (Parke 1977: 146–55; Deubner 1932 [1956]: 179–98). In preparation for a day of sacrificial offerings to Apollo, the Athenians purified their city. Multiple Greek sources, both early and late, suggest the following scenario: two men distinguished by their ugliness and poverty were chosen for the public rite in advance of the festival and fed for some time at the state's expense. On the first day of the festival, both men, one wearing a string of black figs and representing the male inhabitants, the other wearing white figs and representing women, were led in procession around the city, whipped and pelted by the inhabitants, then expelled.

Much like the Israelite go-away goat, the *pharmakoi* (plural) served as the instrument for eliminating community impurities. Likewise, there is a very mechanical transmission of those impurities expressed ritually: the priest laid his hands on the goat; the Athenians physically abused the *pharmakoi*, as the latter processed around the city. What stands out about the Athenian *pharmakos* rite, however, are the status alterations that the *pharmakoi* underwent, from low (ugly, poor) to high (worthy of public welfare) to low (public humiliation and expulsion).

The annual *pharmakos* rite was the quintessential rite of purification for Athens, so familiar that Athenians like the playwright Aristophanes could refer to it proverbially. Moreover, the word *pharmakos* came into common usage as a term of contempt, understandable since *pharmakoi* were chosen from the lowest social level (Harrison 1962: 97).

Other accounts of the *pharmakos* rite indicate that it was practiced widely in the Greek-speaking world and more often as a response to crisis than part of a periodic ritual cycle. The Byzantine grammatician Joannes Tzetzes, writing in the twelfth century, provides a rather full description of the rite, replete with sensational additions like the burning of the *pharmakos* and the sprinkling of his ashes. Yet the account has a historical basis. It rests in part on the work of Hipponax, a sixth-century BCE poet who lived his latter years in Clazomenae, near Ephesus. (Those parts of the quotation that actually come from Hipponax – less than Tzetzes claims – are underlined and introduced by the number under which they appear in the latest critical edition of his fragmentary works [Degani 1991: 29, 43–5]).

> The pharmakos was a purification of this sort of old. If a calamity overtook the city by the wrath of God, whether it were famine or pestilence or any other mischief, they led forth as though to sacrifice the most unsightly of them all as purification and a remedy to the suffering city. They set the sacrifice in the appointed place, and gave him cheese with their hands and a barley cake and figs, and seven times they smote him with leeks and wild figs and other wild plants. Finally they burnt him with fire with the wood of wild trees and scattered the ashes into the sea and to the winds, for a purification, as I said, of the suffering city. Just as, I think, Lycophron records it of the Locrian maidens, speaking somewhat after this manner, I do not remember the exact verse, "when having consumed their limbs with fuel from the fruitless trees, the flame of fire cast into the sea the ashes of the maidens that died on the hill of Taron."
>
> And Hipponax gives us the best complete account of the custom when he says, [26] "to purify the city and strike [the pharmakos] with branches"; and in another place he says in his first iambic poem, [6] "striking him like a storm and beating him with switches and with squills [sea onions, leeks] like a pharmakos"; and again in other places he says as follows: [27] "we must put him out as a pharmakos"; and he says, [28] "offering him figs and a barley cake and cheese such as pharmakoi eat"; and [29] "they have long been waiting agape for them, holding squills in their hands as they do for pharmakoi"; and somewhere else he says in the same iambic poem, [30] "may he be parched with hunger, so that in [their] anger he may be led as pharmakos and beaten seven times."
>
> (Tzetz., *Thousand Histories* 23.726–56; Harrison 1962: 98–9)

If all we had was the fragmentary information from Hipponax, the basic outline of the rite would still be clear: the striking or beating of (a) designee(s), followed by his/their expulsion. The Hipponax fragments also suggest that the *pharmakos/oi* enjoyed a special diet that was withheld as the expulsion drew near.

What could be clearer is the status transformation that the *pharmakos* underwent. Other examples make that aspect of the *pharmakos* rite explicit. The first comes from the poet Callimachus, who lived in third-century BCE Ptolemaic Egypt. A fragment from one of his poems refers to a *pharmakos* rite in Abdera, a city in northern Greece. We would know nothing more about the rite except that Callimachus was very popular and narrative summaries of his poems circulated, some of which have survived. They may have served as an aid to the study of his poems. The line from Callimachus appears underlined (Pfeiffer 1949: frg. 90 = *Aitia* 4.2) and is followed by the summary (*diegesis*), which dates to the first century BCE or first century CE.

> <u>There, Abderos, where now</u> [your city] <u>leads out a scapegoat</u>. . . . In Abdera a slave bought for the purpose provides the purificatory offering on the city's behalf: taking his stand on a plinth of grey stone and partaking of a sumptuous feast, he is led, when he has sated himself, to the gates called Prurides; next, outside the wall, he goes round in a circle, purifying the street thereby, and then he is pelted with stones by the king and the others until he is driven beyond the boundaries.
>
> (Nisetich 2001: 154)

Another example comes from Petronius, a first-century CE Latin author whose description of a *pharmakos* rite was preserved in a fourth-century commentary on Vergil's *Aneid*. The commentator, Maurus Servius Honoratus, quotes from the *Aneid* (underlined below) and reflects on the ambiguity of the Latin term *sacra*. Servius then introduces Petronius's account of a *pharmakos* rite practiced in Massilia (modern Marseilles), originally a Greek colony (*Servius on Aneid* 3.57):

> "<u>The sacred</u> [*sacra*] <u>hunger for gold</u>." "Sacred" means "accursed." This expression is derived from a Gallic custom. For whenever the people of Massilia were burdened with pestilence, one of the poor would volunteer to be fed for an entire year out of public funds on food of special purity. After this period he would be decked with sacred herbs and sacred robes, and would be led through the whole state while people cursed him, in order that the sufferings of the whole state might fall upon him, and so he would be cast out. This account has been given in Petronius.
>
> (Petronius, frg. 1 [Heseltine, LCL])

Much like the equivocal *sacra*, we have a two-sided designee in the *pharmakos* rite. They were from the dregs of society – unsightly, poor, slave – hence the derogatory connotation the word *pharmakos* accrued in the Greek language. Yet in the *pharmakos* rite they enjoyed an elevated status – sumptuous feasting at state expense, dressed in sacred robes. Status transformation came full circle as expulsion approached. What followed – beatings, stonings, cursings at the hands of the entire group – signaled and enacted not only the transfer of community ills to them but also their status degradation, which culminated in their elimination from the community altogether. (Bremmer notes the marginality of the *pharmakoi* but misses their status transformation [Bremmer 2000: 275].)

The preceding examples give some idea of what form curative exit rites took in the ancient Mediterranean. Two things about them stand out: their pervasiveness and their variety. In addition to the foregoing descriptions of *devotio* and *pharmakos* rites, allusions to them appear often enough in Greek and Latin literature, both in prose and poetry, that we are safe in concluding that they were givens in Greek and Roman culture.

Is it also legitimate to conclude that a common ritual structure lay behind such a varied and widespread set of rites? Support for this conclusion comes from the ancients themselves, who reveal the interchangeability of *devotio* and *pharmakos* rites in the way they wrote. For instance, when the Latin poet Ovid refers to the Abdera *pharmakos* rite, the allusion is replete with the vocabulary of devotion: "Or may Abdera call curses [*devoveat*] upon thee on certain days, and stones more numerous than hail seek the object of their cursing [*devotum*]" (*Ibis* 467–8 [Mozley, LCL]). Even more telling is a scene from the Latin epic poem *Thebaid*, composed by Publius Papinius Statius in the first century CE. Statius retells a well-known story from Greek tradition, the conquest of the city of Thebes. In a *devotio*-like scene, prince Menoeceus attempts to relieve the siege of the city by plunging off its wall into the midst of the enemy (10.756–82). Menoeceus's parents lament his loss, and his mother reveals the fear that her noble son will be mistaken for an expendable – a *pharmakos*:

> Here the father laments with tears, overcoming his anger, and at length his mother is given her chance to weep: "Was I rearing you, famous boy, as a sacrifice for fierce Thebes, a devoted head, as though mother of a worthless wight? What sin did I commit, which of the gods so hates me?"
>
> (Stat., *Theb.* 10.791–5 [Shackleton Bailey, LCL])

The mother's anxious questions reveal the correspondence between *devotio* and *pharmakos*, confirming to us how much alike they were in the eyes of the ancients.

What if the author of Mark shared the fear of Menoeceus's mother? Such a fear was warranted, given the logic of the culture: if one died like a slave, then was not the crucified one in reality a slave? This might be a good angle for getting at the question that began this chapter, for it points to the problem the gospels addressed. How could Mark make "good news" out of such a horrendous ending, the humiliating death of Jesus? Mark had to nullify or reverse the negative impact such a death had on Jesus's reputation. To do so, he needed to show how such a shameful ending was necessary and could constitute a beneficial act for many. This goal determined the shape the Marcan passion narrative took.

Vicarious death – the noble act of dying on behalf of another – was a well-known subject in Greek and Roman literature, and some have argued that Mark and the other gospel writers adopted that theme for their portrayal of Jesus. H. S. Versnel, for instance, sees a drama like Euripides's *Alcetis* at work behind the end of the gospels (Versnel 1989a). The gospel of Mark's lack of literary polish, however, tells against appropriation at such a sophisticated level (Marcus 2000: 59–62). More likely, Mark made use of commoner elements in the culture. Ernest Best asks us to picture the gospel writer as a composer making use of traditional folk songs to write a symphony (Best 1983: 121–2).

Evidently, one of those "folk songs" was curative exit ritual, because the Marcan passion narrative bears the telltale earmarks of one: a designee undergoes status transformation and ejection. The Jesus who arrived in Jerusalem at the beginning of the passion narrative as triumphant king (11:1–11), who as authoritative prophet challenged the temple complex and predicted its downfall (11:15–19; 13:1–37), who gained such respect from the populace that his opponents could not publicly check him (11:18; 12:12) and were even won over by him (12:32), is the same Jesus who days later underwent the status degradation rites noted at the beginning of this chapter, rites that culminated in expulsion from Jerusalem and crucifixion.

Mark clearly banked on his listeners and readers understanding such degradation as prerequisite to a beneficial result. The effectiveness of a curative exit rite rested on such degradation, for it was in the acts of spitting, mocking, cursing, deriding, beating, and stoning that the community transferred its ills, impurities, and iniquities to the designee for disposal. The logic of the curative exit rite allowed Mark to make positive sense of Jesus's contemptible end, so that the cruel and bloody manner in which he died became remedial: " 'This is my blood of the covenant, which is poured out for many' " (14:24).

This interpretation of the Marcan passion narrative as a curative exit rite, besides making sense of the ending of Mark, may also help us make sense of the whole gospel. What does the gospel of Mark look like read through a ritual lens? The story of Jesus in Galilee, which leads up to the passion narrative, tells us much about Jesus, but it also reveals a world that is terribly out of order. Illness and demon possession are prevalent, indicating that the land suffers from some malignancy. Likewise, the land has become unholy. The system of purification, with the Jerusalem Temple at its center, has failed, as evidenced by Jesus's devastating critique of both the system (chapter 7) and the Temple (chapter 11).

If the opening and middle chapters of Mark describe a world infected by sickness and impurity, then the passion narrative presents the ritual solution to the crisis: the designation of Jesus, via rites of elevation and degradation, who will bear the land's illness away. This is the gospel of Mark read as a *pharmakos* rite.

The ancient world saw *pharmakos* and *devotio* rites as two sides of the same coin, so we might expect to see elements of the latter rite as well. To do so, we need to consider when the gospel of Mark was written, the events around that date, and the situation of the early church. There is general

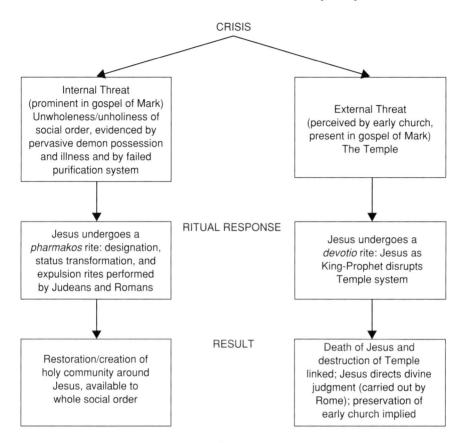

CRISIS

Internal Threat
(prominent in gospel of Mark)
Unwholeness/unholiness of
social order, evidenced by
pervasive demon possession
and illness and by failed
purification system

External Threat
(perceived by early church,
present in gospel of Mark)
The Temple

RITUAL RESPONSE

Jesus undergoes a
pharmakos rite: designation,
status transformation, and
expulsion rites performed
by Judeans and Romans

Jesus undergoes a
devotio rite: Jesus as
King-Prophet disrupts
Temple system

RESULT

Restoration/creation of
holy community around
Jesus, available to
whole social order

Death of Jesus and
destruction of Temple
linked; Jesus directs divine
judgment (carried out by
Rome); preservation of
early church implied

Figure 5.2 Curative Exit Rites in Mark

consensus among scholars that Mark was written around 70 CE or shortly thereafter, as a response to the crisis that arose when Rome put down a rebellion in Palestine in the late 60s. Particularly devastating were the capture of Jerusalem and the destruction of the Temple in 70 CE. But would the early church have seen it as total disaster? Many believers would have decried Rome's brutal treatment of Judea and its desecration of a holy place. At the same time, there was a growing rift and increasing antagonism between Christ followers and their fellow Jews by the late 60s. The disruption of Temple-oriented Judaism undoubtedly took pressure off the early church.

If Mark was a response to the traumatic events of 70 CE, the gospel writer may have employed the *devotio* paradigm to account for what happened. If Jesus's antagonism toward the traditional purification system signals opposition to the Temple early in the gospel (chapter 7), open conflict breaks out when Jesus visits Jerusalem. He physically assaults Temple functionaries (chapter 11) and predicts the Temple's destruction (chapter 13). Later, at the end of the gospel, at the moment Jesus dies, the Temple curtain is torn in two (15:38), which many interpreters read as a symbolic elimination of the temple. Somehow, in the conflict between Jesus and the Temple, their fates have become one.

It is that linkage that gives the passion narrative the look of a *devotio*. If the fledging church of the mid-first century saw the Temple as a threat – an increasingly external enemy – and it understood Rome's destruction of Jerusalem as an expression of divine wrath or judgment, then what happened to Jesus in Jerusalem included, among other things, Jesus acting as emissary to direct divine destruction against the Temple and to preserve the church. While *devotio* is not as explicit as *pharmakos* in the narrative, its presence would account for why the passion narrative is preoccupied with the Temple and, more to the point, how and why Jesus's death and the Temple's destruction become intertwined.

In the decades that followed, believers continued to make sense of Jesus's end through the lens of curative exit rites. The gospel of John articulates the calculus of such rites perfectly on the lips of Jesus's chief opponent, Caiaphas: "You do not understand that it is better for you to have one man die for the people than to have the whole nation destroyed" (11:50). Likewise, Tertullian, the *Epistle of Barnabas*, and other early Christian writers and writings likened Jesus's end to the curative exit rite prescribed in Leviticus 16, as noted earlier in this chapter.

Over time, the rich diversity of curative exit patterns generated a host of redemption scenarios. Origen of Alexandria, a Christian writer of the third century, likened Jesus's death to a *devotio* as he defended the faith against detractors:

> The disciples proclaimed that he who was but recently crucified had willingly accepted that death on behalf of mankind, on the analogy of men who have died for their country to put an end to visitations of plague or famine or tempests. For it seems to be part of the natural order of things that, according to certain recondite principles which are not easy for ordinary men to grasp, the death of one righteous man, voluntarily undertaken for the general good, is effective to avert the power of impious spirits which produces pestilence, dearth, tempests, and the like. Therefore if men deliberately refuse to believe that Jesus died for man by way of the cross they should tell us whether they also refuse to accept the many stories from Greece and from the East which tell of men who died for the general good to free their cities and nations from disasters which had come upon them. Or do they regard these as facts and yet find it incredible that he who was accounted man should have died to destroy the power of the great evil spirit, who is the ruler of the evil spirits, who had subjected all the souls of men which have come upon the earth?
>
> (*Contra Celsum* 1.31; Bettenson 1969: 223–4)

Other *devotio*-inspired scenarios developed over time: (1) the Devil was deceived into accepting Jesus as ransom for humankind; (2) Jesus stemmed the demonic invasion by plunging into Hell and defeating Satan – the harrowing of Hell tradition – and (3) as emissary and surrogate for humankind, Jesus averted divine anger – the satisfaction theory of atonement (Origen, *Commentarium in evangelium Matthaei* 16.8; Aulén 1951).

Early Christian iconography confirms how dominant a ritual paradigm could be. Pre-Constantinian wall frescoes, mosaics, and decorated sarcophagi depicted a host of images and scenes from the Hebrew Bible and Jesus's life, but the most frequent was the Jonah story (Snyder 1985: 43). Jonah's rescue from the great fish after three days in its belly obviously brought Jesus's resurrection to mind, and that scene was depicted often, but not as often as the image that expressed the curative exit rite in the story: Jonah jettisoned from the storm-tossed boat in order to save it.

Bibliography

Achtemeier, Paul J. (1996) "The Continuing Quest for Coherence in St. Paul: An Experiment in Thought," in E. H. Lovering Jr. and J. L. Sumney (eds) *Theology and Ethics in Paul and His Interpreters: Essays in Honor of Victor Paul Furnish*, Nashville, TN: Abingdon, pp. 132–45.

Alcock, Susan E. (1989) "Archaeology and Imperialism: Roman Expansion and the Greek City," *Journal of Mediterranean Archaeology*, 2: 87–135.

—— (1993) *Graecia capta: The Landscapes of Roman Greece*, Cambridge: Cambridge University Press.

—— (1996) "Landscapes of Memory and the Authority of Pausanias," in J. Bingen (ed.) *Pausanias Historien*, Entretiens sur l'Antiquité Classique 41, Geneva: Fondation Hardt, pp. 241–67.

Alexiou, M. (1974) *The Ritual Lament in Greek Tradition*, Cambridge: Cambridge University Press.

Anderson-Stojanović, V. (1988) "Cult and Industry of Isthmia: A Shrine on the Rachi," paper presented at the Archaeological Institute of America 89th General Meeting, New York, 1987; summarized in *AJA*, 92 (1988): 268–9.

Ashton, John (2000) *The Religion of Paul the Apostle*, New Haven, CT: Yale University Press.

Atkins, Stuart (ed. and trans.) (1984) *Johann Wolfgang von Goethe, Faust I & II*, Goethe's Collected Works, vol. 2, Cambridge, MA: Suhrkamp/Insel.

Aulén, Gustaf (1951) *Christus Victor: An Historical Study of the Three Main Types of the Idea of Atonement*, trans. A. G. Hebert, New York: Macmillan.

Aune, David E. (1980) "Magic in Early Christianity," in *ANRW*, part II, vol. 23.2, pp. 1507–57.

Babcock, Barbara A. (1978) "Introduction," in B. A. Babcock (ed.) *The Reversible World: Symbolic Inversion in Art and Society*, Symbol, Myth, and Ritual Series, Ithaca, NY: Cornell University Press, pp. 13–36.

Bammel, Ernst (1997) "Rechtsfindung in Korinth," *ETL*, 73: 107–13.

Barrett, C. K. (1968) *A Commentary on the First Epistle to the Corinthians*, HNTC, New York: Harper & Row.

Bassler, Jouette M. (ed.) (1991) *Pauline Theology, Volume I: Thessalonians, Philippians, Galatians, Philemon*, Minneapolis, MN: Fortress Press.

—— (1993) "Paul's Theology: Whence and Whither?," in D. M. Hay (ed.) *Pauline Theology, Volume II: 1 & 2 Corinthians*, Minneapolis, MN: Fortress Press, pp. 3–17.

Beasley-Murray, G. R. (1962) *Baptism in the New Testament*, New York: St. Martin's Press.

Beezley, William H., Cheryl English Martin, and William E. French (1994) "Introduction: Constructing Consent, Inciting Conflict," in W. Beezley, C. Martin, and W. French (eds) *Rituals of Rule, Rituals of Resistance: Public Celebrations and Popular Culture in Mexico*, Wilmington, DE: Scholarly Resources, pp. xiii–xxxii.

Beker, J. Christiaan (1980) *Paul the Apostle: The Triumph of God in Life and Thought*, Philadelphia, PA: Fortress Press.

Bell, Catherine (1992) *Ritual Theory, Ritual Practice*, New York: Oxford University Press.

—— (1997) *Ritual: Perspectives and Dimensions*, New York: Oxford University Press.

Best, Ernest (1983) *Mark: The Gospel as Story*, Edinburgh: T & T Clark.

Bettenson, Henry (ed. and trans.) (1969) *The Early Christian Fathers: A Selection from the Writings of the Fathers from St. Clement of Rome to St. Athanasius*, Oxford: Oxford University Press.

Betz, Hans Dieter (ed.) (1986) *The Greek Magical Papyri in Translation, including the Demotic Spells*, Chicago: University of Chicago Press.

Biers, Jane C. (1985) *Corinth*, vol. 17: *The Great Bath on the Lechaion Road*, Princeton, NJ: American School of Classical Studies at Athens.

Blegen, Carl W., Hazel Palmer, and Rodney Young (1964) *Corinth*, vol. 13: *The North Cemetery*, Princeton, NJ: American School of Classical Studies at Athens.

Bodel, John (1995) "Minicia Marcella: Taken Before Her Time," *AJP*, 116: 453–60.

Bohren, Rudolf (1952) *Das Problem der Kirchenzucht im Neuen Testament*, Zurich: Evangelischer Verlag.

Bohtz, Carl Helmut (1981) *Das Demeter-Heiligtum*, Deutsches Archäologisches Institut, Altertümer von Pergamum 13, Berlin: Walter de Gruyter.

Bond, George Clement, and Diane M. Ciekawy (eds) (2001) *Witchcraft Dialogues: Anthropological and Philosophical Exchanges*, Research in International Studies, Africa Series No. 76, Athens, OH: Ohio University Center for International Studies.

Bookidis, Nancy (1969) "The Sanctuary of Demeter and Kore on Acrocorinth, Preliminary Report III, 1968," *Hesperia*, 38: 297–310.

—— (1990) "Ritual Dining in the Sanctuary of Demeter and Kore at Corinth: Some Questions," in O. Murray (ed.) *Sympotica: A Symposium on the "Symposium,"* Oxford: Clarendon Press, pp. 86–94.

—— (2005) "Religion in Corinth: 146 B.C. to 100 C.E.," in D. N. Schowalter and S. J. Friesen (eds) *Urban Religion in Roman Corinth: Interdisciplinary Approaches*, HTS 53, Cambridge, MA: Harvard University Press, pp. 141–64.

Bookidis, Nancy, and Joan Fisher (1972) "The Sanctuary of Demeter and Kore on Acrocorinth, Preliminary Report IV: 1969–1970," *Hesperia*, 41: 283–331.

—— and —— (1974) "The Sanctuary of Demeter and Kore on Acrocorinth, Preliminary Report V: 1971–1973," *Hesperia*, 43: 267–91.

Bookidis, Nancy, and Ronald S. Stroud (1987) *Demeter and Persephone in Ancient Corinth*, Corinth Notes 2, Princeton, NJ: American School of Classical Studies at Athens.

—— and —— (1997) *Corinth*, vol. 18.3: *The Sanctuary of Demeter and Kore: Topography and Architecture*, Princeton, NJ: American School of Classical Studies at Athens.

Bourdieu, Pierre (1990) *The Logic of Practice*, trans. R. Nice, Stanford, CA: Stanford University Press.

Bowersock, G. W. (1965) *Augustus and the Greek World*, Oxford: Clarendon Press.

Bowie, Ewen L. (1996) "Past and Present in Pausanias," in J. Bingen (ed.) *Pausanias Historien*, Entretiens sur l'Antiquité Classique 41, Geneva: Fondation Hardt, pp. 207–30.

Bremmer, Jan N. (1992) "The Atonement in the Interaction of Greeks, Jews, and Christians," in J. N. Bremmer and F. G. Martínez (eds) *Sacred History and Sacred Texts in Early Judaism: A Symposium in Honour of A. S. van der Woude*, CBET 5, Kampen: Kok Pharos, pp. 75–93.

—— (2000) "Scapegoat Rituals in Ancient Greece," in R. Buxton (ed.) *Oxford Readings in Greek Religion*, Oxford: Oxford University Press, pp. 271–93.

Broneer, Oscar (1959) "Excavations at Isthmia, Fourth Campaign, 1957–1958," *Hesperia*, 28: 298–343.

—— (1973) *Isthmia*, vol. 2: *Topography and Architecture*, Princeton, NJ: American School of Classical Studies at Athens.

—— (1977) *Isthmia*, vol. 3: *Terracotta Lamps*, Princeton, NJ: American School of Classical Studies at Athens.

Brun, Lyder (1932) *Segen und Fluch im Urchristentum*, Norske Videnskaps-akademi i Oslo, historisk-filosofisk klasse, Skrifter 1932, 1st vol. (1933), no. 1, Oslo: Jacob Dybwad.

Bultmann, Rudolf (1951–5) *The Theology of the New Testament*, Scribner Studies in Contemporary Theology, 2 vols, New York: Charles Scribner's Sons.

Burchard, Christoph (1985) "Joseph and Aseneth: A New Translation and Introduction," in J. H. Charlesworth (ed.) *The Old Testament Pseudepigrapha*, 2 vols, Garden City, NY: Doubleday, vol. 2, pp. 177–247.

Burkert, Walter (1979) *Structure and History in Greek Mythology and Ritual*, Sather Classical Lectures 47, Berkeley, CA: University of California Press.

—— (1983) *Homo Necans: The Anthropology of Ancient Greek Sacrificial Ritual and Myth*, Berkeley, CA: University of California Press.

—— (1985) *Greek Religion: Archaic and Classical*, trans. J. Raffan, Cambridge, MA: Harvard University Press.

—— (1996) *Creation of the Sacred: Tracks of Biology in Early Religions*, Cambridge, MA: Harvard University Press.

Burtt, J. O. (trans.) (1954) *Minor Attic Orators II: Lycurgus, Dinarchus, Demades, Hyperides*, LCL, Cambridge, MA: Harvard University Press.

Byrne, Brendan (2001) "Interpreting Romans Theologically in a Post-'New Perspective' Perspective," *HTR*, 94: 227–41.

Cahill, Thomas J. (2002) "Drinking Blood at a Kosher Eucharist?: The Sound of Scholarly Silence," *BTB*, 32: 168–81.

Calder, William M., III (1991) *The Cambridge Ritualists Reconsidered: Proceedings of the First Oldfather Conference, Held on the Campus of the University of Illinois at Urbana-Champaign, April 27–30, 1989*, Illinois Classical Studies, Supplement 2, Atlanta, GA: Scholars Press.

Cambier, J. (1968–9) "La chair et l'esprit en I Cor. v.5," *NTS*, 15:221–32.

Cameron, Ron (1996) "The Anatomy of a Discourse: On 'Eschatology' as a Category for Explaining Christian Origins," *MTSR*, 8: 231–45.

Campbell, Barth (1993) "Flesh and Spirit in 1 Cor 5:5: An Exercise in Rhetorical Criticism of the NT," *JETS*, 36: 331–42.

Capitolinus, Julius (1921) "Pertinax," in D. Magie (trans.) *The Scriptores Historiae Augustae*, LCL, 3 vols, Cambridge, Mass.: Harvard University Press, vol. 1, pp. 315–47.

Carlson, Richard P. (1993) "The Role of Baptism in Paul's Thought," *Int*, 47: 255–66.

Caskey, John L. (1960) "Objects from a Well at Isthmia," *Hesperia*, 29: 168–76.

Casson, Lionel (1974) *Travel in the Ancient World*, Baltimore, MD: Johns Hopkins University Press.

Chaniotis, Angelos (2005) "Ritual Dynamics in the Eastern Mediterranean: Case Studies in Ancient Greece and Asia Minor," in W. V. Harris (ed.) *Rethinking the Mediterranean*, Oxford: Oxford University Press, pp. 141–66.

Chesnutt, Randall D. (1995) *From Death to Life: Conversion in Joseph and Aseneth*, JSPSup 16, Sheffield: Sheffield Academic Press.

Chilton, Bruce (1992) *The Temple of Jesus: His Sacrificial Program Within a Cultural History of Sacrifice*, University Park, PA: Pennsylvania State University Press.

—— (1995) "The Hungry Knife: Towards a Sense of Sacrifice," in M. Daniel Carroll R., D. J. A. Klines, and P. R. Davies (eds) *The Bible in Human Society: Essays in Honour of John Rogerson*, JSOTSup 200, Sheffield: Sheffield Academic Press, pp. 122–38.

Chwe, Michael Suk-Young (2001) *Rational Ritual: Culture, Coordination, and Common Knowledge*, Princeton, NJ: Princeton University Press.

Clinton, Kevin (1989) "Hadrian's Contribution to the Renaissance of Eleusis," in S. Walker and A. Cameron (eds) *The Greek Renaissance in the Roman Empire: Papers from the Tenth British Museum Classical Colloquium*, Institute of Classical Studies Bulletin Supplement 55, London: Institute of Classical Studies, pp. 56–68.

Collins, Adela Yarbro (1980) "The Function of 'Excommunication' in Paul," *HTR*, 73: 251–63.

Collins, Randall (2004) *Interaction Ritual Chains*, Princeton Studies in Cultural Sociology, Princeton, NJ: Princeton University Press.

Conzelmann, Hans (1975) *1 Corinthians: A Commentary on the First Epistle to the Corinthians*, Hermeneia, Philadelphia, PA: Fortress Press.

Cousar, Charles B. (1993) "The Theological Task of 1 Corinthians: A Conversation with Gordon D. Fee and Victor Paul Furnish," in D. M. Hay (ed.) *Pauline Theology, Volume II: 1 & 2 Corinthians*, Minneapolis, MN: Fortress Press, pp. 90–102.

Crocker, Christopher (1973) "Ritual and the Development of Social Structure: Liminality and Inversion," in J. D. Shaughnessy (ed.) *The Roots of Ritual*, Grand Rapids, MI: Eerdmans, pp. 47–86.

Cross, Anthony R. (2003) "The Meaning of 'Baptisms' in Hebrews 6.2," in S. E. Porter and A. R. Cross (eds) *Dimensions of Baptism: Biblical and Theological Studies*, JSNTSup 234, Sheffield: Sheffield Academic Press, pp. 163–86.

Crossan, John Dominic (1988) *The Cross That Spoke: The Origins of the Passion Narrative*, San Francisco: Harper & Row.

—— (1991) *The Historical Jesus: The Life of a Mediterranean Jewish Peasant*, San Francisco: HarperSanFrancisco.

Cullmann, Oscar (1953) *Early Christian Worship*, Studies in Biblical Theology, First Series, 10. London: SCM Press.

Danby, Herbert (trans.) (1933) *The Mishnah*, Oxford: Oxford University Press.

Das, A. Andrew (2001) *Paul, the Law, and the Covenant*, Peabody, MA: Hendrickson.

Davies, Percival Vaughan (trans.) (1969) *Macrobius, "The Saturnalia,"* Records of Civilization, Sources and Studies 79, New York: Columbia University Press.

Davis, Basil S. (2002) *Christ as Devotio: The Argument of Galatians 3:1–14*, Lanham, MD: University Press of America.

Degani, Enzo (1991) *Hipponactis testimonia et fragmenta*, 2nd ed., Stuttgart: Teubner.

Deissmann, Adolf (1927) *Light from the Ancient East: The New Testament Illustrated by Recently Discovered Texts of the Graeco-Roman World*, rev. ed., London: Hodder and Stoughton.

DeLaine, Janet (1988) "Recent Research on Roman Baths," *Journal of Roman Archaeology*, 1: 11–32.

Delling, Gerhard (1962) *Worship in the New Testament*, Philadelphia, PA: Westminster Press.

DeMaris, Richard E. (2001) Review of *Die liminale Theologie des Paulus: Zugänge zur paulinischen Theologie aus kulturanthropologischer Perspektive*, by Christian Strecker, *BTB*, 31: 79.

—— (2006) Review of *Biblical Mourning: Ritual and Social Dimensions*, by Saul M. Olyan, *BTB*, 36: 42.

Denby, David (2004) "Nailed: Mel Gibson's 'The Passion of the Christ'," *New Yorker*, 1 March: 84–6.

Deubner, Ludwig (1932 [1956]) *Attische Feste*, Berlin: Heinrich Keller; reprint ed.: Berlin: Akademie-Verlag.

de Vos, Craig S. (1998) "Stepmothers, Concubines and the Case of PORNEIA in 1 Corinthians 5," *NTS*, 44: 104–14.

Dibelius, Martin (1966) *Die Formgeschichte des Evangeliums*, 5th ed., G. Bornkamm (ed.), Tübingen: J. C. B. Mohr (Paul Siebeck).

Dio Cassius (1914–27) *Dio's Roman History*, trans. E. Cary, LCL, 9 vols, Cambridge, MA: Harvard University Press.

Dodd, David B., and Christopher A. Faraone (eds) (2003) *Initiation in Ancient Greek Rituals and Narratives: New Critical Perspectives*, London: Routledge.

Donahue, John R. (1973) *Are You the Christ? The Trial Narrative in the Gospel of Mark*, SBLDS 10, Missoula, MT: University of Montana.

Donfried, K. P. (1976) "Justification and Last Judgment in Paul," *Int*, 30: 140–52.

Doskocil, Walter (1958) *Der Bann in der Urkirche: Eine Rechtsgeschichtliche Untersuchung*, Münchener Theologische Studien 3.11, Munich: Karl Zink.

Douglas, Mary (1966) *Purity and Danger: An Analysis of the Concepts of Pollution and Taboo*, London: Routledge & Kegan Paul.

—— (1970a) "Introduction: Thirty Years after *Witchcraft, Oracles and Magic*," in M. Douglas (ed.) *Witchcraft Confessions and Accusations*, Association of Social Anthropologists Monographs 9, London: Tavistock Publications, pp. xiii–xxxviii.

—— (1970b) *Natural Symbols: Explorations in Cosmology*, New York: Random House.

—— (2003) "The Go-away Goat," in R. Rendtorff and R. A. Kugler (eds) *The Book of Leviticus: Composition and Reception*, Leiden: E. J. Brill, pp. 121–41.

Downey, James (1985) "1 Cor 15:29 and the Theology of Baptism," *Euntes Docete*, 38: 23–35.

Driver, Tom F. (1991) *The Magic of Ritual: Our Need for Liberating Rites That Transform Our Lives and Our Communities*, San Francisco: HarperSanFrancisco.

Dunn, James D. G. (1983) "The New Perspective on Paul," *BJRL*, 65: 95–122; reprinted with an Additional Note in *Jesus, Paul, and the Law: Studies in Mark and Galatians* (1990) Louisville, KY: Westminster John Knox Press.

—— (1988a) *Romans 1–8*, WBC 38A, Waco, TX: Word Books.

—— (1988b) *Romans 9–16*, WBC 38B, Waco, TX: Word Books.

—— (1990) *Unity and Diversity in the New Testament: An Inquiry into the Character of Earliest Christianity*, 2nd ed., Philadelphia, PA: Trinity Press International.

—— (1993) *The Epistle to the Galatians*, Peabody, MA: Hendrickson.

—— (1998) *The Theology of Paul the Apostle*, Grand Rapids, MI: Eerdmans.

Eilberg-Schwartz, Howard (1990) *The Savage in Judaism: An Anthropology of Israelite Religion and Ancient Judaism*, Bloomington, IN: Indiana University Press.

Elliott, J. K. (1993) *The Apocryphal New Testament: A Collection of Apocryphal Christian Literature in an English Translation*, Oxford: Clarendon Press.

Elliott, John H. (1991) "Household and Meals vs. Temple Purity: Replication Patterns in Luke-Acts," *BTB*, 21: 102–8.

—— (1993) *What Is Social-Scientific Criticism?* GBS: New Testament Series. Minneapolis, MN: Fortress Press.

Engels, Donald (1990) *Roman Corinth: An Alternative Model for the Classical City*, Chicago: University of Chicago Press.

Estrada, Nelson P. (2004) *From Followers to Leaders: The Apostles in the Ritual Status Transformation in Acts 1–2.*

Evans, Ernest (1964) *Tertullian's Homily on Baptism: The Text Edited with an Introduction, Translation and Commentary*, London: SPCK.

Fagan, Garrett G. (1999) *Bathing in Public in the Roman World*, Ann Arbor, MI: University of Michigan Press.

Ferguson, J. (1970) *The Religions of the Roman Empire*, Aspects of Greek and Roman Life, London: Thames and Hudson.

Finlan, Stephen (2004) *The Background and Content of Paul's Cultic Atonement Metaphors*, Academia Biblica 19, Atlanta, GA: Society of Biblical Literature.

Finn, Thomas M. (1997) *From Death to Rebirth: Ritual and Conversion in Antiquity*, New York: Paulist Press.

Fitzmyer, Joseph A. (1967) *Pauline Theology: A Brief Sketch*, Englewood Cliffs, NJ: Prentice-Hall.

Forkman, Göran (1972) *The Limits of the Religious Community: Expulsion from the Religious Community within the Qumran Sect, within Rabbinic Judaism, and within Primitive Christianity*, ConBNT 5, Lund: Gleerup.

Foschini, Bernard M. (1951) *"Those Who Are Baptized for the Dead" I Cor. 15:29: An Exegetical Historical Dissertation*, Worcester, MA: Heffernan Press.

Fuller, Reginald H. (1976) "Christian Initiation in the New Testament," in *Made, Not Born: New Perspectives on Christian Initiation and the Catechumenate*, Murphy Center for Liturgical Research, Liturgical Studies, Notre Dame, IN: University of Notre Dame Press, pp. 7–31.

Furnish, Victor Paul (1984) *II Corinthians*, AB 32A, Garden City, NY: Doubleday.

Gane, Roy E. (2005) *Cult and Character: Purification Offerings, Day of Atonement, and Theodicy*, Winona Lake, IN: Eisenbrauns.

Garfinkel, Harold (1956) "Conditions of Successful Degradation Ceremonies," *American Journal of Sociology*, 61: 420–4.

Garland, Robert (1985) *The Greek Way of Death*, London: Duckworth.

Gathercole, Simon (2001) "After the New Perspective: Works, Justification and Boasting in Early Judaism and Romans 1–5," *TynBul*, 52: 303–6.

Geagan, Daniel J. (1989) "The Isthmian Dossier of P. Licinius Priscus Juventianus," *Hesperia*, 58: 351–60.

Gebhard, Elizabeth R. (1993a) "The Evolution of a Pan-Hellenic Sanctuary: From Archaeology towards History at Isthmia," in N. Marinatos and R. Hägg (eds) *Greek Sanctuaries: New Approaches*, London: Routledge, pp. 154–77.

—— (1993b) "The Isthmian Games and the Sanctuary of Poseidon in the Early Empire," in T. E. Gregory (ed.) *The Corinthia in the Roman Period*, Journal of Roman Archaeology Supplementary Series 8, Ann Arbor, MI: Journal of Roman Archaeology, pp. 78–94.

—— (2005) "Rites for Melikertes-Palaimon in the Early Roman Corinthia," in D. N. Schowalter and S. J. Friesen (eds) *Urban Religion in Roman Corinth: Interdisciplinary Approaches*, HTS 53. Cambridge, MA: Harvard University Press, pp. 165–203.

Geertz, Clifford (1973) *The Interpretation of Cultures: Selected Essays*, New York: Basic Books.

Gilders, William K. (2004) *Blood Ritual in the Hebrew Bible: Meaning and Power*, Baltimore, MD: Johns Hopkins University Press.

Girard, René (1977) *Violence and the Sacred*, trans. P. Gregory, Baltimore, MD: Johns Hopkins University Press.

—— (1986) *The Scapegoat*, trans. Y. Freccero, Baltimore, MD: Johns Hopkins University Press.

Giraud, Demosthenis (1989) "The Greater Propylaia at Eleusis, a Copy of Mnesikles' Propylaia," in S. Walker and A. Cameron (eds) *The Greek Renaissance in the Roman Empire: Papers from the Tenth British Museum Classical Colloquium*, Institute of Classical Studies Bulletin Supplement 55, London: Institute of Classical Studies, pp. 69–75.

Glare, P. G. W. (1968 [1982]) *Oxford Latin Dictionary*, Oxford: Clarendon Press.

Goetze, Albrecht (trans.) (1955) "Hittite Rituals, Incantation, and Description of Festivals," in J. B. Pritchard (ed.) *Ancient Near Eastern Texts Relating to the Old Testament*, 2nd ed., Princeton, NJ: Princeton University Press, pp. 346–61.

Gorman, Frank H., Jr. (1994) "Ritual Studies and Biblical Studies: Assessment of the Past, Prospects for the Future," *Semeia*, 67: 13–36.

—— (1997) *Divine Presence and Community: A Commentary on the Book of Leviticus*, Grand Rapids, MI: Eerdmans.

Grimes, Ronald L. (1982) "Defining Nascent Ritual," *JAAR*, 50: 539–55.

—— (1984) "Sources for the Study of Ritual," *RelSRev*, 10: 134–45.

—— (1985) "Research in Ritual Studies: A Programmatic Essay," in R. Grimes, *Research in Ritual Studies: A Programmatic Essay and Bibliography*, ATLA Bibliography Series 14. Metuchen, NJ: ATLA and Scarecrow Press, pp. 1–33.

—— (1988) "Infelicitous Performances and Ritual Criticism," *Semeia*, 41: 103–22.

—— (1990) *Ritual Criticism: Case Studies in Its Practice, Essays on Its Theory*, Studies in Comparative Religion, Columbia, SC: University of South Carolina Press.

—— (1995) *Beginnings in Ritual Studies*, Studies in Comparative Religion, rev. ed., Columbia, SC: University of South Carolina Press.

Gruenwald, Ithamar (2003) *Rituals and Ritual Theory in Ancient Israel*, BRLJ 10, Leiden: Brill.

Gurney, Oliver Robert (1977) *Some Aspects of Hittite Religion*, Schweich Lectures of the British Academy 1976, Oxford: Oxford University Press.

Habicht, Christian (1985) *Pausanias' Guide to Ancient Greece*, Sather Classical Lectures 50, Berkeley, CA: University of California Press.

Hahn, Ferdinand (1973) *The Worship of the Early Church*, Philadelphia, PA: Fortress Press.

Hamerton-Kelly, Robert G. (1994) *The Gospel and the Sacred: Poetics of Violence in Mark*, Minneapolis, MN: Fortress Press.

Hancher, Michael (1988) "Performative Utterance, the Word of God, and the Death of the Author," *Semeia*, 41: 27–40.

Handelman, Don (1998) *Models and Mirrors: Towards an Anthropology of Public Events*, New York: Berghahn Books; originally published without preface by Cambridge University Press (1990).

Handelman, Don, and Galina Lindquist (eds) (2005) *Ritual in Its Own Right: Exploring the Dynamics of Transformation*, New York: Berghahn Books.

Hanson, K. C. (1994) "Transformed on the Mountain: Ritual Analysis and the Gospel of Matthew," *Semeia*, 67: 147–70.

Harrison, Jane Ellen (1962) *Prolegomena to the Study of Greek Religion*, London: Merlin Press.

Hartman, Lars (1997) *'Into the Name of the Lord Jesus': Baptism in the Early Church*, Studies of the New Testament and Its World, Edinburgh: T & T Clark.

Hawthorne, John G. (1958) "The Myth of Palaemon," *TAPA*, 89: 92–8.

Hays, Richard B. (1996) *The Moral Vision of the New Testament: Community, Cross, New Creation: A Contemporary Introduction to New Testament Ethics*, New York: HarperSanFrancisco.

Henninger, Joseph (1987a) "Sacrifice," in M. Eliade (ed.) *Encyclopedia of Religion*, 16 vols, New York: Macmillan, vol. 12, pp. 544–57.

—— (1987b) "Scapegoat," in M. Eliade (ed.) *Encyclopedia of Religion*, 16 vols, New York: Macmillan, vol. 13, pp. 92–5.

Hill, Bert Hodge (1964) *Corinth*, vol. 1.6: *The Springs: Peirene, Sacred Spring, Glauke*, Princeton, NJ: American School of Classical Studies at Athens.

Hoff, M. C. (1989) "Civil Disobedience and Unrest in Augustan Athens," *Hesperia*, 59: 267–76.

Hopkins, Keith (1983) *Death and Renewal*, Sociological Studies in Roman History 2, Cambridge: Cambridge University Press.

Horace (1926) *Satires, Epistles and Ars Poetica*, trans. H. R. Fairclough, LCL, London: W. Heinemann.

Horden, Peregrine, and Nicholas Purcell (2000) *The Corrupting Sea: A Study of Mediterranean History*, Malden, MA: Blackwell Publishers.

Horrell, David G. (1996) *The Social Ethos of the Corinthian Correspondence: Interests and Ideology from 1 Corinthians to 1 Clement*, Studies of the New Testament and Its World, Edinburgh: T & T Clark.

Horsley, Richard A. (1994) "Innovation in Search of Reorientation: New Testament Studies Rediscovering Its Subject Matter," *JAAR*, 62: 1127–66.

—— (1997) "1 Corinthians: A Case Study of Paul's Assembly as an Alternative Society," in R. A. Horsley (ed.) *Paul and Empire: Religion and Power in Roman Imperial Society*, Harrisburg, PA: Trinity Press International, pp. 242–52.

—— (2000) "Rhetoric and Empire – and 1 Corinthians," in R. A. Horsley (ed.) *Paul and Politics: Ekklesia, Israel, Imperium, Interpretation: Essays in Honor of Krister Stendahl*, Harrisburg, PA: Trinity Press International, pp. 72–102.

Howard, J. K. (1965) "Baptism for the Dead: A Study of 1 Corinthians 15:29," *EvQ*, 37: 137–41.

Hübner, H. (1987) "Paulusforschung seit 1945: Ein kritischer Literaturbericht," in *ANRW*, part II, vol. 25.4, pp. 2649–840.

Hughes, Philip E. (1962) *Paul's Second Letter to the Corinthians*, NICNT, Grand Rapids, MI: Eerdmans.

Hui, C. Harry, and Harry C. Triandis (1986) "Individualism-Collectivism: A Study of Cross-Cultural Researchers," *Journal of Cross-Cultural Psychology*, 17: 225–48.

Hull, Michael F. (2005) *Baptism on Account of the Dead (1 Cor 15:29): An Act of Faith in the Resurrection*, Academica Biblica 22, Atlanta, GA: Society of Biblical Literature.

Humphrey, Caroline, and James Laidlaw (1994) *The Archetypal Actions of Ritual: A Theory of Ritual Illustrated by the Jain Rite of Worship*, Oxford Studies in Social and Cultural Anthropology, Oxford: Clarendon Press.

Humphrey, Edith McEwan (2000) *Joseph and Aseneth*, Guides to Apocrypha and Pseudepigrapha, Sheffield: Sheffield Academic Press.

Hunter, Archibald M. (1961) *Paul and His Predecessors*, rev. ed., Philadelphia, PA: Westminster Press.

Hurd, J. C., Jr. (1965) *The Origin of I Corinthians*, New York: Seabury.

Iozzo, M. (1987) "Corinthian Basins on High Stands," *Hesperia*, 56: 355–416.

Janowski, Bernd, and Gernot Wilhelm (1993) "Der Bock, der die Sünden hinausträgt: Zur Religionsgeschichte des Azazel-Ritus Lev 16,10.21f," in B. Janowski, K. Klaus, and G. Wilhelm (eds) *Religionsgeschichtliche Beziehungen zwischen Kleinasien, Nordsyrien und dem Alten Testament: Internationales Symposion Hamburg, 17.–21. März 1990*, OBO 129, Göttingen: Vandehoeck & Ruprecht, pp. 109–69.

Janssen, L. F. (1981) "Some Unexplored Aspects of *Devotio Deciana*," *Mnemosyne*, 4th ser., 34: 357–81.

Johnson, Luke Timothy (1998) *Religion Experience in Earliest Christianity: A Missing Dimension in New Testament Studies*, Minneapolis, MN: Fortress Press.

Jordan, David (1985) "A Survey of Greek Defixiones Not Included in the Special Corpora," *GRBS*, 26: 151–97.

—— (1994) "Inscribed Lamps from a Cult at Corinth in Late Antiquity," *HTR*, 87: 223–9.

Joy, N. George (1988) "Is the Body Really to Be Destroyed? (1 Corinthians 5:5)," *BT*, 39: 429–36.

Judge, Edwin A. (1980) "The Social Identity of the First Christians: A Question of Method in Religious History," *Journal of Religious History*, 11: 201–17.

Kapferer, Bruce (2005) "Ritual Dynamics and Virtual Practice: Beyond Representation and Meaning," in D. Handelman and Galina Lindquist (eds) *Ritual in Its Own Right: Exploring the Dynamics of Transformation*, New York: Berghahn Books, pp. 35–54.

Käsemann, Ernst (1969) "Sentences of Holy Law in the New Testament," in *New Testament Questions of Today*, Philadelphia, PA: Fortress Press, pp. 66–81.

Katz, Paul R. (2005) "Festivals and the Recreation of Identity in South China: A Case Study of Processions and Expulsion Rites in Pucheng Zhejiang," *JRitSt*, 19/1: 67–85.

Kelber, Werner H. (1976a) "Conclusion: From Passion Narrative to Gospel," in W. H. Kelber (ed.) *The Passion in Mark: Studies on Mark 14–16*, Philadelphia, PA: Fortress Press, pp. 153–80.

—— (ed.) (1976b) *The Passion in Mark: Studies on Mark 14–16*, Philadelphia, PA: Fortress Press.

Kelly, John N. D. (1960) *Early Christian Doctrines*, 2nd ed., New York: Harper & Row.

Kennedy, Charles (1987) "The Cult of the Dead in Corinth," in J. Marks and R. Good (eds) *Love and Death in the Ancient Near East: Essays in Honor of Marvin H. Pope*, Guilford, CT: Four Quarters, pp. 227–36.

Kennedy, George A. (1984) *New Testament Interpretation through Rhetorical Criticism*, Studies in Religion, Chapel Hill, NC: University of North Carolina Press.

Kim, Seyoon (2002) *Paul and the New Perspective: Second Thoughts on the Origin of Paul's Gospel*, Grand Rapids, MI: Eerdmans.

Kinnes, Ian (1981) "Dialogues with Death," in R. Chapman, I. Kinnes, and L. Randsborg (eds) *The Archaeology of Death*, New Directions in Archaeology, Cambridge: Cambridge University Press, pp. 83–91.

Klawans, Jonathan (2005) *Purity, Sacrifice, and the Temple: Symbolism and Supersessionism in the Study of Ancient Judaism*, Oxford: Oxford University Press.

Kleiner, F. S. (1991) "The Trophy on the Bridge and the Roman Triumph over Nature," *L'Antiquitâe classique*, 60: 182–192.

Klingbeil, Gerald A. (2007) *Bridging the Gap: Ritual and Ritual Texts in the Bible*, BBR, Supplements 1, Winona Lake, IN: Eisenbrauns.

Kloppenborg, John S. (2005) "*Evocatio deorum* and the Date of Mark," *JBL*, 124: 419–50.

Koester, Helmut (1990) "Melikertes at Isthmia: A Roman Mystery Cult," in D. Balch, E. Ferguson, and W. Meeks (eds) *Greeks, Romans, and Christians: Essays in Honor of Abraham J. Malherbe*, Minneapolis, MN: Augsburg-Fortress, pp. 355–66.

Koperski, Veronica (2001) *What Are They Saying about Paul and the Law?* New York: Paulist Press.

Kraemer, Ross Shepard (1998) *When Aseneth Met Joseph: A Late Antique Tale of the Biblical Patriarch and His Egyptian Wife*, New York: Oxford University Press.

Krentz, Peter, and Everett L. Wheeler (trans.) (1994) *Polyaenus, "Stratagems of War,"* 2 vols, Chicago: Ares Publishers.

Kurtz, Donna C., and John Boardman (1971) *Greek Burial Customs*, Aspects of Greek and Roman Life, London: Thames and Hudson.

Lake, Kirsopp (trans.) (1912) *The Apostolic Fathers*, LCL, 2 vols, Cambridge, MA: Harvard University Press.

Lampe, G. W. H. (1967) "Church Discipline and the Interpretation of the Epistles to the Corinthians," in W. R. Farmer, C. F. D. Moule, and R. R. Niebuhr (eds) *Christian History and Interpretation: Studies Presented to John Knox*, Cambridge: Cambridge University Press, pp. 337–61.

Lau, D. C. (1970) *Mencius: Translated with an Introduction*, London: Penguin Books.

Leach, Edmund R. (1968) "Ritual," in D. L. Sills (ed.) *International Encyclopedia of the Social Sciences*, 17 vols, New York: Macmillan and Free Press, vol. 13, pp. 520–6.

—— (1976) *Culture and Communication: The Logic by Which Symbols Are Connected: An Introduction to the Use of Structuralist Analysis in Social Anthropology*, Themes in the Social Sciences, New York: Cambridge University Press.

Levi, Peter (trans.) (1971) *Pausanias, Guide to Greece, Volume 1: Central Greece*, Penguin Classics, London: Penguin Books.

Levine, Baruch A. (1989) *The JPS Torah Commentary: Leviticus*, Philadelphia, PA: Jewish Publication Society.

Lewis, Charlton T., and Charles Short (1897) *A Latin Dictionary*. Oxford: Clarendon Press.

Lewis, John G. (2005) *Looking for Life: The Role of "Theo-Ethical Reasoning" in Paul's Religion*, JSNTSup 291, London: T & T Clark.

Liddell, Henry G., and Robert Scott (1996) *A Greek–English Lexicon*, rev. H. S. Jones with R. McKenzie, 9th ed. with supplement, Oxford: Clarendon Press.

Lietzmann, Hans (1979 [1926]) *Mass and Lord's Supper: A Study in the History of the Liturgy*, with *Introduction and Further Inquiry*, by Robert D. Richardson, trans. (with appendices) D. H. G. Reeve, Leiden: Brill; translation (with supplements) of *Messe und Herrenmahl: Eine Studie zur Geschichte der Liturgie*, Arbeiten zur Kirchengeschichte 8, Berlin: Walter de Gruyter.

Livy, Titus (1919–59) *Livy*, trans. B. O. Foster *et al.*, LCL, 14 vols, London: W. Heinemann.

Lolos, Yannis A. (1997) "The Hadrianic Aqueduct of Corinth (with an Appendix on the Roman Aqueducts in Greece)," *Hesperia*, 66: 271–314 and plates 66–76.

McCauley, Robert N., and E. Thomas Lawson (2002) *Bringing Ritual to Mind: Psychological Foundations of Cultural Forms*, Cambridge: Cambridge University Press.

MacDonald, Dennis R. (2000) *The Homeric Epics and the Gospel of Mark*, New Haven, CT: Yale University Press.

Mack, Burton L. (1988) *A Myth of Innocence: Mark and Christian Origins*, Philadelphia, PA: Fortress Press.

—— (1996) "On Redescribing Christian Origins," *MTSR*, 8: 247–69.

McLean, B. Hudson (1990) "On the Revision of Scapegoat Terminology," *Numen*, 37: 168–73.

—— (1996) *The Cursed Christ: Mediterranean Expulsion Rituals and Pauline Soteriology*, JSNTSup 126, Sheffield: Sheffield Academic Press.

McVann, Mark (1988) "The Passion in Mark: Transformation Ritual," *BTB*, 18: 96–101.

—— (1991) "Baptism, Miracles, and Boundary Jumping in Mark," *BTB*, 21: 151–7.

—— (1994a) "Introduction," *Semeia*, 67: 7–12.

—— (1994b) "Reading Mark Ritually: Honor–Shame and the Ritual of Baptism," *Semeia*, 67: 179–98.

Malina, Bruce J. (1996) "Mediterranean Sacrifice: Dimensions of Domestic and Political Religion," *BTB*, 26: 26–44.

Malina, Bruce J., and Jerome H. Neyrey (1988) *Calling Jesus Names: The Social Value of Labels in Matthew*, Foundations and Facets: Social Facets, Sonoma, CA: Polebridge Press.

Manderscheid, Hubertus (1988) *Bibliographie zum römischen Badewesen unter besonderer Berücksichtigung der öffentlichen Thermen*, Munich: H. Manderscheid.

Marcus, Joel (2000) *Mark 1–8: A New Translation with Introduction and Commentary*, AB 27, New York: Doubleday.

Martin, Dale (1995) *The Corinthian Body*, New Haven, CT: Yale University Press.

Mead, Margaret (1973) "Ritual and Social Crisis," in J. D. Shaughnessy (ed.) *The Roots of Ritual*, Grand Rapids, MI: Eerdmans, pp. 87–101.

Meeks, Wayne A. (ed.) (1972) *The Writings of St. Paul*, Norton Critical Editions in the History of Ideas, New York: W. W. Norton.

—— (1983) *The First Urban Christians: The Social World of the Apostle Paul*, New Haven, CT: Yale University Press.

Meyer, Paul W. (1997) "Pauline Theology: A Proposal for a Pause in Its Pursuit," in E. E. Johnson and D. M. Hay (eds) *Pauline Theology, Volume IV: Looking Back, Pressing On*, SBLSymS 4, Atlanta, GA: Scholars Press, pp. 140–60.

Milgrom, Jacob (1991) *Leviticus 1–16: A New Translation with Introduction and Commentary*, AB 3, New York: Doubleday.

Mitchell, Margaret M. (1991) *Paul and the Rhetoric of Reconciliation: An Exegetical Investigation of the Language and Composition of 1 Corinthians*, HUT 28, Tübingen: J. C. B. Mohr (Paul Siebeck).

Modéus, Martin (2005) *Sacrifice and Symbol: Biblical Šĕlāmîm in a Ritual Perspective*, ConBOT 52, Stockholm: Almqvist & Wiksell International.

Moore, Henrietta L., and Todd Sanders (2001) "Magical Interpretations and Material Realties: An Introduction," in H. Moore and T. Sanders (eds) *Magical Interpretations, Material Realties: Modernity, Witchcraft and the Occult in Postcolonial Africa*, London: Routledge, pp. 1–27.

Morris, Ian (1992) *Death-Ritual and Social Structure in Classical Antiquity*, Key Themes in Ancient History, Cambridge: Cambridge University Press.

Moule, C. F. D. (1961) *Worship in the New Testament*, Ecumenical Studies in Worship 9, Richmond, VA: John Knox Press; reprinted (1983) as Grove Liturgical Study 12–13, Bramcote, Notts: Grove Books.

Moulton, J. M.; W. F. Howard, and N. Turner (1906–76) *A Grammar of New Testament Greek*, 4 vols, Edinburgh: T & T Clark.

Murphy-O'Connor, Jerome (1979) *1 Corinthians*, New Testament Message 10, Wilmington, DE: Glazier.

Musurillo, Herbert (1972) *The Acts of the Christian Martyrs: Introduction, Texts and Translations*, Oxford: Clarendon Press.

Myerhoff, Barbara (1982) "Rites of Passage: Process and Paradox," in V. Turner (ed.) *Celebration: Studies in Festivity and Ritual*, Washington, DC: Smithsonian Institution Press, pp. 109–35.

Myers, Ched (1988) *Binding the Strong Man: A Political Reading of Mark's Story of Jesus*, Maryknoll, NY: Orbis.

Nash, R. Scott (2000) "Death Becomes Him: Memorializing Untimely Death in the Ancient Korinthia and Paul's Foolish Preaching of the Cross," presidential address, National Association of Baptist Professors of Religion, Southeast Region (USA), March 2000.

Neyrey, Jerome H. (1990) *Paul, in Other Words: A Cultural Reading of His Letters*, Louisville, KY: Westminster John Knox Press.

—— (1998) *Honor and Shame in the Gospel of Matthew*, Louisville, KY: Westminster John Knox Press.

Nickelsburg, George (1980) "The Genre and Function of the Markan Passion Narrative," *HTR*, 73: 153–84.

Nielsen, Inge (1990) *Thermae et balnea: The Architecture and Cultural History of Roman Public Baths*, 2 vols, Aarhus: Aarhus University Press.

Nisetich, Frank (trans.) (2001) *The Poems of Callimachus*, Oxford: Oxford University Press.

Nock, A. D. (1972) "The Cult of Heroes," in Z. Stewart (ed.) *Essays on Religion and the Ancient World*, 2 vols, Cambridge, MA: Harvard University Press, vol. 2, pp. 575–602.

Olyan, Saul M. (2004) *Biblical Mourning: Ritual and Social Dimensions*, Oxford: Oxford University Press.

Orr, William F., and James Arthur Walther (1976) *I Corinthians: A New Translation: Introduction with a Study of the Life of Paul, Notes, and Commentary*, AB 32, Garden City, NY: Doubleday, 1976.

Osiek, Carolyn (1992) *What Are They Saying about the Social Setting of the New Testament?* rev. ed., New York: Paulist Press.

Ovid (1929) *The Art of Love, and Other Poems*, trans. J. H. Mozley, LCL, London: W. Heinemann.

Parke, H. W. (1977) *Festivals of the Athenians*, Aspects of Greek and Roman Life, Ithaca, NY: Cornell University Press.

Parker, Robert (1983) *Miasma: Pollution and Purification in Early Greek Religion*, Oxford: Clarendon Press.

Pascuzzi, Maria (1997) *Ethics, Ecclesiology and Church Discipline: A Rhetorical Analysis of 1 Corinthians 5*, Tesi Gregoriana, Serie Teologia 32, Rome: Editrice Pontificia Università Gregoriana.

Paton, W. R. (trans.) (1915–18) *The Greek Anthology*, LCL, 5 vols, London: W. Heinemann.

Patrick, James E. (2006) "Living Rewards for Dead Apostles: 'Baptised for the Dead' in 1 Corinthians 15.29," *NTS*, 52: 71–85.

Pausanias (1918–35) *Description of Greece*, trans. W. H. S. Jones, H. A. Ormerod, and R. E. Wycherley, LCL, 5 vols, London: W. Heinemann.

Pemberton, E. (1989) *Corinth*, vol. 18.1: *The Sanctuary of Demeter and Kore: The Greek Pottery*, Princeton, NJ: American School of Classical Studies at Athens.

Penner, Hans (1971) "The Poverty of Functionalism," *HR*, 11: 91–7.

Peterson, Dwight N. (2000) *The Origins of Mark: The Markan Community in Current Debate*, Biblical Interpretation Series 48, Leiden: E. J. Brill.

Petronius, Arbiter (1913) *Petronius* trans. M. Heseltine, LCL, Cambridge, MA: Harvard University Press.

Pfeiffer, Rudolf (ed.) (1949) *Callimachus*, vol. 1, *Fragmenta*, Oxford: Clarendon Press.

Pilch, John J. (1995) "Death with Honor: The Mediterranean Style Death of Jesus in Mark," *BTB*, 25:65–70.

Plevnik, Joseph (1986) *What Are They Saying about Paul?* New York: Paulist Press.

Pliny (1915) *Letters*, trans. W. Melmoth, LCL, 2 vols, London: W. Heinemann.

Porter, S. E., and A. R. Cross (eds) (2003) *Dimensions of Baptism: Biblical and Theological Studies*, JSNTSup 234, Sheffield: Sheffield Academic Press.

Preisendanz, Karl (1973–4) *Papyri graecae magicae: Die griechischen Zauberpapyri*, Sammlung Wissenschaftlicher Commentare, 2nd ed., Stuttgart: Teubner.

Purcell, Nicholas (1996) "Rome and the Management of Water: Environment, Culture and Power," in G. Shipley and J. Salmon (eds) *Human Landscapes in Classical Antiquity: Environment and Culture*, Leicester-Nottingham Studies in Ancient Society 6, New York: Routledge, pp. 180–212.

Raeder, Maria (1955) "Vikariatstaufe in I Cor 15:29?" *ZNW*, 46: 258–60.

Räisänen, Heikki (1986) *Paul and the Law*, Philadelphia, PA: Fortress Press.

Rappaport, Roy A. (1979) *Ecology, Meaning, and Religion*, Berkeley, CA: North Atlantic Books.

—— (1999) *Ritual and Religion in the Making of Humanity*, Cambridge Studies in Social and Cultural Anthropology 110, Cambridge: Cambridge University Press.

Ray, Benjamin C. (1991) "The Koyukon Bear Party and the 'Bare Facts' of Ritual," *Numen*, 38: 151–76.

Rehm, Rush (1994) *Marriage to Death: The Conflation of Wedding and Funeral Rituals in Greek Tragedy*, Princeton, NJ: Princeton University Press.

Reinders, Eric (1997) "Ritual Topography: Embodiment and Vertical Space in Buddhist Monastic Practice," *HR*, 36: 244–64.

Reitzenstein, Richard (1978 [1910]) *Hellenistic Mystery-Religions: Their Basic Ideas and Significance*, trans. J. E. Steely, PTMS 18, Pittsburgh, PA: Pickwick Press; translation of *Die hellenistischen Mysterienreligionen: Ihre Grundgedanken und Wirkungen*, Leipzig: B. G. Teubner.

Richardson, Rufus B. (1900) "The Fountain of Glauce at Corinth," *AJA*, 4: 458–75 and plate VII.

Rife, Joseph Lee (1999) "Death, Ritual and Memory in Greek Society during the Early and Middle Roman Empire," Ph.D. dissertation, University of Michigan.

Riley, Gregory J. (1997) *One Jesus, Many Christs: How Jesus Inspired Not One True Christianity, But Many*, New York: HarperCollins.

Rissi, Mathis (1962) *Die Taufe für die Toten: Ein Beitrag zur paulinischen Tauflehre*, ATANT 42. Zurich: Zwingli.

Robinson, Betsey A. (2001) "Fountains and the Culture of Water at Roman Corinth," Ph.D. dissertation, University of Pennsylvania.

—— (2005) "Fountains and the Formation of Culture Identity at Roman Corinth," in D. N. Schowalter and S. J. Friesen (eds) *Urban Religion in Roman Corinth: Interdisciplinary Approaches*, HTS 53, Cambridge, MA: Harvard University Press, pp. 111–40.

Robinson, Henry S. (1964) *Corinth: A Brief History of the City and a Guide to the Excavations*, Athens, Greece: American School of Classical Studies.

Roebuck, Carl (1951) *Corinth*, vol. 14: *The Asklepieion and Lerna*, Princeton, NJ: American School of Classical Studies at Athens.

Roetzel, Calvin J. (1969) "The Judgment Form in Paul's Letters," *JBL*, 88: 305–12.

—— (1998) *The Letters of Paul: Conversations in Context*, 4th ed., Louisville, KY: Westminster John Knox Press.

Romano, David G. (2005) "Urban and Rural Planning in Roman Corinth," in D. N. Schowalter and S. J. Friesen (eds) *Urban Religion in Roman Corinth: Interdisciplinary Approaches*, HTS 53, Cambridge, MA: Harvard University Press, pp. 25–59.

Romano, Irene B. (1994) "A Hellenistic Deposit from Corinth: Evidence for Interim Activity (146–44 B.C.)," *Hesperia*, 63: 57–104 and plates 14–32.

Roo, Jacqueline C. R. De (2000) "Was the Goat for Azazel Destined for the Wrath of God?" *Biblica*, 81: 233–42.

Rosen, Leora Nadine (1972) "An Ideal Typology of Witchcraft Beliefs and Accusations," *African Studies*, 31: 25–30.

—— (1991) "Temple and Holiness in 1 Corinthians 5," *TynBul*, 42: 137–45.

Rosner, Brian S. (1992) "'OUCHI MALLON EPENTHESATE': Corporate Responsibility in 1 Corinthians 5," *NTS*, 38: 470–3.

Rothaus, Richard M. (1995) "Lechaion, Western Port of Corinth: A Preliminary Archaeology and History," *Oxford Journal of Archaeology*, 14: 293–306.

—— (2000) *Corinth: The First City of Greece: An Urban History of Late Antique Cult and Religion*, Religions in the Graeco-Roman World 139, Leiden: Brill.

Rudman, Dominic (2004) "A Note on the Azazel-goat Ritual," *ZAW*, 116: 396–401.

Salamon, Sonya (1992) *Prairie Patrimony: Family, Farming, and Community in the Midwest*, Studies in Rural Culture, Chapel Hill, NC: University of North Carolina Press.

Salom, A. P. (1958) "The Imperatival Use of *hina* in the New Testament," *ABR*, 6: 123–41.

Sanders, E. P. (1977) *Paul and Palestinian Judaism: A Comparison of Patterns of Religion*, Philadelphia, PA: Fortress Press.

Sandes, Karl Olav (2005) "*Imitatio Homeri*? An Appraisal of Dennis R. MacDonald's 'Mimesis Criticism'," *JBL*, 124:715–32.

Schilbrack, Kevin (ed.) (2004) *Thinking through Rituals: Philosophical Perspectives*, New York: Routledge.

Schnackenburg, Rudolf (1964) *Baptism in the Thought of St. Paul: A Study in Pauline Theology*, trans. G. R. Beasley-Murray, New York: Herder and Herder.

Schüssler Fiorenza, Elisabeth (1983) *In Memory of Her: A Feminist Theological Reconstruction of Christian Origins*, New York: Crossroad.

Scott, James C. (1985) *Weapons of the Weak: Everyday Forms of Peasant Resistance*, New Haven, CT: Yale University Press.

Scranton, Robert L. (1951) *Corinth*, vol. 1.3: *Monuments in the Lower Agora and North of the Archaic Temple*, Princeton, NJ: American School of Classical Studies at Athens.

Seeman, Don (2005) "Otherwise Than Meaning: On the Generosity of Ritual," in D. Handelman and Galina Lindquist (eds) *Ritual in Its Own Right: Exploring the Dynamics of Transformation*, New York: Berghahn Books, pp. 55–71.

Segal, Alan F. (1998) "Paul and the Beginning of Christian Conversion," in P. Borgen, V. K. Robbins, and D. Gowler (eds) *Recruitment, Conquest, and Conflict: Strategies in Judaism, Early Christianity, and the Greco-Roman World*, Emory Studies in Early Christianity 6, Atlanta, GA: Scholars Press, pp. 79–111.

Sellin, Gerhard (1986) *Der Streit um die Auferstehung der Toten: Eine religions-geschichtliche und exegetische Untersuchung von 1 Korinther 15*, FRLANT 138, Göttingen: Vandenhoeck and Ruprecht.

—— (1987) "Hauptprobleme des Ersten Korintherbriefes," in *ANRW*, part II, vol. 25.4, pp. 2940–3044.

Seneca (1917–25) *Ad Lucilium Epistulae Morales*, trans. R. M. Gummere, LCL, 3 vols, Cambridge, MA: Harvard University Press.

—— (1928–35) *Moral Essays*, trans. J. W. Basore, LCL, 3 vols, Cambridge, MA: Harvard University Press.

Senft, C. (1990) *La Première Épitre de Saint Paul aux Corinthiens*, CNT, 2nd series, 7, 2nd ed., Geneva: Labor et Fides.

Shear, T. L. (1931) "The Excavation of Roman Chamber Tombs at Corinth in 1931," *AJA*, 35: 424–41.

Smith, Dennis E. (2003) *From Symposium to Eucharist: The Banquet in the Early Christian World*, Minneapolis, MN: Fortress Press.

Smith, Jonathan Z. (1980) "The Bare Facts of Ritual," *HR*, 20: 112–27; reprinted in *Imagining Religion: From Babylon to Jonestown*, CSHJ, Chicago: University of Chicago Press, 1982, pp. 53–65.

—— (1987) *To Take Place: Toward Theory in Ritual*, CSHJ, Chicago: University of Chicago Press.

—— (1990) *Drudgery Divine: On the Comparison of Early Christianities and the Religions of Late Antiquity*, CSHJ, Chicago: University of Chicago Press.

—— (2004) *Relating Religion: Essays in the Study of Religion*, Chicago: University of Chicago Press.

Smith, Morton (1980) "Pauline Worship as Seen by Pagans," *HTR*, 73: 241–9.

Smyth, Herbert W. (1956) *Greek Grammar*, rev. ed., Cambridge, MA: Harvard University Press.

Snyder, Graydon F. (1985) *Ante Pacem: Archaeological Evidence of Church Life before Constantine*, Macon, GA: Mercer University Press.

South, James T. (1992) *Disciplinary Practices in Pauline Texts*, Lewiston, NY: Edwin Mellen Press.

Sperber, Dan (1975) *Rethinking Symbolism*, Cambridge Studies in Social Anthropology, Cambridge: Cambridge University Press.

Spinks, Bryan D. (2006) *Early and Medieval Rituals and Theologies of Baptism*, Liturgy, Worship and Society, Burlington, VT: Ashgate.

Staal, Frits (1979) "The Meaninglessness of Ritual," *Numen*, 26: 2–22.

—— (1989) *Rules Without Meaning: Ritual, Mantras and the Human Sciences*, Toronto Studies in Religion 4, New York: Peter Lang.

Statius (1928) *Silvae, Thebaid, and Achilleid*, trans. J. H. Mozley, LCL, 2 vols, London: W. Heinemann; new trans. D. R. Shackleton Bailey (2003) Cambridge, MA: Harvard University Press.

Steiner, Ann (1992) "Pottery and Cult in Corinth: Oil and Water at the Sacred Spring," *Hesperia*, 61: 385–408 and plate 87.

Stendahl, Krister (1963) "The Apostle Paul and the Introspective Conscience of the West," *HTR*, 56: 199–215.

Stewart, Charles, and Rosalind Shaw (1994) "Introduction: Problematizing Syncretism," in C. Stewart and R. Shaw (eds) *Syncretism/Anti-syncretism: The Politics of Religious Synthesis*, European Association of Social Anthropologists, London: Routledge, pp. 1–26.

Stillwell, Richard, Robert L. Scranton, and Sarah Elizabeth Freeman (1941) *Corinth*, vol. 1. 2: *Architecture*, Cambridge, MA: Harvard University Press.

Strecker, Christian (1999) *Die liminale Theologie des Paulus: Zugänge zur paulinischen Theologie aus kulturanthropologischer Perspecktive*, FRLANT 185, Göttingen: Vanderhoeck & Ruprecht.

Stroud, Ronald (1993) "The Sanctuary of Demeter on Acrocorinth in the Roman Period," in T. E. Gregory (ed.) *The Corinthia in the Roman Period*, Journal of Roman Archaeology, Supplementary Series 8, Ann Arbor, MI: Journal of Roman Archaeology, pp. 65–74.

Stuhlmacher, Peter (2001) *Revisiting Paul's Doctrine of Justification: A Challenge to the New Perspective*, with an essay by Donald A. Hagner, Downers Grove, IL: InterVarsity Press.

Tacitus, Cornelius (1914) *Dialogus, Agricola, Germania*, trans. M. Hutton, LCL, London: W. Heinemann.

—— (1925–37) *The Histories, The Annals*, trans. C. H. Moore and J. Jackson, LCL, 4 vols, Cambridge, MA: Harvard University Press.

Tambiah, Stanley J. (1985) *Culture, Thought, and Social Action: An Anthropological Perspective*, Cambridge, MA: Harvard University Press.

Tannehill, Robert C. (1967) *Dying and Rising with Christ: A Study in Pauline Theology*, BZNW 32. Berlin: Alfred Töpelmann.

Tertullian (1951) *Latin Christianity: Its Founder, Tertullian*, trans. A. Roberts and J. Donaldson, ANF 3, Grand Rapids, MI: Eerdmans.

Theissen, Gerd (1974) "Soziale Schichtung in der korinthischen Gemeinde: Ein Beitrag zur Soziologie des hellenistischen Urchristentums," *ZNW*, 65: 232–72.

—— (1982) *The Social Setting of Pauline Christianity: Essays on Corinth*, Philadelphia, PA: Fortress Press.

ThesCRA (2004–6) *Thesaurus cultus et rituum antiquorum*, 6 vols, Los Angeles, CA: J. Paul Getty Museum.

Thiselton, Anthony C. (2000) *The First Epistle to the Corinthians: A Commentary on the Greek Text*, NIGTC, Grand Rapids, MI: Eerdmans.

Thompson, Cynthia L. (1988) "Hairstyle, Head-coverings, and St. Paul: Portraits from Roman Corinth," *BA*, 51: 99–115.

Thompson, K. C. (1964) "I Corinthians 15, 29 and Baptism for the Dead," in F. Cross (ed.) *Studia Evangelica, Vol. II: Papers Presented to the Second International Congress on New Testament Studies held at Christ Church, Oxford, 1961*, TU 87, Berlin: Akademie-Verlag, pp. 647–59.

Thornton, Timothy C. G. (1972) "Satan – God's Agent for Punishing," *ExpTim*, 83: 151–2.

Thrall, Margaret E. (1994) *Introduction and Commentary on II Corinthians I–VII*, vol. 1 of *The Second Epistle to the Corinthians*, ICC 8, Edinburgh: T & T Clark.

Toynbee, J. M. C. (1971) *Death and Burial in the Roman World. Aspects of Greek and Roman Life*, London: Thames and Hudson.

Triandis, Harry C. (1990) "Cross-Cultural Studies of Individualism and Collectivism," in J. J. Berman (ed.) *Cross-Cultural Perspectives: Nebraska Symposium on Motivation 1989*, Nebraska Symposium on Motivation 37, Lincoln, NE: University of Nebraska Press, pp. 41–133.

Turner, Victor W. (1967) *The Forest of Symbols: Aspects of Ndembu Ritual*, Ithaca, NY: Cornell University Press.

—— (1969) *The Ritual Process: Structure and Anti-Structure*, Chicago: Aldine Publishing Company.

—— (1980) "Social Dramas and Stories about Them," *Critical Inquiry*, 7: 141–68.

Turner, Victor W., and Edith Turner (1978) *Image and Pilgrimage in Christian Culture: Anthropological Perspectives*. Lectures on the History of Religions, n. s., 11. New York: Columbia University Press.

Uro, Risto (forthcoming) "Towards a Cognitive History of Early Christian Rituals," in I. Czachesz and T. Biro (eds) *Changing Minds: Religion and Cognition through the Ages*, Groningen Studies in Cultural Change, Leuven: Peeters.

Van Gennep, Arnold (1960) *The Rites of Passage*, trans. M. Vizedom and G. Caffee, Chicago: University of Chicago Press.

Versnel, H. S. (1976) "Two Types of Roman Devotio," *Mnemosyne*, 4th ser., 29: 365–410.

—— (1981) "Self-Sacrifice, Compensation and the Anonymous Gods," in J. Rudhardt and O. Reverdin (eds) *Le sacrifice dans l'antiquité*, Entretiens sur l'antiquité classique 27, Geneva: Fondation Hardt, pp. 135–94.

—— (1989a) "Jesus Soter – Neos Alkestis? Over de niet-joodse achtergrond van een christelijke doctrine," *Lampas*, 22: 219–42.

—— (1989b) "Quid Athenis et Hierosolymis? Bemerkungen über die Herkunft von Aspekten des 'Effective Death'," in J. W. van Henten with B. A. G. M. Dehandschutter and H. J. W. van der Klaauw (eds) *Die Entstehung der jüdischen Martyrologie*, StPB 38, Leiden: E. J. Brill, pp. 162–96.

Walbank, Mary E. Hoskins (1989) "Pausanias, Octavia and Temple E at Corinth," *Annual of the British School at Athens*, 84: 361–94.

—— (1997) "The Foundation and Planning of Early Roman Corinth," *Journal of Roman Archaeology*, 10: 95–130.

—— (2005) "Unquiet Graves: Burial Practices of the Roman Corinthians," in D. N. Schowalter and S. J. Friesen (eds) *Urban Religion in Roman Corinth: Interdisciplinary Approaches*, HTS 53, Cambridge, MA: Harvard University Press, pp. 249–280.

Walls, Jeannette, with Ashley Pearson (16 Sept. 2005) "Mel Gibson Says His Wife May Be Going to Hell," MSNBC Online, Gossip section. Available HTTP: <http//:www.msnbc.msn.com/id/4224452/>.

Ward, Richard F. (1994) "Pauline Voice and Presence as Strategic Communication," *Semeia*, 65: 95–107.

Wedderburn, A. J. M. (1987) *Baptism and Resurrection: Studies in Pauline Theology against Its Graeco-Roman Background*, WUNT 44, Tübingen: Mohr, 1987.

West, A. B. (1931) *Corinth*, vol. 8.2: *Latin Inscriptions 1896–1926*, Cambridge, MA: Harvard University Press.

Wheelock, Wade T. (1982) "The Problem of Ritual Language: From Information to Situation," *JAAR*, 50: 49–71.

White, Joel R. (1997) " 'Baptized on account of the Dead': The Meaning of 1 Corinthians 15:29 in its Context," *JBL*, 116: 487–99.

Whitehouse, Harvey (2004) *Modes of Religiosity: A Cognitive Theory of Religious Transmission*, Walnut Creek, CA: AltaMira Press.

Wiles, Gordon P. (1974) *Paul's Intercessory Prayers: The Significance of the Intercessory Prayer Passages in the Letters of St Paul*, SNTSMS 24, Cambridge: Cambridge University Press.

Williams, Charles K., II (1987) "The Refounding of Corinth: Some Roman Religious Attitudes," in S. Macready and F. H. Thompson (eds) *Roman Architecture in the Greek World*, Occasional Papers, n.s., 10. London: Society of Antiquaries of London, pp. 26–37.

—— (1989) "A Re-Evaluation of Temple E and the West End of the Forum of Corinth," in S. Walker and A. Cameron (eds) *The Greek Renaissance in the Roman Empire: Papers from the Tenth British Museum Classical Colloquium*, Institute of Classical Studies Bulletin Supplement 55, London: Institute of Classical Studies, pp. 156–62.

—— (1993) "Roman Corinth as a Commercial Center," in T. E. Gregory (ed.) *The Corinthia in the Roman Period*, Journal of Roman Archaeology Supplementary Series 8, Ann Arbor, MI: Journal of Roman Archaeology, pp. 31–46.

—— (2005) "Roman Corinth: The Final Years of Pagan Cult Facilities along East Theater Street," in D. N. Schowalter and S. J. Friesen (eds) *Urban Religion in Roman Corinth: Interdisciplinary Approaches*, HTS 53, Cambridge, MA: Harvard University Press, pp. 221–47.

Williams, Charles K., II, and Joan E. Fisher (1975) "Corinth, 1974: Forum Southwest," *Hesperia*, 44: 1–50 and plates 1–11.

Wiseman, James (1972) "The Gymnasium Area at Corinth, 1969–1970," *Hesperia*, 41: 1–42 and plates 1–11.

—— (1978) *The Land of the Ancient Corinthians*, Studies in Mediterranean Archaeology 50, Göteburg: Åström.

—— (1979) "Corinth and Rome I: 228 B.C.–A.D. 267," in *ANRW*, part II, vol. 7.1, pp. 438–548.

Wright, David P. (2001) *Ritual in Narrative: The Dynamics of Feasting, Mourning, and Retaliation Rites in the Ugaritic Tale of Aqhat*, Winona Lake, IN: Eisenbrauns.

Yarbrough, O. Larry (1995) "Parents and Children in the Letters of Paul" in L. M. White and O. L. Yarbrough (eds) *The Social World of the First Christians: Essay in Honor of Wayne A. Meeks*, Minneapolis, MN: Augsburg Fortress, pp. 126–41.

Yegül, Fikret (1992) *Baths and Bathing in Classical Antiquity*, Cambridge, MA: MIT Press.

Zuesse, Evan M. (2005) "Ritual [First Edition]," in L. Jones (ed.) *Encyclopedia of Religion*, 2nd ed., 15 vols, Detroit: Macmillan, pp. 7833–48.

Index of Ancient Sources

Old Testament

Gen
  41:45 26

Exod
  12:5 96
  12:8 85
  12:15–20 85

Lev
  16 96–7, 100, 110
  16:5–10 96
  16:10 100
  16:21–2 96
  16:34 96, 100

Isa
  34:8–15 100

New Testament

Matt
  5:4 82
  9:15 82
  18:15–17 81
  18:15–19 74
  28:19 14

Mark
  1:9–11 6, 94
  2:18–20 6
  2:23–8 6
  7 108, 109
  7:1–23 6
  8:23–5 28

  8:31 95
  9:2–8 94
  9:17–18 28
  9:31 95
  10:29–30 25
  10:33–4 95
  11 108, 109
  11:1–11 108
  11:8–9 94
  11:15–19 108
  11:18 108
  12:12 108
  12:32 108
  13 109
  13:1–37 108
  13:2 101
  14–16 92
  14:22–5 6
  14:24 95, 96, 108
  14:53–65 94
  15:1–15 94
  15:16–20 94
  15:25–32 94
  15:38 110
  15:39 93
  16:10 82

Luke
  6:25 82
  14:26 25
  23:47 93

John
  3:3–6 60
  3:22 17
  4:2 17

5:3–4 55
11:50 110

Acts
  2:38 14
  2:41 14
  5:1–11 74
  6:1–6 6
  8:13 14
  8:16 14
  8:35–9 24
  8:36 14
  9:1–19 3
  9:18 14
  10:46b–48a 17
  10:47 14
  10:48 6
  18:25 17
  19:3 14, 17

Rom
  6:1–14 19
  6:3 14
  6:3–4 18, 64, 83
  6:4 65
  6:6 18, 65
  8:1–17 87

1 Cor
  1–4 79, 88, 89
  1:10 88
  1:10–11 29
  1:10–13 16
  1:10–16 30
  1:13 52
  1:14–16 16
  1:17 16
  1:21–5 69
  2:2 69
  3:5–6 16
  3:14–17 89
  3:16–17 87
  4 88
  4:8 31
  4–5 89
  5 79–80, 84–90
  5–16 79, 88
  5:1–8 89
  5:1–5 79–84

5:2 81–84
5:3 84
5:3–5 85
5:4 81
5:4–5 81, 84
5:5 86–7, 89
5:6–8 84
5:7 84, 85, 87, 89
5:9 85, 87
5:11 85, 87
6:11 14
6:12–20 89
7:1–9 89
7:10–16 89
7:14 59
7:25–40 89
8 31, 70, 89
8:10 31
10 31, 70, 89
10:1–2 52
10:1–5 31
10:5 31
10:11 31
10:16 6
10:16–17 31
10:20–1 31
10:21 32
10:22 31
11:2–16 89
11:4 33
11:5–6 33
11:7 33
11:13 33
11:17 81
11:17–20 29
11:17–34 69, 83, 89
11:18 81
11:20 81
11:21–2 29
11:24 6
11:26 69
11:28–30 59
11:29 81
11:31–2 81
11:33 81
11:33–4 29
11:34 81
12 16
12–14 89

12:12–13 15
12:13 14, 52
14 33
14:23 81
14:26 81
15 59
15:29 53, 57–61, 83
15:30–4 58
15:35–58 89

2 Cor
2:5 86
2:6–8, 10a 85
4:10–11 19
6:8–9 19
10–13 78

Gal
1:11–17 3
2:19–20 19
3:3 87
3:26 25
3:26–8 18
3:27 14
3:27–8 25
4:6–7 25
5:16–26 87

Eph
4:4–6 17
4:5 14, 17

Phil
2:6–11 6
2:17–18 6
3:2–21 3
3:10–11 19
4:21–3 6

Col
1:15–20 6
2:10–12 19
2:11–12 32
2:12 14, 60
3:1–17 19
3:9–10 18
3:10–11 18

1 Thess
4–5 78

Titus
3:5 14

Heb
4:14–5:10 96
6:2 14, 17
6:4 14
6:4, 6 28
9:23–10:18 96

1 Pet
1:18–19 96
3:21 14

Rev
18:11 82
18: 15 82
18:19 82

Old Testament Pseudepigrapha

1 Enoch
9:6 100

Jos. Asen.
7:7–8 26
11:5 26
11:16 26
12:5 26
12:12 26
12:14 26

Qumran Literature

1QS
5:24–6:1 81
7:18–19 84
7:25–7 84

New Testament Apocrypha

Acts of Andr. (Epitome)
27 55

Early Christian Writings

Barnabas
7.7–8 97

Didache
　7:1–4　34
　7:2　50
　9:1–10:7　34

John Chrysostom

Catech. illum.
　1　29

Hom. Jo.
　18　29, 55

Hom. Act.
　1　29

Hermas

Vision
　2.2.4　28
　3.5.5　28

Mandate
　4.3.3–5　28

Origen

Comm. Matt.
　16.8　111

Cels.
　1.31　110

Pass. Perp. et Fel.
　21.9　53
　21.1–3　54

Tertullian

Adv. Jud.
　14.9　97

Bapt.
　5　55–6
　15　49
　16　54

Marc.
　3.7.7　97

Jewish Writings

Mishnah

m. Yoma
　4:2　101
　6:4　101
　6:5–6　101

Babylonian Talmud

b. Bava Metzi'a
　59b　83

Classical Literature

Antipater of Sidon　51

Apuleius

Golden Ass
　4:28–6:24　26
　11:23　28
　11:25　26

Callimachus
　frg. 90　106

Cicero

Fin.
　2.19 §61　102

Quinct.
　15 §50　63

Tusc.
　1.37.89　102
　3.22.53　51

Dio Cassius
　21　51
　54.7.2–3　53
　74.13.1–2　61
　75.4.2–3　61
　75.5.5　61

Euripides

Alcetis　108

Fragmente der griechischen Historiker
   323a F23 104

Hipponax 105

Homer

Iliad
   22 93
   24 93

Odyssey 93

Horace

Epist.
   2.1.156 38

Inscriptiones graecae
   IV, 203, 20–1 68

Inscriptiones Latinae Selectae
   §7212, II, 3–4 62

Julius Capitolinus
   14.9 61
   15.1 61

Livy
   8.9 102
   8.9.4–12 103
   10.28 102

Lycurgus

Leoc.
   84–7 103

Macrobius

Saturnalia
   3.9.7–8 101
   3.9.11 101

Ovid

Ibis
   467–8 107

Papyri graecae magicae
   V.334–6 87

Pausanias

Descr.
   1.43.3 57
   2.2.6–8 42
   2.3.1 42
   2.3.5 46
   2.3.6 41
   2.3.6–7 40
   2.3.8–11 40
   6.24.10 53
   8.22.3 46

Petronius
   frg. 1 106

Satyricon
   §§71–8 63

Philostratus

Imagines
   2.16 67

Pliny the Younger

Ep.
   8.4.1–2 46

Plutarch

Quaest. rom.
   109 (289E–F) 84

Theseus
   25 67

Polyaneus

Strat.
   1.18 104
   43 99

Seneca

Brev. Vit.
   20.3–4 62

Helv. 63

Lucil.
  12.6 62
  12.8 63
  12.9 63

Servius

Servius on Aneid
  3.57 106

Statius

Silvae
  4.3.81–4 46
  4.3.134–5 46

Thebaid
  10.756–82 107
  10.791–5 107

Tacitus

Agricola
  21 37, 45

Annales
  4.45 83

Tzetzes

Thousand Histories
  23.726–56 105

Velleius Paterculus
  1.2.1 104

Vergil

Aneid 106

Index of Modern Authors

Achtemeier, Paul J. 78
Alcock, Susan E. 37, 39, 40, 44, 48–50, 53
Alexiou, M. 65
Anderson-Stojanović, V. 67
Ashton, John 20, 77–8
Atkins, Stuart 10
Aulén, Gustaf 111
Aune, David E. 87

Babcock, Barbara A. 50
Bammel, Ernst 81
Barrett, C. K. 16, 58, 69, 87
Bassler, Jouette M. 76, 77, 78
Beasley-Murray, G. R. 17, 58
Beezley, William H. 53
Beker, J. Christiaan 78
Bell, Catherine 4, 30, 32, 36
Best, Ernest 108
Bettenson, Henry 110
Betz, Hans Dieter 87
Biers, Jane C. 46
Blegen, Carl W. 52, 66, 70
Boardman, John 65, 66
Bodel, John vi, 60
Bohren, Rudolf 81
Bohtz, Carl Helmut 42
Bond, George Clement 74
Bookidis, Nancy vii, 49, 51, 67, 68, 69
Bourdieu, Pierre 30
Bowersock, G. W. 53
Bowie, Ewen L. 38, 39
Bremmer, Jan N. 101, 106
Broneer, Oscar 66, 67, 68
Brun, Lyder 87

Bultmann, Rudolf 20
Burchard, Christoph 26
Burkert, Walter 1, 22, 66, 67, 101
Burtt, J. O. 103
Byrne, Brendan 77

Cahill, Thomas J. 32
Calder, William M., III 1
Cambier, J. 85
Cameron, Ron 2
Campbell, Barth 82, 87
Carlson, Richard P. 18, 58
Caskey, John L. 68
Casson, Lionel 38, 39, 40, 42
Chaniotis, Angelos 1
Chesnutt, Randall D. 26
Chilton, Bruce 8, 95
Chwe, Michael Suk-Young 5
Ciekawy, Diane M. 74
Clinton, Kevin 42
Collins, Adela Yarbro 87
Collins, Randall 5
Conzelmann, Hans 58, 79, 81, 87
Cousar, Charles B. 78
Crocker, Christopher 22
Cross, Anthony R. 3, 17
Crossan, John Dominic 93, 97
Cullmann, Oscar 59

Danby, Herbert 101
Das, A. Andrew 77
Davies, Percival Vaughan 101
Davis, Basil S. 3
Degani, Enzo 105
Deissmann, Adolf 87
DeLaine, Janet 45

Delling, Gerhard 59
DeMaris, Richard E. 3
Denby, David 91, 93, 95
Deubner, Ludwig 104
de Vos, Craig S. vii, 80
Dibelius, Martin 78
Dodd, David B. 20
Donahue, John R. 92
Donaldson, J. 97
Donfried, K. P. 87
Doskocil, Walter 81
Douglas, Mary 1, 5, 22, 35, 36, 74, 88–9, 99
Downey, James 58
Driver, Tom F. 30
Dunn, James D. G. 18, 19, 20, 76–7

Eilberg-Schwartz, Howard 35
Elliott, J. K. 55
Elliott, John H. vii, 2
Engels, Donald 69
Estrada, Nelson P. 3
Evans, Ernest 55, 56

Fagan, Garrett G. 45
Faraone, Christopher A. 20
Ferguson, J. 65
Finlan, Stephen 3
Finn, Thomas M. 3
Fisher, Joan E. 43, 49, 68
Fitzmyer, Joseph A. 18
Forkman, Göran 81
Foschini, Bernard M. 57, 58
Frazer, James G. 1
Freeman, Sarah Elizabeth 41, 43
French, William E. 53
Fuller, Reginald H. 18
Furnish, Victor Paul 85

Gane, Roy E. 4
Garfinkel, Harold 94
Garland, Robert 65, 66, 67, 68
Gathercole, Simon 77
Geagan, Daniel J. 67, 68
Gebhard, Elizabeth R. 52, 66, 67
Geertz, Clifford 12, 30, 32
Gilders, William K. 3
Girard, René 8
Giraud, Demosthenis 42

Glare, P. G. W. 101
Goetze, Albrecht 100
Gorman, Frank H., Jr. 1, 7, 8, 9, 35, 73, 97
Gregory, Timothy E. vi, vii
Grimes, Ronald L. 2, 4, 6–9, 21–22, 27, 32, 34, 36
Gruenwald, Ithamar 4, 9
Gurney, Oliver Robert 100

Habicht, Christian 38
Hahn, Ferdinand 59
Hamerton-Kelly, Robert G. 8
Hancher, Michael 2
Handelman, Don 5, 8
Hanson, K. C. 2
Harrison, Jane Ellen 1, 104, 105
Hartman, Lars 14–15, 27, 34
Hawthorne, John G. 66
Hays, Richard B. 78–80
Henninger, Joseph 95, 97
Hill, Bert Hodge 41, 48
Hoff, M. C. 53
Hopkins, Keith 62, 65
Horden, Peregrine 1
Horrell, David G. 15, 18, 21
Horsley, Richard A. 50, 76
Howard, J. K. 58
Howard, W. F. 82
Hübner, Hans 76
Hughes, Philip E. 85
Hui, C. Harry 86
Hull, Michael F. 58, 59
Humphrey, Caroline 4
Humphrey, Edith McEwan 26
Hunter, Archibald M. 17
Hurd, J. C., Jr. 58

Iozzo, M. 48

Janowski, Bernd 100
Janssen, L. F. 102
Johnson, Luke Timothy 9, 81
Jordan, David 54, 69
Joy, N. George 85
Judge, Edwin A. 33

Käsemann, Ernst 81
Kapferer, Bruce 8

Katz, Paul R. 99
Kelber, Werner H. 92
Kelly, John N. D. 28
Kennedy, Charles 70
Kennedy, George A. 88
Kim, Seyoon 77
Kinnes, Ian 57
Klawans, Jonathan 4
Kleiner, F. S. 45
Klingbeil, Gerald A. 4, 8
Kloppenborg, John S. vii, 101, 102
Koester, Helmut 66, 67
Koperski, Veronica 76
Kraemer, Ross Shepard 26
Krentz, Peter 99
Kurtz, Donna C. 65, 66

Laidlaw, James 4
Lake, Kirsopp 97
Lampe, G. W. H. 85
Lau, D. C. 1
Lawson, E. Thomas 3
Leach, Edmund R. 22, 30
Levi, Peter 57
Levine, Baruch A. 97
Lewis, Charlton T. 101
Lewis, John G. 78
Liddell, Henry G. 101
Lietzmann, Hans 2, 69
Lindquist, Galina 8
Lolos, Yannis A. 46

McCauley, Robert N. 3
MacDonald, Dennis R. 93
Mack, Burton L. 2, 93
McLean, B. Hudson 3, 97
McVann, Mark 2, 3
Malina, Bruce J. vii, 2, 93–4, 95
Manderscheid, Hubertus 46
Marcus, Joel 108
Martin, Cheryl English 53
Martin, Dale 87
Mead, Margaret 22
Meeks, Wayne A. 18–19, 21, 59–60, 64, 78
Meyer, Paul W. 77
Milgrom, Jacob 4, 8, 97
Mitchell, Margaret M. 88
Modéus, Martin 4

Moore, Henrietta L. 74
Morris, Ian 70
Moule, C. F. D. 14–15, 27
Moulton, J. M. 82
Murphy-O'Connor, Jerome 58, 81, 82, 85
Musurillo, Herbert 54
Myerhoff, Barbara 18, 22
Myers, Ched 92, 93

Nash, R. Scott vi, 70
Neyrey, Jerome H. vii, 3, 80, 89, 93–4, 95
Nickelsburg, George 93
Nielsen, Inge 46
Nisetich, Frank 106
Nock, A. D. 68

Olyan, Saul M. 3
Orr, William F. 16
Osiek, Carolyn vii, 37

Palmer, Hazel 52, 66, 70
Parke, H. W. 104
Parker, Robert 88
Pascuzzi, Maria 80
Paton, W. R. 51
Patrick, James E. 59
Pearson, Ashley 91
Pemberton, E. 48
Penner, Hans 7
Peterson, Dwight N. 93
Pfeiffer, Rudolf 106
Pilch, John J. vii, 95
Plevnik, Joseph 76
Porter, Stanley E. 3
Purcell, Nicholas 1, 45

Raeder, Maria 58, 59
Räisänen, Heikki 77
Rappaport, Roy A. 4, 5, 8, 27, 30
Ray, Benjamin C. 8
Rehm, Rush 60
Reinders, Eric 30
Reitzenstein, Richard 2
Richardson, Rufus B. 39
Rife, Joseph Lee 52, 66, 70
Riley, Gregory J. 70
Rissi, Mathis 58, 59

Roberts, A. 97
Robinson, Betsey A. 46, 48
Robinson, Henry S. 41
Roebuck, Carl 48, 49
Roetzel, Calvin J. 78, 81
Romano, David G. 43
Romano, Irene B. 51
Roo, Jacqueline C. R. De 100
Rosen, Leora Nadine 74
Rosner, Brian S. 81, 89
Rothaus, Richard M. vi, vii, 46, 54

Salamon, Sonya 22–3
Salom, A. P. 82
Sanders, E. P. 77
Sanders, Todd 74
Sandes, Karl Olav 93
Schilbrack, Kevin 5
Schnackenburg, Rudolf 59–60
Schüssler Fiorenza, Elisabeth 76
Scott, James C. 50
Scott, Robert 101
Scranton, Robert L. 41, 43
Seeman, Don 8
Segal, Alan F. 28
Sellin, Gerhard 52, 59, 79
Senft, C. 58
Shaw, Rosalind 42
Shear, T. L. 66
Short, Charles 101
Small, A. vii
Smith, Dennis E. 3
Smith, Jonathan Z. 1, 2, 8, 29, 31, 35, 70
Smith, Morton 59
Smyth, Herbert W. 82
Snyder, Graydon F. 111
South, James T. 85
Sperber, Dan 7
Spinks, Bryan D. 49
Staal, Frits 4, 7
Steiner, Ann 49
Stendahl, Krister 75, 77
Stewart, Charles 42
Stillwell, Richard 41, 43
Strecker, Christian 3, 5–6, 9, 20

Stroud, Ronald S. 49, 67, 68, 69
Stuhlmacher, Peter 77

Tambiah, Stanley J. 7, 32, 36
Tannehill, Robert C. 19
Theissen, Gerd 52, 71
Thiselton, Anthony C. 82
Thompson, Cynthia L. 33
Thompson, K. C. 58
Thornton, Timothy C. G. 85
Thrall, Margaret E. 78, 85
Toynbee, J. M. C. 65, 66
Triandis, Harry C. 86
Turner, Edith 20
Turner, N. 82
Turner, Victor W. 2, 3, 5, 18–20, 22, 27, 60

Uro, Risto 3

Van Gennep, Arnold 5, 18, 22, 60
Versnel, H. S. 101, 102, 108

Walbank, Mary E. Hoskins 43, 44, 52, 66, 70, 71
Walls, Jeannette 91
Walther, James Arthur 16
Ward, Richard F. 2
Wedderburn, A. J. M. 18, 19, 58
West, A. B. 68
Wheeler, Everett L. 99
Wheelock, Wade T. 30
White, Joel R. 59
Whitehouse, Harvey 3
Wiles, Gordon P. 81
Wilhelm, Gernot 100
Williams, Charles K., II vii, 41–2, 43, 51, 52, 69
Wiseman, James vii, 41, 43, 46, 51, 54
Wright, David P. 4, 34

Yarbrough, O. Larry 80
Yegül, Fikret 54
Young, Rodney 52, 66, 70

Zuesse, Evan M. 34

Index of Subjects

Acrocorinth 47, 48, 68
Acts of the Apostles 15, 17, 24, 35, 52
atonement 96–7, 100, 111; *see also* exit rites

baptism 2, 3, 7, 12, 14–21, 24, 27–30, 32, 34–5, 37, 49–52, 55–6, 59–61, 63–5, 81; as burial 60, 64–5; on behalf of the dead 12, 53, 57–61, 63–5, 69–70, 83; kinship-making and -breaking *see* entry rites; martyrdom as second baptism 54; postponed 29; *see also* entry rites
bathing *see* water
biblical scholarship and interpretive method: cognitive science 3; history-of-religion 1; orality/oral performance 2; ritual theory 3–8, 11–12; social-scientific 2–3, 5; speech-act theory 2

Cambridge ritualists 1
conversion *see* entry rites
Corinth, Greek-period 38; Asklepieion *see* temple; bath near gymnasium 46, 54; north cemetery 47, 66; Peirene (lower) fountain 46; sacred spring 49; sanctuary of Demeter and Kore (Persephone) 48–9, 67; south stoa 51; temples *see* temple
Corinth, interim-period 50–2
Corinth, Roman-period 37–45, 46–9; Asklepieion *see* temple; bath near

gymnasium 46, 54; baths 46, 50; forum 40, 42–4, 47; fountain of Poseidon 40, 43, 46; fountain of the lamps 47, 54–6; Glauke fountain 40–2, 44, 48; harbor at Lechaion 46–7; north cemetery 47, 66, 70; Peirene (lower) fountain 40, 46–7; sanctuary of Demeter and Kore (Persephone) 46, 47, 68–70; south stoa 40, 46, 51; temples *see* temple
curative exit rites *see* exit rites
curse tablets/defixiones 54, 69, 87

devotio *see* exit rites
dining *see* meals

early church ritual 3, 5, 29, 34, 54–5; penance 28
entry rites 9, 12, 24, 28, 35, 53, 64, 73; and bathing 28; initiation 3, 6, 17–21, 26, 28, 35, 60; kinship-making and -breaking 24–7, 30–1, 34; *see also* baptism *and* rites/rituals
eucharist *see* meals
execration *see* exit rites
exile *see* exit rites
exit rites 9, 73–5, 80–5, 87–8, 94–111; curative 9, 74, 97–104, 107–11; devotio 98, 101–3, 107–11; execration 83, 87–8; exile, banishment 63, 74; expulsion 74–5, 81–5, 94, 97–8, 104–6, 108–9; funerals *see* funerary/burial practices; ostracism 74, 97; pharmakos 98, 101, 104–10;

scapegoat 8, 96–7, 99–101, 106;
   see also baptism *and* rites/rituals
expulsion *see* exit rites

First Corinthians 15–16, 31, 50, 52,
   57–61, 69–70, 74, 75, 79–80,
   88–9
funerary/burial practices 60–6, 88;
   body orientation 52; Corinthian 52,
   66, 70–1; cremation/inhumation
   52, 70; grave goods 66; Greek 65,
   70; hero cult 66–7; imaginary
   (honorary, mock) 61–5, 83;
   marriage to death 60; mourning 3,
   62, 81–3, 88; Roman 65, 70; for
   the living 62–4; *see also* baptism

gospel of Mark 74, 92–5, 107–10;
   passion narrative 8–9, 74, 92–7,
   107–8, 110

holiness *see* purity

initiation *see* entry rites
Isthmia: Demeter-Persephone cult
   67–8; Palaimon-Melikertes cult 52,
   66–70; roman bath 46; temple of
   Poseidon 46, 66–7

meals: creating solidarity 29; dining at
   temples/sanctuaries 31–2; eucharist
   7, 32, 34, 59–60, 69, 81, 89;
   funerary 61, 65, 69–70, 83;
   marking difference 29
Mummius 49, 51, 68

New Testament scholarship: focus on
   early Christian communities 2, 11;
   neglect of ritual 1–2, 4, 11, 34–5

ostracism *see* exit rites

passion narrative *see* gospel of Mark
Paul, the apostle: and baptism 15–16,
   18–19, 30–1, 52–3, 83; and
   community purity 9, 74, 79–80,
   84–5, 87–90; and meals 29, 31–2,
   59, 90; and worship 33, 81, 88, 90;

center of thought 75–8; funerary
   orientation 64–5, 69–70, 83
Pausanias 38–44, 46, 51
pharmakos *see* exit rites
pollution 74, 80, 84–5, 88–9, 100,
   108
purification *see* rites/rituals
purity 9, 74, 79–80, 84–5, 87–90, 99

religion: Greek 1, 54; chthonic 67–9
rites of passage 17–21, 60; *see also*
   entry rites *and* exit rites
rites/rituals: and crisis 21–3, 27–9,
   32–3; as action/performance 7–8,
   31; context 7, 32–3; bodiliness 34,
   90; boundary-crossing 9, 12, 18,
   22–3, 25–7, 31, 33–4, 60, 64,
   73; characteristics 7, 12, 18,
   21–34; defective/failed 27–8; of
   degradation 93–5, 106, 108; of
   inversion 32–3, 49–50, 54; making/
   maintaining boundaries 3; neglect of
   1, 35–6; primacy of 1–2, 7, 8–9,
   36, 73, 95; purification 4, 6, 28–9,
   34, 48, 85–8, 90, 97–100, 104–5,
   108–9; of resistance 49–50, 53; of
   status transformation 3, 18–19, 31,
   64, 93–6, 98, 103–6, 108–9; in
   texts 4–6, 9, 34, 73–4; unintended
   consequences 27–8; vicarious 58–9,
   61–4, 98, 102–4, 107; *see also*
   entry rites *and* exit rites
ritual studies 4–8
Roman fountains (nymphaea) *see*
   water
Romanization 37–8, 42–6, 48–9, 53

sacrifice 1, 4, 8, 33, 35, 48, 63, 65,
   67, 95–6, 99, 102, 104–5, 107
scapegoat *see* exit rites

temple: of Asklepios 47, 48–9;
   Archaic 40, 42, 44; C 40–1;
   community as 89; D 40, 43;
   E 40, 42–4; F 40, 43; G 40, 43;
   Jewish/Jerusalem 4, 93, 108–10; of
   Palaimon *see* Isthmia; of Poseidon
   see Isthmia

water: and demons 55; and healing
56; and nymphs 54, 56; and
Roman culture 12, 37, 45–50, 53;
aqueduct 46, 50; bathing 7, 12, 28,
45, 48–9, 54–5; civic use of 45–8;
cultic use of 37, 48–9, 52–3, 55;
Roman baths 37, 54–5; Roman

fountains (nymphaea) 12, 37, 43,
46, 50
wedding/marriage 25–7, 60, 63
see also entry rites
witchcraft accusation 74; *see also* exit
rites
worship *see* Paul, the apostle

Archaeology, Ritual, Religion
Timothy Insoll

The archaeology of religion is a much neglected area, yet religious sites and artefacts constitute a major area of archaeological evidence. Timothy Insoll presents an introductory statement on the archaeology of religion, examining what archaeology can tell us about religion, the problems of defining and theorizing religion in archaeology, and the methodology, or how to 'do', the archaeology of religion.

This volume assesses religion and ritual through a range of examples from around the world and across time, including prehistoric religions, shamanism, African religions, death, landscape and even food. Insoll also discusses the history of research and varying theories in this field before looking to future research directions. This book will be a valuable guide for students and archaeologists, and initiate a major area of debate.

Hb: 978–0–415–25312–3
Pb: 978–0–415–25313–0

Available at all good bookshops
For ordering and further information please visit:
www.routledge.com

Related titles from Routledge

Early Christianity
Mark Humphries

Examining sources and case studies, this accessible book explores early Christianity, how it was studied, how it is studied now, and how Judaeo-Christian values came to form the ideological bedrock of modern western culture.

Looking at the diverse source materials available, from the earliest New Testament texts and the complex treaties of third century authors such as Lactantius, to archaeology, epigraphy and papyrology, the book examines what is needed to study the subject, what materials are available, how useful they are, and how the study of the subject may be approached.

Case study chapters focus on important problems in the study of early Christianity including:

- the book of Acts as a text revelatory of the social dynamics of cities and as a text about the inherent tensions in Hellenistic Judaism
- Orthodoxy and Organization in early Christianity
- Early Christianity and the Roman Empire.

Also including a comprehensive guide for students that lists major collections of literary and non-literary sources, major journals and series, and major text books, it is an excellent aid to the study of Christianity in history.

ISBN13: 978–0–415–20538–2 (hbk)
ISBN13: 978–0–415–20539–9 (pbk)

Available at all good bookshops
For ordering and further information please visit:
www.routledge.com

Related titles from Routledge

The Early Christian World
Edited by Philip F. Esler

'This is a splendid collection of essays by renowned scholars in the field that presents a coherent, authoritative and yet readable account of how a small Jewish sect became a major world religion . . . A useful resource that any graduate or undergraduate library would do well to have on its shelves.' – *Kenneth G.C. Newport, Theological Book Review*

The Early Christian World presents an exhaustive, erudite, and lavishly-illustrated treatment of how a small movement formed around Jesus in Galilee became the pre-eminent religion of the ancient world.

Situating early Christianity within its Mediterranean social, political and religious contexts,the book charts the history of the first Christian centuries. The creation and perpetuation of Christian communities through means including mission and monasticism is then explored, as is the everyday experience of early Christians, through discussion of gender and sexuality, religious practice, communication and social structures. The intellectual (particularly theological) and artistic heritage of the period is fully considered, and a vivid picture provided of the internal and external challenges faced by early Christianity.

With profiles of the most notable figures of the age, up-to-date coverage of the most important topics in the study of early Christianity and an invaluable collection of visual material. *The Early Christian World* is a comprehensive, accessible and indispensable resource for everyone studying this period.

ISBN13: 978–0–415–24114–0 (hbk)
ISBN13: 978–0–415–33312–2 (pbk)

Available at all good bookshops
For ordering and further information please visit:
www.routledge.com